Yesterday's Papers
Volume Five.

Life on the Isle of Wight in the 1950's.

*From the archives of
The Isle of Wight County Press.*

by
Alan Stroud

Now and Then Books

ISBN   978-0-9565076-2-4
© Alan Stroud 2011
Typeset by Alan Stroud.

Printed by
Short Run Press Limited
25 Bittern Road
Sowton Industrial Estate
EXETER
EX2 7LW

Once again I need to thank my wife Sue, son Tom and friend Richard Brimson for their initial read through and helpful suggestions. The proof reading skills of Gay and David Baldwin were much appreciated and I'm grateful to them both.

My thanks also go to all at the County Press for their usual assistance, and to the County Club and Roger Silsbury for assistance with photographs.

Published by Now and Then Books. Cowes, Isle of Wight.
E-mail: nowandthenbooksiw@googlemail.com

Volumes 1, 2 and 3 were published by The Oakwood Press, P.O.Box 13, Usk, Mon. NP15 1YS, from whom they are still available at www.oakwoodpress.co.uk or through local bookshops.

When the phrase, 'affluent society' was used to describe Britain in the 1950's it was used with some justification. There was more money to spend and there were more things to spend it on. Productivity rose, wages increased and there were opportunities to earn, spend and consume as never before and when Harold Macmillan, the Prime Minister, told the public in 1957, "You've never had it so good," it was, as a statement of fact, true.

To illustrate the point a few statistics are unavoidable. Between 1952 and 1963 the number of cars in Britain rose from 2 to 7 million while the number of homes with television soared from 10 to 85 per cent and in the same period personal spending rose by 20 per cent. Washing machines, refrigerators and vacuum cleaners appeared for the first time in more and more homes and many of these purchases were funded by credit. Hire purchase, or 'HP,' had quickly become a part of everyday life and well over half of the cars and televisions bought in the 1950's were paid for using "buy now, pay later" plans.

Cars and televisions, perhaps more than anything else, were to change people's lives and the arrival of both had a marked effect on the Island. Over the past twenty years there had been a huge increase in car ownership which led to a dramatic fall in railway passenger numbers and as a direct result four of the Island's branch lines were closed during the 1950's. The first line to go was the Merstone to Ventnor line in 1952, followed by the Brading to Bembridge, and Newport to Freshwater lines in 1953, and three years later, the Newport to Sandown line. In all instances it is fair to say that the public were neither surprised nor even particularly bothered by the closures. While sorry to see the lines go, the closures were mostly accepted with quiet resignation, indeed when the inevitable protest letters appeared in the County Press, many came not from Island addresses but mainland ones. The only public outcry came when British Railways was accused of massaging passenger figures to make the already substantial losses appear even worse than they actually were. If that was indeed the case, it was a futile exercise. It was universally acknowledged that all four lines were running at a loss, in some instances the takings not even paying the staff wages. Trains on the Brading to Bembridge line in particular, sometimes ran with only the driver, fireman and guard on board. By mutual agreement, the end had come; new bus routes were introduced to take the railways' place and the little branch lines passed quietly into history.

At the same time, television slowly began to overtake the printed word to become the major cultural force in Britain and as more and more people stayed in to watch it, cinemas all across the country, the Island included, were forced to close. The first to go on the Island was the King's Cinema at East Cowes. The vacant building was absorbed into the nearby Saunders-Roe factory as office space and was known until its recent demolition as "King's Building."

The recent war had brought people together in that way that wars do and some wartime values were still very strong. For some, respectability, restraint and conformity were what underpinned the Fifties while many others saw 1950's society as oppressive, prurient and prim. Either way, there was little doubt that attitudes in post-war Britain had changed a good deal and by the end of the 1950's British society had become noticeably more casual.

The 'teenager' and 'rock and roll' both arrived in the mid 1950's to the tune of Bill Haley's 'Rock Around the Clock.' Haley, far from a teenager himself, was amongst the first to set adult alarm bells ringing, a sound which grew the following year with the arrival of Elvis Presley; but the time was right and rock and roll proved an unstoppable force. In response to this American invasion a wave of British acts appeared almost overnight, leading to that other phenomenon of the Fifties, the coffee bar. They sprang up in towns across the Island where teenagers would gather to enjoy frothy coffee as they listened to records played on the other new arrival from America, the jukebox. Local dance-hall owners could see there was an honest penny to be made from rock and roll and slowly but surely the traditional dance bands disappeared, to be replaced by rock and roll or skiffle groups. And not just local ones. From the mid-Fifties to the mid-Seventies the youth of the Island was very well served as far as musical entertainment was concerned and the list of well-known national acts who appeared here is a fairly impressive one, the Fifties names including Tommy Steele, Lonnie Donegan and Marty Wilde, not to mention Newport's very own milkman-turned-pop star, Craig Douglas.

Also well represented on the Island were the armed forces. Conscription remained in place until 1960 and for the most part, the forts and batteries on the Island were still fully manned at the beginning of the 1950's, including Fort Victoria, Northwood Camp, Albany Barracks and Golden Hill Fort. The many court cases involving drunken soldiers in local dance-hall brawls bear silent testimony to their presence.

In Britain, the Fifties saw the introduction of motorways, CND, the Mini and the hovercraft, while into the shops came Windolene, tinned sweetcorn and Silvikrin. Children brought up on Big Chief I-Spy, Tri-ang trains and Dinky toys tuned in each Saturday morning to hear Uncle Mac play 'Nellie the Elephant' and 'Tubby the Tuba' before going off to spend their pocket money on sherbert fountains, Spangles and sweet tobacco.

The hovercraft made its first appearance in 1959 and was very much an Island affair. Conceived and built at the Saunders-Roe factory at East Cowes, the hovercraft put the Island on the map. It was also a well-timed arrival, providing much needed employment just as J.S. White's shipyard at Cowes began to go into a long period of terminal decline, losing contracts to overseas shipbuilders and slowly laying off more and more of its workers as time went on.

Over the next 25 years a wide range of hovercraft were built at East Cowes, both for military purposes and for passenger services, including the huge SRN4 craft which operated the Dover to Calais car ferry service from 1968 to 2000. Unfortunately the hovercraft never captured the imagination of the Ministry of Defence and no meaningful military sales were ever forthcoming. Eventually, cheaper modes of sea transport combined with the arrival of the Channel Tunnel signalled the end for the hovercraft and production ceased in the mid-80s.

Unemployment, which was at its lowest ever level during the war years, remained low during the 1950's; in August 1951 the official unemployment figures for the Island show just 208 men and 110 women out of work. In 1951 a farm worker's wage was £5 for a 47 hour week, 3s 4d for every hour worked on a Sunday and 2s 8d for every hour worked over the 47 which could bring in as much as £6 or £7. Average wages elsewhere were about £5 or £5 10s a week but they slowly began to grow and in 1954 the Island council was advertising for a 'rodent officer' to be paid £6 16s a week, and for a secretary, to be paid £7.

The Labour Government which took office at the end of the war won a majority of 5 in the February 1950 election, prompting the newspaper headline, "They're in - but for how long?" The answer was just a few months, and in October the Conservatives won the second election that year with a majority of 17. While various governments came and went, the Island bucked the national trend and remained Conservative. Sir Peter Macdonald was the Island's MP for 35 unbroken years, eventually standing down in the general election of 1959 to make way for Mark Woodnutt, who in turn went on to hold the seat for the Conservatives until 1974.

The constraints of utility fashion and style were gone. Culture and the Arts had blossomed since the end of the war and the bland but practical war-time styles made way for bold new designs in architecture and fashion, but without doubt the single most radical change in the nation's cultural life was the arrival of television.

Available in the London area since 1936, television finally came to the Island in 1954 with the opening of the BBC transmitter at Rowridge. The reaction of the County Press and public alike was one of keen anticipation and from the outset there was an extraordinary and relentless interest in the newcomer. In the lead-up to the opening of the service there was a succession of articles about television in all its aspects; where to buy one, how to install it and even how to watch it. To accompany the big switch-on which took place in November of 1954, that week's issue included a 12 page supplement completely devoted to the new arrival and for months to come the merits, or otherwise, of television became a talking point in the columns of the County Press. Advertisements for televisions began to appear on the front page and for a while it seemed as if every shop in the Island's high streets had branched into the television business, so numerous were all manner of unlikely shops which briefly took to selling them. When ITV, in the form of Southern Television, launched in 1958 the interest in television was undiminished. The County Press reaped the benefits as both retailers and Southern Television itself placed large amounts of advertising as the new channel prepared to take to the air. With two channels to choose from now, articles appeared comparing their presentation virtues (some readers found the ITV presentation "too brash") and even comparing picture quality. To receive the new ITV transmissions a separate aerial was required and so a momentary glance to one's neighbour's roof revealed at an instant who was, and who was not, keeping up with the Jones.

Passing quietly into history during the 1950's, although not actually demolished until 1960, were East Cowes Castle and the Victoria Pier at Cowes Parade. Both slowly fell to pieces while discussions took place regarding their future, until eventually they reached the point where repair ceased to be an economic proposition. The grounds of East Cowes Castle became a housing estate while a curved section of balustrade on Cowes Parade today acts as a rough guide to where the pier entrance was once located.

Arrivals in the 1950's included myxomatosis, a disease that almost eradicated the wild rabbit from the Island and is still carried in local rabbits today, and Decca Radar, who with the encouragement of the government, purchased the old Somerton Aerodrome at Cowes to build their new state-of-the-art factory. The manufacture of radar at Cowes continues to this day, with the site currently in the ownership of BAE Systems.

One other arrival during the Fifties meant that overnight, the public had to get used to referring to their monarch as, *"Her"* Majesty, when King George died in 1952 and Queen Elizabeth came to the throne.

Much to the relief of most Islanders, there was one arrival which did not materialise. For the best part of a year, in 1959, the Island was one of six south coast locations under serious consideration as a suitable site for a nuclear power station. The proposed location was Hamstead, alongside Newtown Creek, and inevitably the subject of an atomic power station in the unspoilt Newtown estuary received extensive coverage in the County Press as Islanders expressed their almost universal opposition. The long running debate was a revealing indicator of how attitudes to the countryside were slowly changing. More people were now likely to visit the countryside for leisure than to actually work in it. Slowly the public became more aware of its virtues and correspondingly, more protective towards it, and for the first time Islanders made clear their desire for unspoilt countryside rather than any potential jobs.

For the managers of the countryside, the farmers, life had changed beyond recognition and a revolution had taken place in agriculture, fuelled by chemicals and tractors. Farming practices had remained virtually unchanged for hundreds of years and a farm worker from the Middle Ages would have no difficulty in identifying the tools hanging in an early 20th century barn, but in just one generation those tools had all but disappeared. So too had their users, all swept aside by mechanisation. A glance at any County Press of the 1950's will confirm the changes that were sweeping over agriculture. Large and expensive adverts appeared regularly for chemical manufacturers such as Fisons, Shell and ICI, all keen to sell farmers their latest pesticides and fertilisers to boost crop yields. Alongside, equally numerous advertisements appeared for labour saving tractors and farm machinery of every kind.

For the County Press itself, the decade was, by and large, a trouble-free and profitable one. Brief paper shortages in 1950 meant smaller papers for several months, while a national newspaper strike in 1954 brought the paper perilously close to not appearing for the first time in its history when the print room staff were instructed by their London union headquarters to withdraw their labour. Management and office workers rose to the challenge, donned aprons and in the absence of the striking print workers learned how to operate the presses and for several weeks produced the newspaper themselves.

Apart from that, while the 1950's winds of change swirled around them, for the County Press it was business as usual.

————————◆————————

This volume covers the 1950's, beginning with the first issue of 1950 and ending with the last issue of 1959.

For the most part the items are in their entirety and appear exactly as they did when they were originally published. For considerations of space, some longer items have been edited and where this has occurred it is indicated by dotted lines.

The items variously headed 'The Week's News,' 'Island Notes' or 'Town and County Notes' are compilations. They are undated for the most part as the date is usually superfluous but they are always placed within five or six weeks of their original appearance. On the odd occasion where the date of an item has been considered relevant it appears in brackets.

As in the previous four volumes contemporary spellings and printing conventions have been retained and are *not* misprints. Throughout the book the titles used for the articles are those that accompanied them on the day they first appeared in the County Press; none have been altered or modified in any way.

Extracts from the weekly column 'An Islander's Notes by Vectensis' can be found at various points throughout the book. 'Vectensis' was the pen-name of Walter Sibbick, who joined the County Press as a 13-year-old boy in 1902 and eventually rose to become the editor, a position he held from 1945 to his retirement in 1960. His delightful and excellent column began in the 1920's and continued many years after his retirement, covering every subject under the sun as the mood took him but always having its roots in Island life. His weekly column was a mine of local information and miscellany so rich and varied that it deserves a book of its own.

Where possible, the photographs used in this volume are ones which actually appeared in the County Press during the 1950's. They have been produced by going back to the bound volumes of original copies of the County Press and photographing them as they appeared in the paper at the time (the original photographs no longer existing). As a result, some of them show clear signs of their origin but they have been included because of their rarity value, usually being unavailable elsewhere and hopefully, their historical interest outweighs any technical shortcomings. The captions for each photograph are those that originally accompanied them when they first appeared but the dates shown alongside the photographs are the date of publication, not the date of the event. Some photographs have come from the author's collection or elsewhere and are marked correspondingly.

Finally, the prices throughout the book appear in their original pre-decimal form of pounds, shillings and pence. For those unfamiliar with the system, twelve old pennies made a shilling and twenty of those shillings made a pound.

1950

The County Press of the 1950's still had an eye for the more unusual news items. The adventures of a wandering pair of glasses were just the thing...

January 21st, 1950

LONG-DISTANCE SPECTACLES!

While repairing a conveyor belt at a pit at a Northumberland colliery a month ago, Alfred Thompson, of Ashington, took off his spectacles and, putting them into their case, rested them on the canvas strip for a moment. Suddenly the belt started up and carried them through the screens among tons of coal. The spectacles, with the coal, dropped into a tub from where they were tipped into a railway wagon and taken to Blyth, where they were shot into the hold of a waiting collier. The collier, the Eleanor Brook, then sailed for the Island and landed the coal at Cowes last week. A load was then sent to Freshwater where the spectacle case was discovered by Mr. A. Speed, of Totland, yard foreman of Messrs. Wood and Jolliffe's Freshwater depot. The spectacles were intact, and the case bore the name of the owner. They are now on their way back to Mr. Thompson after a round journey of 1000 miles.

———————————◆———————————

An eight inch nail was found inside a tree felled at Calbourne. According to Moreys' staff who felled the tree, foreign objects found inside growing trees were not unheard of and they went on to tell of even more unusual finds. The last line of the report was to generate correspondence for several weeks to come...

January 28th, 1950

PECULIAR FINDS IN TREES.

An eight inch nail in a horizontal position was found in the middle of the trunk of an old elm tree cut down at the Rectory, Calbourne. Members of the staff of Messrs. H.W. Morey and Sons, who felled the tree, say that although at least 200 years of growth surrounded the nail the discovery was not very unusual. They once found a three foot length of steel chain inside a tree trunk, and other items "swallowed" by trees which they have discovered have included glass beads and a pair of scissors. They state that occasionally, right in the heart of a tree, they come across something far more strange - a little hollow space occupied by a large species of grub or caterpillar, still alive. How the grub survives under centuries of growth, in a cavity without any opening, is a mystery - similar to that of live frogs or toads which are sometimes found embedded in solid blocks of chalk.

———————————◆———————————

THE WEEK'S NEWS.

During 1949 the County Fire Brigade received 497 calls at the 11 stations in the Island - 200 more than in the previous year. There were four false alarms, all of which were malicious.

HOUSEBREAKING IN THE COWES AREA. – After listening to a news broadcast about the large number of Borstal escapes in the Island, Mr. Ben Edwards, of Maree, Newport Road, Northwood, went to meet a relative off a bus and on his return found that his home had been broken into... Borstal clothing was left in the house.

NOTES BY VECTENSIS – I have received from Mr. F.C.W. Reed of 17, Well Street, Ryde his indentures as a cabinet-maker's apprentice to Henry Mills, dated February 1st, 1896. He undertook during the five years "not to contract matrimony, play at cards or dice tables, or any other unlawful games, haunt taverns or play-houses, or absent himself from his master's service day or night unlawfully." His pay was to be 4s. 6d a week, with an annual increase of a shilling a week.

The "Parliamentary Gazette" of 1842 records a big landslide near Blackgang Chine in February, 1790, when "the whole of the farm called Pitlands, consisting of 100 acres of land, was observed to be in motion and continued so for two days, moving towards the sea. The changes which took place were extremely curious. There was scarcely a square yard but what had altered its appearance, both rocks and trees shifting their situations and forming as confused a scene as if the ground had been convulsed by an earthquake. In many places the earth sank 30 or 40 feet, and a new cottage about to be occupied was thrown down and buried in the fissures."

———————————◆———————————

An aviation correspondent in the Daily Express dared to suggest that the Princess flying boats* currently under construction on the Island had been so long on the production line that they would be outdated by the time they were finished...

February 11th, 1950

THE PRINCESS FLYING BOATS.
SUGGESTION THAT THEY MAY BE "WHITE ELEPHANTS."

In an article in Tuesday's "Daily Express," Wing Commander Paul Richey, writing about the Princess flying boats, which are under construction by Messrs. Saunders-Roe at East Cowes, comments that after three and a half years of work they threaten to become another Government white elephant for the British taxpayer. The writer states that two serious snags have impeded the work - the stopping of the work on the original engines and the slumping of the estimated performance of the substitute engines, and a big jump in the estimated cost, from £2,800,000 to £4,500,000 without engines. Summing up the situation, Wing Commander Richey states that the earliest delivery date is given as 1953... In five years jet planes will be regularly flying the Atlantic in almost half the time to be taken by the Princesses... All the money spent, plus any operating losses in the future, must ultimately be borne by the taxpayer. On

---

* The Princess was a huge flying boat, over 40 metres in length and with a wingspan of nearly 70 metres. With four propellors over five metres in diameter, it was designed to carry over over 100 passengers at speeds of up to 360mph.

enquiring of Saunders-Roe's Press agents in London, the "County Press" was informed that a conference had been held to consider the article, and it had been decided to ignore it. An official of Messrs. Saunders-Roe described the article as "all nonsense." *

———————————◆———————————

The County Press was a paper of record and scrupulously impartial in its news coverage, always confining opinion to the editorial column where, it is fair to say, they would speak their mind. As the nation approached the 1950 general election, the County Press, being a staunch supporter of the Conservative party, left its readers in no doubt as to where their duties lay when they visited the ballot box, pointing out to its readers, "the Conservative manifesto has a heartening, tonic quality"...

February 4th, 1950

TAKE YOUR CHOICE.

The Socialists are evidently trying to shelve the nation's financial crisis until this election is over. Their manifesto is mainly compounded of misrepresentation of carefully chosen pieces of past history and evasiveness about the future. It states the need to expand our trade till we can pay for our necessities but does not say how this is to be done. The measures of nationalisation which it outlines would merely add to our difficulties. There is not a word about the succession of crises in building or the health service... It is a certainty that a Socialist Chancellor must introduce as unpopular budget as Britain has ever known. By contrast, the Conservative manifesto has a heartening, tonic quality. It is positive and constructive. It sees a salvation not in further repression of initiative and earnings but in expansion... The homeless can derive fresh hope from the declared intention to let the building industry get on with the job. The housewife will be cheered by the knowledge that prices can be lowered and queues made a nightmare of the past... Assured that the Tory policy is to combine the protection of the weak with the encouragement of the strong, and aware that, despite Socialist lies, the Tories yield to no one in their determination to maintain full employment, no elector who is guided by reason and not by ingrained prejudice, need hesitate to vote Conservative.

———————————◆———————————

In the same issue, an elderly Newport resident shared his memories of elections gone by...

February 4th, 1950

LIVELY ELECTION BATTLES OF THE PAST.
AN OCTOGENARIAN'S REMINISCENCES.

Mr. W.H. Baker, of Clatterford Road, Carisbrooke, who is 86, sent us the following interesting account of his reminiscences of general election incidents at Newport in his early days:

---

* Unfortunately, Wing Commander Richey's predictions proved to be all too accurate. In 1953, with no solution in sight to the underpowered engines problem, the three planes were mothballed; two at Calshot and the third parked on a concrete slipway on the foreshore at Medina Road, Cowes, where it became a local landmark for some years until all three were scrapped in 1967.

"My memory takes me back to the last open voting election in 1868, when I was five years old. Wooden huts were erected in several places in the town as polling stations. One was on the pavement between Morris's shop and the Parish Church, and I remember sitting on my father's shoulder watching the men going in to vote, and at four o'clock, when the poll closed, seeing the mob of roughs make a rush for the hut and smash it up and fight like devils for the wood and carry it away. Votes were bought and sold, sometimes twice over, but the man who sold his vote to both Tory and Radical never dared to enter the polling booth as he would have been pretty roughly handled by both... Tories and Radicals used to organise processions, and once both, unknown to each other, had arranged to have their processions on the same night. The Tories went up the High Street and the Radicals up Pyle Street, and when they got to the top of the town they met, and then the sparks began to fly! A "free for all" ensued, and the ground was covered with struggling men... All the roughs of the town used to be rounded up and sworn in as special constables and locked up in the Town Hall until the poll closed, to keep them out of mischief. While they were locked up they held mock courts and charged each other with supposed offences, and imposed fines of quarts or gallons of beer. When they were released the fun started; there were fights all over the town... Political meetings were very rowdy affairs with frequent fights, and those on the platform were often pelted with rotten eggs and rotten oranges, and all kinds of rotten vegetables... Those were the days! But were they?"

The recent remark about live toads jumping from the centre of blocks of chalk had not gone unnoticed. A Mr. Saunt had written to the editor the following week explaining in fairly sarcastic terms why the whole thing was implausible, but quite a few readers disagreed with him, among them, Mr. Cross of Brook, who wrote back to champion the cause of entombed frogs...

February 11th, 1950
FROGS IN "SUSPENDED ANIMATION."

I did not see "Rural Notes" but I should like to question the comments made by Mr. Saunt in last week's issue. May I first quote the case of the frog which now rests in the museum attached to the public library at Brentford. Some 25 years ago an old building on property owned by my father was being demolished having become unusable through old age. As a plaster wall was broken into, a frog jumped out of the plaster in which it had been embedded. The man working there called his mates to see the extraordinary phenomenon; they watched the frog breathe heavily for about three minutes, after which time it died. As it had been entombed for well over a century the men naturally considered the frog a sufficient curiosity to warrant its being brought to my father. He placed it in a convenient spot and the frog was forgotten for a couple of days and when my father again noticed it he was amazed to find that the body had set as hard as a piece of stone. And so it remains to this day without any other vestige of alterations from the moment it jumped from the plaster. As to attempting to explain this extraordinary case, first one must assume that the fully grown frog was in the water with which the plaster was being mixed. Once the plaster had set it is possible that it was sufficiently porous to permit a minute quantity of air to penetrate. One can then only surmise that since it was completely immobile, the frog needed no nourishment with which to sustain the spark of life. How far such a theory can be applied to frogs found embedded in chalk I hesitate to suggest, but I do not think that we can dismiss out of hand stories of such a nature. F.C. CROSS. Old Myrtle Cottage, Brook.

Five years after the end of the war, the housing shortage, both here and on the mainland, showed no sign of improving...

February 18th, 1950

VENTNOR - POSSIBLY ONLY TWO COUNCIL HOUSES THIS YEAR.
MINISTRY CHARGED WITH "WICKED FRUSTRATION."

What amounted to almost complete cancellation of the Ventnor Council's housing programme for 1950, as the result of a cut in the allocation of houses by the Ministry of Health, was referred to as a very grave situation at the meeting at the Town Hall on Monday. Mr. H.J. Beaumont (Chairman of the Housing Committee) gave the startling information that the effect of the cuts would mean that only two council houses could be built in Ventnor this year... The committee was of the opinion that the allocation was ridiculously low... The tragedy was that 14 houses for West Street, Wroxall, for which plans had been prepared and tenders invited, had not been accepted by the Ministry... the net result was the magnificent total of two council houses for Ventnor for the whole of 1950. In explaining his committee's hard work to house, at the earliest opportunity, those living under crowded and in some instances, disgusting conditions, Mr. Beaumont said that... 61 applicants on the housing list might have to wait at least another year before they could ever hope to be offered accommodation. He wondered if the independent members of the council were going to be blamed for that wicked example of frustration on the part of the Ministry. The blame rested fairly and squarely on the shoulders of the Ministry...

Wing Commander Richey's recent pronouncements regarding the Princess flying boats had not gone down well with some readers. With more than a whiff of class predjudice in the air, a Mr. Boston of East Cowes vigorously challenged not only the Wing Commander's facts, but also his mentality...

February 18th, 1950

THE PRINCESS FLYING BOATS.

I was surprised to read the article taken from the "Daily Express" re the above. The statements made by Wing Commander Richey are a lot of piffle, in keeping with the type of his mentality and that of a good number of his commissioned comrades whom I had the misfortune to contact during the late war. Richey has not the actual knowledge of the facts and his reflections are illusionary. Paul wants to pull up his socks and cast his mind back to the day when he joined the RAF. The same applies to others of his standing. When puffed up frogs are croaking they make much noise and it is pleasant to the ear, but when the likes of Paul start, it is an insult to the intelligence of the illiterate, and causes the person of average knowledge of the true facts to smile with contempt.

THOMAS BOSTON. 9 Yarborough Road, East Cowes.

———————————◆———————————

As an object lesson in how far the lives of working class people had come in the last fifty years, this reader's letter can hardly be bettered...

February 18th, 1950

"WE ARE CERTAINLY BETTER OFF."

Re your statement in the editorial in last Saturday's issue - "ask the housewife if the average wage of £6 a week to-day is better than the £3 per week before the war" - the average skilled worker would have indeed felt well off if his wages were £3 per week in 1939. My husband is a skilled fitter and when we married his wages were £2 14s. 6d. a week. He did ask for a rise once and received a farthing an hour more. Insurance and unemployment were deducted from this amount. A week's holiday with pay was only wishful thinking on our part. Take Christmas, the time of good cheer, with two or three days' pay deducted from an already meagre wage packet. How right Mr. J.B. Priestley was when he said our Christmases are better than ever before. My husband now earns almost 3 times as much as in 1939 (not at his trade). He does not lose any pay through sickness, his Christmas-box is more than his week's wages were in 1939, he is paid for all bank holidays, and, above all, we go away each year to enjoy our fortnight's holiday with pay. I think, Mr. Editor, you will agree that we are certainly better off, and that it takes a war to make the Tories realise that the workers are underpaid. My husband and I often talk about the hard times we had before the war, and, like Mr. Hill of Shanklin, we think this Government has served the country and the workers well, so, being two more sports, we shall vote Labour.

A MERE HOUSEWIFE (A.K. THEARLEY). Hurst Cottage, Ryde.

———————————◆———————————

TOWN AND COUNTY NOTES.

Approval was given to a resolution to prevent rebuilding on the bomb damaged sites of 1-9 Bernard Road, Cowes, and 22 and 24 Mill Hill Road, Cowes. Control of development of the site had been requested by the General Post Office for the erection of a new telephone exchange. Mr. L.S. Jay (County Planning officer) said it would not be a matter which would be hanging about for years.*

* The telephone exchange was not built for another 14 years.

THE CANDIDATE AND THE "COUNTY PRESS." – At Whitwell on Saturday Mr. Conbeer, the Labour candidate for the Island, said he had attacked the "County Press" in the past, but he was always willing to give credit when it was due. He had expected the worst, but he had to congratulate them on their fairness in reporting the speeches. They had given the whole of Labour's case as well as the Tory side.

PARISH COUNCILS AND PUBLIC RIGHTS OF WAY. – Every parish council in England and Wales is being asked to take steps now to help in preparing the greatest survey of public rights of way ever to be made in this country... Parish councils are recommended to consult maps and records, to collect evidence from old inhabitants, and themselves to walk over all reputed public ways in their parishes. They are advised to prepare maps showing foot paths, bridle roads, park roads, and green lanes, driftways and metalled paths, as well as the position and condition of all stiles, stepping stones, kissing gates, footbridges, and other means of passage... Full advantage should be taken of the knowledge and enthusiasm of local inhabitants...(February 25)

FROGS IN SUSPENDED ANIMATION. – Poor Mr. Saunt! What a lot of pleasure he must miss in life by not believing what he has not himself seen! Perhaps he just hates frogs and doubts any story which suggests they are leading anything but the most mundane existences. Turning to Mr. Saunt's very simple explanation of the Brentford frog, of course, we are only simple people, but does he really think that such explanations were not exhaustively tested by the curators of the museum - if not by my father himself? ... Perhaps my father made it all up! What fun if he did, because the frog is still there! F.C. CROSS. Old Myrtle Cottage, Brook.

———————————◆———————————

Air travel to and from the Island had proved a surprising success in the pre-war years. Brought to a halt by the war, some local entrepreneurs were now attempting to restore the services at Ryde Airport...

February 25th, 1950

RE-OPENING RYDE AIRPORT.

The directors of Ryde airport, which is to be reopened after having been inoperative for over 10 years, met Press representatives at Yelf's Hotel, Ryde, on Tuesday, when they outlined their proposals for developments. Although not the largest airfield, it was, until the outbreak of war, recognised by the Air Ministry as being No. 1 aerodrome here, on account of altitude and freedom from mist. During the war the airfield was littered with old cars and other vehicles to prevent enemy landings, and with the establishment of the Home Guard the control tower and buildings were commandeered as a post. So far as the airfield is concerned a clearance of derelict vehicles was made a year or so after the cessation of hostilities, but owing to many hampering restrictions the company previously operating the services were unable to resume. It seemed for a long time that there was little hope of reopening but this has now come about by the enterprise of two Island airmen, Messrs. J. Sinclair and L. Chester Lawrence, who have acquired the airfield and intend to restore all of the pre-war services... The airport will be open to civilian traffic within the next few days... So far as the air services are concerned the Ryde-Portsmouth ferry will be reinstated in the late Spring, and there is every possibility of the Ryde-Croydon service being revived. Arrangements have been made with Warner's Holiday Camp at Puckpool for the conveyance of visitors wishing to travel from London by air.

———————————◆———————————

A licence to explore for oil underneath the Island had been granted back in 1935, the County Press stating at the time, "The discovery of oil in the Island would be a serious matter as the countryside in the region of the wells would immediately become industrialised. The vast majority of Vectensians will hope that the prospectors will draw a blank here." The drilling licence had recently been renewed and the search was on again. This time the County Press expressed no such reservations...

March 4th, 1950

OIL UNDER THE ISLAND?
PROMISING EXPERIMENTS IN S.E. WIGHT.

The arrival of convoys of drilling apparatus and a van carrying high explosive charges has caused considerable interest in the Arreton district this week, and some colourful but inaccurate rumours have been circulated regarding the project under way. As a result of facilities granted to the "County Press" by the Anglo-Iranian Oil Company, London, we are able to give the following account of the actual work being carried out. License to prospect for oil in this district was first granted as long ago as 1935... The licence was renewed in 1946 and last year a party toured the Island to make an initial survey by a series of gravity tests and the results indicated that favourable conditions might exist in the south-eastern part of the Island... The party numbers 32 men, with headquarters at Standen House, near Newport... The system on which the apparatus is worked is based on measurements of "echoes" received from oscillations started from a known point, employing a shock wave started underground by the explosion of a small charge of dynamite... A small hole is drilled to a depth of between 50 and 300 feet, at the bottom of which a light charge varying from a few ounces to about 20lb. of dynamite is placed. Two mobile rigs, consisting of miniature replicas of the normal large-scale derricks mounted on lorries, are carrying out the drilling operations. In line with the firing point, about 350 yards away, is placed a number of geophones which send signals to a master receiver in the recording van... A "County Press" representative watched one of the explosions in the Perreton district on Wednesday. A charge of 10lb. of dynamite was lowered to a depth of 60 ft. underwater and was set off, causing a dull thud, felt rather than heard, and hurling a stream of water and gravel about 60 ft. into the air, like a miniature geyser. As each operation is completed the borehole is filled in and safely plugged and the surrounding ground put in good order...

Dorothy O'Grady, a Sandown landlady, was famously sentenced to death for spying during the war. Whether she was or wasn't a Nazi spy is still a matter for conjecture (see volume 4, pages 88 and 90). In 1950 she was released from jail and returned to the Island to live, where she died in 1985, aged 87. Unfortunately, her given reasons for her wartime behaviour do little to dissuade the conspiracy theorists...

March 11th, 1950

SENTENCED TO DEATH "FOR FUN."
SANDOWN WOMAN'S NINE YEARS IN GAOL.

Mrs. Dorothy Pamela O'Grady, formerly a boarding-housekeeper, of Osborne Villa, the Broadway, Sandown, returned to the Island this week after her release from Aylesbury Gaol, where she has served nine years of a 14 year sentence on charges concerned with public security in war-time. Mrs. O'Grady was tried at Winchester in 1941 for various offences including some contravening the Treachery Act, 1940. She pleaded not guilty, but was sentenced to death. On appeal, the conviction under the capital charge was quashed, and a sentence of 14 years' penal servitude ... was passed. She now claims that the acts which led to her arrest and conviction were all part of an elaborate game of make-believe to attract the attention of the authorities so that she could enjoy the thrill of a reputation of a spy and of standing trial for her life. In an interview with a London Sunday newspaper, Mrs. O' Grady said that she had learned that because of her manoeuvres most of the defence plans for the Island had been changed. She wanted Islanders to know the truth about her, as it was better to be thought a fool than a traitor. Mrs. O'Grady, who has served the longest sentence in the history of Aylesbury Gaol, where most women with life sentences are released after five years, now plans to reopen her boarding house.

———————◆———————

Over a month had gone by but frogs and toads encased in various substances were still taking up space on the letters page...

March 18th, 1950

FROGS IN "SUSPENDED ANIMATION."

Sir, Many years ago a large piece of chalk, weighing half a ton, was broken up in Garstons chalk pit, Gatcombe. Embedded in the centre was a small frog, which made several slight movements after liberation. Nothing is known as to what happened to it afterwards. This can be verified by Mr. Charles Cheverton of Gatcombe Hill Farm Cottages who saw this amazing occurrence.
ARTHUR WILLIAMS. The Orchard, Gatcombe.

———————◆———————

The national housing shortage showed no signs of coming to an end. As part of the problem was believed to be a shortage of cement, the Island Chamber of Commerce investigated the possibilities of reopening the Medina cement mills at Stag Lane...

March 18th, 1950
A BRAKE ON BUILDING.

At the meeting of the IW Chamber of Commerce at Newport this week, officials of the Cement Marketing Board dashed the hopes that supplies of cement to the Island might be increased, and that the disused cement works on the River Medina, near Newport, might be brought back into production... it was stated that this was a hopeless proposition on economic grounds... On the question of the reopening of the Medina Works, Mr. Binnion (area manager of the Cement Marketing Co.) said he did not hold out the slightest hope. The works had been demolished and "cannibalised" to supply fitments which were required at other works and could not be obtained, due to present-day restrictions. When the Medina Works were open they probably produced 40,000 tons a year, and the Island consumed 10,000 tons... In 1949 the Island had received preferential treatment ... and had received 33% more cement than in 1938, against only 10% for the rest of the country... and had very few grounds for complaint. Mr. Binnion said it was well known that the main preoccupation of the country was with exports, and his firm had instructions that their product was to be exported after essential needs in this country had been met. He would emphasise the word "essential," and add that there was little hope of any increased supplies until output was increased, and that would not be for some considerable time.

------------◆------------

These were the days when potholes in the road were dealt with by simply throwing a handful of tarmac in the hole and patting it down with the back of a shovel. If only...

April 22nd, 1950
"A PLEA FOR BETTER ROADS."

Sir, Mr. R. A. Hudson, commenting on the state of the roads through Cowes, suggests that we suffer from a lack of equipment. Evidently he missed seeing the horse and cart with the two men in attendance! One man leads the horse, making appropriate sounds to stop and start it, the other takes a shovel full of tarmac from the cart, puts it in a pothole, pats it with the back of the shovel, and moves on to the next hole. Lack of equipment indeed! What does Mr. Hudson think we pay the highest rate in the Island for? He will be saying next that the street-cleaners use wheelbarrows.

JOHN STONES. 1 Arctic Road, Cowes.

------------◆------------

Many readers will remember the grocers Upward and Rich, situated in Pyle Street, Newport, who traded well into the 1970s. The company had been there since 1650 and were now celebrating their 300th birthday....

May 13th, 1950
OLDEST PROVISION MERCHANTS IN ENGLAND.
NEWPORT FIRM'S TERCENTENARY.

This week Messrs. Upward and Rich Ltd., wholesale grocers, provision merchants, and confectioners, of 50 Pyle Street, Newport, who enjoy the distinction of being the oldest firm of that character in England, celebrated the 300th anniversary of their foundation, and to mark the occasion, perhaps for the first time in its long history, the business was closed on an ordinary working day and the staff of 45 were the guests of the directors on the IW Grocers' Council excursion to Cadbury's Bournville factory near Birmingham.

Records show that the business was started on the same site in 1650, by whom it is not certain, but John Upward owned it in 1702, and members of the Upward family were actively associated with it until recently... The Rich family association still continues, as Miss Rich, of Carisbrooke, is one of the directors.

From the commencement to today the business has flourished and developed, the extensive premises now running through to South Street. In the last few years it has absorbed the wholesale sections of the former firms of Messrs. Jordan and Stanley (grocers and provision merchants) and the Central Confectionery Co. In 1935 the old front was replaced by a handsome erection in Tudor style, which is one of the features of the business architecture of Newport.

Up to about 30 years ago the establishment was more famed in Newport for its smell than its expanding business. Up to that time one of its activities was the melting down of fat to form tallow (originally for tallow candles), and the pungent smell was the cause of frequent complaints,* but to-day, in keeping with its high standing as a business house, the pleasant aroma of roasting coffee beans arises from the exact spot where the evil smelling fat was formerly treated.

The firm has rendered outstanding service to the Island people, particularly in supplying their needs during the shortages of the two world wars, and to-day it enjoys a reputation and measure of trade second to none in the South of England.

———————————————◆———————————————

Over the next twenty years the car was to completely take over Britain's roads, sweeping aside all other forms of transport. With hindsight, this report of the Whitsun holiday rush shows quite clearly that the process was already well underway ...

June 3rd, 1950

NO WHITSUN HOLIDAY RUSH
WEATHER PROPHETS RESPONSIBLE?

"A moderate Whitsun" is the main impression provided by a summing up of reports from "County Press" observers at Island holiday centres. Generally speaking, transport facilities proved more than adequate, beaches were only thinly populated, and caterers of all kinds had a comparatively slack time. For many Islanders it was largely a stay-at-home Whitsun, and this may be attributed to somewhat unfortunate weather forecasts broadcast by the BBC, which proved to err on the gloomy side. In fact, there was no rain the whole

---

* From Victorian times through to the 1920's, the company made several appearances in court as a result of their candle making activities, being charged on more than one occasion with making 'noisome smells.'

weekend, and Saturday and Sunday provided many hours of sunshine, although there was a stiff and rather chilly wind. Monday was dull until evening, when clear skies and brilliant sunshine proved to be the forerunner of two days of real summer weather. While it is appreciated that forecasts prepared on a regional basis cannot take account of local variations, there can be little doubt that many Islanders and intending day trippers from the mainland were discouraged from having a day out by the adverse forecast.

The freeing of petrol gave a considerable fillip to local traffic, which still, however, fell far short of a pre-war Whitsun, but many more visitors would have brought cars had the announcement been made in time for the necessary arrangements to be made.

DROP IN BOAT TRAFFIC.

The number of passengers travelling on the Ryde-Portsmouth boats showed a considerable decrease on last year's figures... The total figures for the four days were: incoming 29,771, outgoing 27,236, compared with 35,888 and 31,152 respectively last Whitsun...

RYDE AND EAST WIGHT.

Following the de-rationing of petrol, motorists were, of course, much more in evidence, and the northern side of the Canoe Lake Road in Ryde on Monday afternoon was a parking place for hundreds of vehicles. The local garages reported heavy business on Saturday when people were "filling up" for the weekend, and it was obvious that the traffic on the roads in this part of the Island was much heavier than for many years... The air rally at Bembridge Airport was a popular attraction for many on Sunday afternoon, and hundreds of motorists during their first holiday of freedom for over ten years made it their Mecca. An even larger number appeared to favour the top of Bembridge Down where many cars were parked.... The cricket match on the village green at St Helens was watched by hundreds of spectators including many motorists who parked around the village green.

SANDOWN-SHANKLIN.

Although the announcement on Friday of the de-rationing of petrol had some effect on the weekend holiday traffic, the full benefits of the announcement will not be felt in the district until later in the season... Returns at both Sandown and Shanklin railway stations were considerably lower than for the same holiday weekend last year. At Shanklin only 3100 tickets were collected, 1200 fewer than last year and at Shanklin a total of 3900 was a decrease of 900. At both stations there was a notable difference in the numbers of daytrippers on Monday. Motor traffic was certainly considerably greater than for some years and most noticeable was the increase in the number of motorcyclists... Two families already on holiday in the district are reported to have returned home to fetch their cars for use during the remainder of their stay. Local garages reported petrol sales as having increased by 100% during the weekend.

THE LADY OF THE CHEQUERS

Miss Bella Reynolds, the esteemed landlady of the The Chequers Inn, Rookley, with whom much sympathy is felt in the death, on Christmas Day, of her sister May, (Miss Elizabeth May Reynolds), who had assisted her in the management of the inn for 20 years. [*Cartoon by Tom Smitch.*]
(Jan 1, 1950)

Cowes Pier in its heyday. By the early 1950's it had fallen into disrepair and was finally demolished in 1960. (See page 76)   *[Author's collection]*

THE FIRST PRINCESS FLYING BOAT MOVED FROM HANGAR

On Tuesday the first Princess flying boat was moved from the hangar in which she was erected. It is hoped that she will be ready for her first trial flight in June next, provided there is no further delay in supplying the engines. (Nov 3, 1951)
(See page 48)

RURAL NOTES.

NEW PETS - GOLDEN HAMSTERS. – Mrs. T. Rickard, of the New Inn, Norton Green, Freshwater, has bred from a pair of Golden Hamsters. Hamsters are rodents, and those in this country are descended from the family of one adult female and her 12 young discovered in Syria in 1930... They have a large cheek pouch in which they carry food or bedding to their nest. The customers at the New Inn have taken a great interest in these pets, who are full of amusing tricks. One recently nibbled through the cord on which the cash box key was suspended, and was sneaking back to the nest when a piece of string dangling from its mouth led to the discovery that it had pouched the key.

A Rhode Island Red hen, owned by Mrs. G.H. Downer, of Corfe Farm, Shalfleet, has hatched out nine healthy chicks in a nest in the hollowed top of a tree stump about 12 feet above the ground.

An Alsatian owned by a Norton Green, Freshwater, resident is rearing a kitten along with her two eight-day-old puppies.

A Freshwater man's two-year-old pet jackdaw was drowned in a jug this week. The bird was very fond of a bath, and a large water jug was kept at hand to replenish the supply in his bowl. Jack often perched on the handle of the jug, and he must have overbalanced and fallen into it.

IRONFOUNDERS' BUSINESS CHANGES HANDS. – The business of Messrs. W. Hurst and Son, agricultural engineers and iron founders, established in 1859, has changed hands following the death of the late Mr. Arthur Hurst. It has been purchased by two local businessmen (Messrs. R.G.W. Reed and A. Henton, jun.), who will continue to run it under the same name as hitherto. The sale, embracing extensive freehold properties in Holyrood Street and Sea Street, was negotiated through Messrs. Henry J. Way and Son. (June 17)

AN "ISLAND" SKATE. – Much interest was caused at Mr. A.H. Cooper's fish shop in the High Street on Saturday by the exhibition of a skate, about the size of a desk blotter, which was almost exactly the same shape as the Isle of Wight. The outline was almost identical to the Island's coastline, and to make the resemblance more realistic Mr. Cooper decorated the skate with parsley to denote the forests and woods and exhibited name cards to mark the towns.

———————◆———————

The Island managed to support a moderate otter population in the 1950's. But only just...

July 1st, 1950

WHY KILL OTTERS?

Sir, I wish to protest against the recent killing of two otter cubs in the marsh at Freshwater Bay. One, it is reported, was killed by an employee of the Catchment Board engaged on drainage work and its corpse was left at the side of the road by the bridge in Blackbridge Lane. The other was killed by one of the gangs of youths who roam this neighbourhood accompanied by a pack of mongrel dogs. It would be interesting to know what motives inspired the employee of the Catchment Board to kill a young and defenceless animal which could do nobody any harm, and whether the board approve of their men destroying our varied forms of wildlife in the course of their duties.* With regard to the boys (one of whom was handling the body of the cub, making it perform lifelike movements for the edification of his friends), when I protested they laughed and jeered, saying that otters killed chickens. I keep chickens within 100 yards of the marsh and my only losses have been through the depredations of two-legged animals!† My neighbours have had the same experience. Nobody's property here is immune from the visitations of these youths and their dogs. They are quite pitiless, and day in and day out, Sundays included, in season and out, rabbits are mercilessly hunted, and this, coupled with the destruction of birds' nests and eggs in the spring, seems to be their main occupation. I have on several occasions given their names when found with their dogs on my property to the police, and I reported the ringleaders of the otter incident. Apparently, however, the police have little influence with them or their parents. To my mind the prevention of this constant persecution of the wildlife of the Island is largely a matter of education. When something as innocent and helpless as a baby otter makes no appeal to the protective instincts of young people, then the teaching methods and curriculum of the schools must be wrong.   S.H. CROW. Lt-Col. Easton Farm Cottage, Freshwater Bay.

◆

RURAL NOTES.

In "A Folklore Survey of the Isle of Wight," compiled by Mr. S. Jackson Coleman, it says that there are still people in the Island who can remember when raw cat's flesh was regarded as a certain cure for asthma and the swallowing of a spider to be a remedy for those suffering from ague. Reference is made to the times when the boys of Freshwater played "Zagger-Zagger-Zee," and other peculiarities of the Vectensian dialect, including those surrounding such personages as "Sal Hatch," "Lazy Larrance," and "Sam Hatchet." "Lazy Larrance" was a term applied to the very tired ones...

A SNAKE IN THE NEST. – When collecting eggs at Kingate's Dairy, Whitwell, on Friday week, Mrs. G.A. Millmore found a grass snake, a yard long, curled up under a broody hen which was sitting on three eggs.

VISITOR BITTEN BY ADDER. – Mrs. E. Dark, of Greenford, Middlesex was bitten by an adder on Tuesday afternoon. Accompanied by her friend Miss Joyce Hood, of Walthamstow, she went for a walk across The Warren, where they sat down for a rest. The adder, which was only about a foot in length, bit Mrs. Dark in the left forearm. Showing commendable presence of mind, she

---

* In a letter published the following week, the clerk of the Water Authority denied that any member of their staff had been responsible.

† A few weeks previously, a farmer at Newbridge had shot a pair of otters which had taken many of his chickens.

jumped to her feet and crushed the reptile to death with her shoe. She then applied a tourniquet above the wound and walked to Totland in search of a doctor. The doctor treated her with anti-viper venom serum, imported from Paris by a local chemist only a few days ago in readiness for such an emergency. When the tourniquet was removed Mrs. Dark suffered rather badly, and later in the evening became delirious. On Wednesday morning, however, Miss Hood stated that her friend was making a good recovery, although still in great pain.

AIR CRASH AT COWES – PILOT KILLED AND PLANE BURNT. – Shortly after taking off from Cowes Airport on Tuesday afternoon, a Miles Magister aircraft crashed, and the pilot, Mr. Anthony Peter Corke (22), of Surrey was killed. Mr. Corke who had arrived at the airfield in the plane just after 2.30 p.m. took off again at about 3.35 p.m. but he had only gone about a quarter of a mile when his machine crashed in a Cockleton Farm field, at the rear of Kingsmead, Place Road...It immediately burst into flames and although several people rushed to render assistance they were unable to approach near enough to extricate the pilot, as the plane was burning so fiercely... By about 3.55p.m. the plane had been almost destroyed... The Inquest was held on Monday in the Birmingham Road Methodist Church and found that the cause of the accident was a stall through a climbing turn, carried out at a very low altitude. (July 22)

———————◆———————

Despite the war being over for five years, newsprint shortages not only continued but actually grew worse. The County Press, no great friend of the 'Socialist' Government, felt hard done by and got things off their chest in an editorial...

July 22nd, 1950

MORE BAD PLANNING

On July 2nd the size of newspapers was cut to six pages for dailies and an average of nine pages for weeklies. That was a bad enough injustice on the people, placing them in the unenviable position of having the smallest newspapers of the world, but worse is likely to follow. It was announced this week that the newsprint situation had become so serious that unless the Government take action to increase supplies, daily newspapers will be cut to four pages and weeklies to eight pages or less. If that happens it will mean that the newspapers of this country will be back to wartime size, while those of other countries, including Germany, will be considerably larger... With an average of nine pages the "County Press" has found it increasingly difficult to give adequate publicity to Island events and cater fully for advertisers. Almost every week we have to omit a considerable number of advertisements, and news has often had to be curtailed to a degree which has dissatisfied both the staff of this paper and various organisations who deserve full publicity... We cannot go into details here as to the cause of the newsprint shortage, but it is due in part to the bad planning of the Government... Had the majority of Britain's newspapers been favourable to them politically their appreciation might have been greater, but they have been unfair in their dealings with the newspapers in the matter of newsprint, and we hope that the reading public will show their resentment...

THE WEEK'S NEWS.

PORPOISES IN THE MEDINA. – Mrs. Coghlan, of East Medina Mill Cottage, informs us that just before 7 p.m. on Wednesday she saw a school of eight or nine porpoises going up the River Medina. Watching them through binoculars it was evident that they were chasing fish, probably mackerel, as she could occasionally see a fish in the disturbed water as the porpoises broke the surface. The porpoises went up to beyond Dodnor, before returning about three quarters of an hour later. Although porpoises are often seen in the summer in the Medina and Wootton Creek, they usually appear singly or in pairs. So large a school in inland waters is unusual.

An Island local paper[*] this week stated "The heaviest rainfall was on August 2nd, when 95 inches was recorded." It only seemed like that, of course.

Four hundred people die each week in Britain from tuberculosis, while waiting lists for treatment have risen to 11,000.

CALBOURNE - BEES HOLD UP CHURCH REPAIR. – Mr. A. Downer found himself confronted with an unusual problem when commissioned to carry out repair work on the east roof of the Parish Church. For at least a century the space between the rafters and tiles has been the home of many colonies of bees, which fiercely resent any intrusion. A Northwood bee-keeping expert was called in, and he extracted a large quantity of honey before using cyanide to destroy the insects. After two attempts there were still many survivors, and when Mr. Downer inspected the roof on Tuesday morning the bees were everywhere. He placed cyanide powder under the tiles, but later in the day the roof was still alive with bees. The cyanide treatment will be continued, but it will spoil the large store of honey still in the roof.

A TRAPPED BUZZARD. – Sir, with mixed feelings of interest and disgust I read the account of the capture of a common buzzard at Porchfield in a vermin trap. These abominable instruments of torture should be abolished, and if the use of them is not illegal then it is high time something was done to stop this wanton cruelty and destruction of our wildlife, even so-called vermin... That this rare visitor to the Island should meet with such a fate is most regrettable. I should appreciate the printing of this letter, which I'm sure will be welcomed by all bird and nature lovers. P. SLEIGHTSHOLME. Park Lodge, Woodside, Wootton.

———————————◆———————————

The economy was struggling and for the moment austerity ruled the day. Ironically, at the same time, the demand from London dealers for expensive Newtown oysters was insatiable. "If we could supply three times the quantity," said the manager of the Newtown oyster fisheries, "it still would not be enough"...

[*] In 1950 the County Press still had competition from the Isle of Wight Times and the Isle of Wight Chronicle.

September 9th, 1950.
NEWTOWN OYSTERS IN GREAT DEMAND.

If conditions are favourable next week the Newtown oyster beds will start to yield a rich harvest which will eventually find its way to the tables of gourmets throughout the country. The Newtown oyster fishery is possibly the Island's oldest industry. Thanks to the enterprise of Sir John Simeon, Bt., the Swainston Estate has put down nearly a million spats (two-year-old oysters) imported from Brittany since 1945 to replace the now almost extinct local oyster. The Simeon family's interest in the fisheries is of long standing. In the 1870s they were being run by a Mr. T. Abrook, whose father took the beds on a 999 year lease from the Swainston Estate. Mr. Abrook was persuaded to forego the lease, and the Simeon family formed a company to develop the fisheries... In 1877 it was estimated that there were between five and six million oysters in the Newtown and Medina Rivers.

Breeding Beds Wiped out.

Tragedy overtook the enterprise in 1880, when a severe frost, lasting some six weeks, exterminated the stock in the breeding beds. In those beds, which are no longer in use, it was necessary to change the water every 48 hours, as it is estimated that an oyster pumps 10 gallons of water daily through its valves. Although an oyster can live up to 10 days out of water, it cannot stand extremes of temperature and frost is invariably fatal to exposed oysters... Sometime later the oyster beds were taken over by Messrs. Paskin Brothers of Cowes, but once again disaster overtook the fishery when oil pollution from the Solent during the First World War, was blamed for the loss of practically the whole stock. The Cowes firm continued to operate on a small scale until midway through the last war, when owing to family bereavement, the lease was returned to the Swainston Estate.

Mr. J. A. Chalmers, of Ashen Grove, Calbourne, manager of the Swainston Estate is in charge of the present operations... In an interview this week with a "County Press" reporter, Mr. Chalmers spoke with pride of the fact that the Newtown oysters had been given a 100% purity certificate by the public analyst. He pointed out that the oysters were particularly fine because no sewage entered the river, and there was always a good flow of fresh water, and the oysters were covered to a depth of six inches even at the lowest spring tide.

Cannot Meet the Demand.

He considered it a waste of time and money to return to the old methods of breeding, preferring the present system of buying spat, about the size of a five shilling piece, and allowing it to mature for two years, when it measures between three and three and a half inches in diameter. The demand for Newtown oysters was so great that London dealers were anxious to take all they could supply. "If we could supply three times the quantity," he said, "it still would not be enough." Mr. Chalmers said... at present there were three acres of beds in use in Clamerkin Lake, but these could be extended by using the Ningwood Lake where the gravel bottom was ideal for the purpose... "But it would be no use putting them down in the Medina today," he added, "because of the amount of pollution. They would be dead within an hour."

The present-day method of dredging, which could raise 10,000 in a day, was

THE FIRST EASTER VISITOR

"Smarten up, mates! We've got a passenger!"

by means of two drags hauled by a motor boat... Of the total haul, possibly 10% would be dead - a highly satisfactory result when compared with the figures of a few years ago when the loss was as high as 70%... As well as being an expert in their cultivation, Mr. Chalmers is a connoisseur of the finished product. His advice is to cook them in their own juice in half of the shell, or to stew them in butter - "about a dozen makes a nice supper!"

THE WEEK'S NEWS.

BORSTAL ESCAPES - HOME SECRETARY'S APOLOGY. – In the nine days previous to Wednesday 16 Borstal boys from the Camp Hill Institution absconded, but all are now safely back.... On Friday week six boys had escaped in four days. On Sunday five more were missed at roll call. One was re-taken at Merstone during Monday night and the remaining four were recaptured on Tuesday morning, after a chase across Godshill Park... There have been 67 escapes from the institution this year... In the House of Commons on Thursday Sir Peter Macdonald MP said that the large number of escapes were causing great alarm. The Home Secretary expressed his regret to the inhabitants of the Island. (October 21)

SUGGESTED REMOVAL OF VICTORIA MONUMENT. – The chief subject before the council on Wednesday was the suggestion that in connection with the proposal to lay out the Church Litten Burial Ground as a garden of rest, as a Festival of Britain Year commemoration, the Victoria Monument in St James's Square should be removed to some part of the proposed garden... Mr. S. Wendes ... said that without the memorial to lend dignity, St James's Square would look poor and commercialised... Ald Mrs. E.R. Chandler said ... it had been a most dignified square, but no one could say it fitted that description today. The thought of the traffic sign recently installed in front of the memorial left her quite speechless...(November 18)

NEWTOWN OYSTERS - PROMISE OF A VERY GOOD SEASON. – The oyster season in the fisheries of the Swainston Estate has now commenced, and Mr. Chalmers, manager, stated this week that there were indications that the season would be a very good one... Referring to the troubles being experienced at Falmouth, where the oyster fisheries are being spoiled by a boring insect, Mr. Chalmers said that the Newtown beds were remarkably free of all things which preyed on oysters.[*]

COWES - VICTORIA PIER TO BE RESTORED. – After a lengthy discussion which showed that opinion was very divided, the Cowes Council decided by nine votes to seven that the Victoria Pier should be restored at a cost, including a pavilion, of nearly £18,000. A petition against the restoration had so far been signed by nearly 2000 ratepayers and 3000 workers in the Cowes area.

---

[*] In January 2010 the County Press reported a "catastrophic decline" in Newtown oyster numbers and that none of the eight-boat oyster fleet had put to sea since the beginning of the season in November the previous year. Fishermen blamed the tingle - a snail-like creature which bores into the oyster to suck out the contents.

Eggs had long since ceased to come from small flocks of hens scratching around in picturesque farmyards. Beginning in the 1930's, the industrialisation of egg production had been raised to a fine art by the beginning of the 1950's. So many were now being produced on the Island from commercially reared birds that it was granted its own egg packing station...

October 28th, 1950

HANDLING ISLAND EGG PRODUCTION
NEW TESTING AND GRADING STATION AT NEWPORT.

Housewives receiving eggs with the number "105" stamped on them will know that they are from local poultry farms, and have passed through Messrs. Pittis and Way's new packing station in South Street, Newport. The station has a staff of 15 and is at present handling between 250 and 300 cases of eggs a week, each case containing 30 dozen. These are mainly pullets' eggs.

EXAMINATION AND WEIGHING

The receiving and despatching of cases of eggs is made by conveyors, smooth-running rollers. Defects in the eggs are discovered by the "candling" process, when they are examined under points of light in a dark compartment. The women who do this job manipulate two eggs in each hand in a way which would prove disastrous if tried by the uninitiated. One egg is held in the palm of each hand while two others are inspected, each being turned by the thumb and first two fingers. Adroit handling then transfers the inspected eggs to the palms of the hands, and the uninspected between the fingers. Breakages are almost unknown. The eggs, apart from the defective ones, are then placed on a moving belt and deposited individually into each of 12 small cups... and a stamping device marks the eggs "MF105"... Much has been heard of eggs being weeks old when placed on sale, but Mr. R. Gay (manager) assured our reporter that the station can deal with any number of eggs sent in within two days.

————————◆————————

Just when the Island's tourist trade was beginning to recover from the war it was stopped in its tracks by an outbreak of polio. The outbreak, which led to five deaths, received prolonged and excited coverage in the national dailies, the Island being branded "Polio Isle." Doctor Wallace, Officer of Health for the Island commented "Although the number of cases did not justify the use of the word 'epidemic' the notice which was taken of the disease by the Press ... was responsible for a campaign which was ruinous to the tourist season." The County Press used the word "polio" as little as possible in its reports, ironically preferring the strictly correct but arguably more alarming synonym 'infantile paralysis'...

November 11th, 1950

FINAL RECKONING ON INFANTILE PARALYSIS.
"WE HAVE BEEN LUCKY."

Mr. L. H. Baines, Clerk of the County Council reported on the recent all-Island conference on poliomyelitis where it was revealed that in the recent epidemic there were 50 paralytic and 38 non-paralytic cases affecting residents, and in addition 16 visitors caught the disease. There had been five deaths, three in the Island, and two of visitors on their return to the mainland.

The Clerk said that the conference were agreed that the medical staff had done all that was right and proper in their treatment of the outbreak, and in the statements which were made. He would not comment on the ultimate form in which they appeared in print. It was agreed that it would be better for the Press to obtain authoritative information at one central point and that in future there should be Press conferences at which a written statement would be handed out, and the Press would be able to ask supplementary questions... It had to be remembered that if the Press could not obtain the information they wanted when they asked for it, then they would go to other sources which might not be so trustworthy. The result was likely to be far more damaging than if immediate and accurate information were available...

———————————◆———————————

Since the nationalisation of the railways in 1948 the Government had carefully looked at the profitability or otherwise of each separate line. On the Island the first rumours of line closures began to circulate...

December 9th, 1950

ISLAND RAILWAYS.
ALD THOMPSON AND A CLOSING RUMOUR.

Ald. W. Thompson stated that he had heard on good authority that officials of British Railways had been in the Island to consider the closing down of the lines from Newport to Sandown and Merstone to Ventnor West.

He said that there was a rumour going around that British Railways were contemplating closing the main line from Sandown to Newport. One could easily visualise the effect of such a drastic action. It was not difficult to visualise the great confusion there would be during the summer months if the railway authorities relied only on buses to convey the visitors. An official of British Railways at Waterloo informed the "County Press" that the whole of the Island's railways were coming under review in connection with the national policy of closing down unremunerative lines, but that consideration was still in the preliminary stage.

1951.

In 1950 the British Wool Marketing Board, still in existence today, was established and run by Britain's farmers with the aim of achieving the best possible price for wool. Within a year the Island's wool fair was no more...

January 6th, 1951

NO MORE ISLAND WOOL FAIRS.
CLIP TO BE SOLD AT CHICHESTER.

At the monthly meeting of the Island branch of the NFU it was announced that the Island Wool Fairs, which have been a valued institution in local agricultural life for over 70 years, would no longer be held. Mr. S.A. Watson reported that the last wool fair had been held in the Island. The first wool fair was held in 1878. From 1940 onwards the wool had been collected jointly by the two local firms of auctioneers (Sir Francis Pittis and Son and Messrs. Henry J Way and Son Ltd), appraised by the Wool Control, and taken over on Government account. The auctioneers had been paid one half-penny per pound, out of which they were required to pay the whole of the expenses, including labour, tolls, etc. The result had been the income did not meet expenditure and each firm had had to contribute out of their own pockets to meet the deficiency. During the war they were prepared to do this to help the country, but in times of peace they did not consider themselves called upon to do so.... The Wool Control, loathe to lose the knowledge, organisation, and ability of the local auctioneers, had suggested that the wool clip for 1951 be taken to Chichester, whither the bulk has, in recent years, been sent. The auctioneers would, prior to loading on Newport Quay, lot and weigh each bail. They would be in attendance at Chichester at the appraisal and in due course pay out each producer as they had done in the past. The auctioneers had agreed to this. The wool would, therefore, not be offered for sale in the Island...

RURAL NOTES.

BEATING THE BLACK-OUT. – Now that Government regulations have prohibited the use of electricity for shop window lighting, the High Street and other shopping centres have resumed that depressing blacked-out look. But there will be one bright spot - the windows of Messrs. Sherratt and Son. Mr. Sherratt is engaged at the moment in the completion of a wind generator. The wind-driven wheel will be geared to a generator and the current produced is hoped to be enough to light all the shop windows.

MEAT RATION AGAIN REDUCED. – The Minister of Food announced in the House of Commons yesterday morning that the fresh meat ration will be reduced from 10d. to 8d. worth from Sunday February 4th.

Mr. A.T. Sheath, of 36 College Road, Newport, writes: "You may be interested to hear of the piece of wood I have in my possession which has a unique though rather morbid history. It is one of the original black shutters used by the late firm of Edwin Way and Co. Ltd., corn merchants of Newport. It bears a list of 111 persons for whose funerals it was displayed. Heading the list is HRH Prince Henry of Battenberg, and other names include well-known local business and professional figures... Two rather amusing entries are 'Our Cat' and 'Our Blackbird,' but whether the board was put up for their funerals I cannot say."

Rabbits on the Island, as elsewhere, have increased to such an extent that they have become "Public Enemy No 1." The NFU is to stage a very interesting demonstration on Forestry Commission land at Brighstone on Wednesday at 2 p.m. The correct method of snaring, trapping, and long netting will be demonstrated and a bulldozer will show how to push out a troublesome warren, and the correct technique of gassing will be shown.

A national coal shortage had led to economies in its use throughout the country. One immediate target was the number of unprofitable railway lines, some of which were consuming large amounts of coal for little or no return. On the Island the Brading to Bembridge railway line was felt to fall into this category and in a surprise move the line was closed by the Railway Executive. Although it was a temporary measure, it was suggested by some that perhaps the Executive were testing the water for a permanent closure in the near future ...

February 10th, 1951

ISLAND RAILWAY ECONOMY CUTS.
BEMBRIDGE BRANCH TO CLOSE.

As the Island's contribution to the railway fuel economy cuts which are being made throughout the country, it has been announced that the Bembridge branch line will be closed from Sunday until further notice, and that cuts have been made in other services. The Merstone-Ventnor West line bears the brunt of the remaining economies with the 9.12 a.m., 11.27 a.m., 1.25 p.m., 6.27 p.m., and 7.27 p.m. cancelled on weekdays...

In a previous issue, a correspondent to the letters column had asked if the words of any Isle of Wight songs had been recorded for posterity and had enquired about Isle of Wight cheese and mutton...

February 17th, 1951

"ISLAND SONGS, CHEESE AND PIES."

I was much interested in your correspondent's letter in the last issue especially as my recollections carry me back to the 1870s... I remember a short play in the Isle of Wight dialect which used to be performed by a number of young men calling themselves "Christmas Boys," who were dressed in various fancy garb and visited the large private houses and hotels to give their performance during the Christmas season. Regarding cheese, butter was made on most of the farms in those days, and skimmed milk was utilised for the manufacture of cheese, which had quite an agreeable taste though apt to go hard after a time... Another Island speciality was the doughnut which was highly appreciated. It was well cooked and had a small nest of currants in the centre. The present article bearing that name is generally insipid and uninteresting, with a coating of sugar and a pinch of jam in the centre - a travesty of the real thing...

ARTHUR HARVEY. Sunnymead, Freshwater Bay.

Your lady correspondent enquires about real Isle of Wight songs. I know of none, but about 40 years ago an octogenarian friend of mine, in broad Isle of Wight dialect, quoted me: "Old Ben Chessel built a vessel, Tommy Last he made the mast, Peter Hayles he sowed the sails, Billy Pope spliced the rope, And Henry Warder took her up harbour." This refers to a Yarmouth vessel. Henry Warder was, in the 1870s, our harbourmaster here...I have mislaid a poem I used to have about Isle of Wight cheese, which was always of a very hard variety. The verses were about a woman who stored the cheeses he had made in an oak chest. "The rats gnawed through the chest with ease, but they could not bite the cheese!"

A.G. COLE. Landguard. Yarmouth.

Your correspondent, Margaret Melhuish, wants to know where she can get Isle of Wight mutton pies. Alas they are no more, but I can remember the joke about the noted pie shop in Newport, where a cat was never known to pass; also the skimmed milk cheese we used to cut with hatchets. Isle Of Wight sauce was made by Mrs. Cheverton, of The Bedford, The Mall, and Newport doughnuts at a half-penny each would make you bilious. Those were the days! If one had a golden sovereign in those days one wouldn't call the King his uncle. But all things good and bad come to an end. Good porter could be had for three halfpence a pint, and if one had twopence to lift the latch "he was well away."

ARTHUR WILLIAMS. Gatcombe.

TOWN AND COUNTY NOTES

DEATH OF ISLAND'S PIONEER LADY MOTORIST. – Mrs Margaret Harrison, widow of Mr. George Harrison, JP, died at Thornton, near Ryde, on Wednesday, aged 88. She was the first lady motorist in the Island, having owned a Cadillac, which bore the registration number DL 2. She drove the vehicle regularly until during the First World War, when she disposed of it, although she still retained the number plates.

NEW LIGHT INDUSTRY AT COWES. – Messrs. Readers of Somerton Aerodrome, Cowes, makers of lampshades, have recently extended their activities to include household utensils of wire construction. At present they are fulfilling a £15,000 trial order placed by a large chain store for potato and vegetable cutters, skewers, eggbeaters, extending toasting forks, and fireguards. These articles, labelled "A Reader Product." will be on sale in some 50 stores, and if the demand reaches expectations a further order about 10 times the size of the present one is to be given.

The abrupt closure of the Brading to Bembridge railway line had generated protests from all quarters but when Brading Parish Council voiced their opposition they were forced to concede that only 60 people a day used the service and that their needs could, in fact, be satisfied by only four or five trains a day. Damned with faint praise, the closure of the line moved a little closer ...

February 17th, 1951

BRADING-BEMBRIDGE RAILWAY CLOSING.
PARISH COUNCIL'S PROTEST.

At a special meeting of the Brading Parish Council on Tuesday to consider the closing of the Brading-Bembridge railway line it was decided to send a strong letter of protest to British Railways requesting that a modified service should be run. The council suggested that two trains before 9 a.m. and three trains after 4 p.m. would cater for quite 90% of the public concerned. No request was made for the opening of the Sunday service... Our Bembridge correspondent writes: The decision to suspend until further notice the train services on the Brading-Bembridge line from Sunday last has met with complaints from all sides. The decision has caused a great deal of inconvenience and a certain amount of hardship, particularly in view of the fact that normally more trains run over this route daily than on any other part of the Island system. The last train over the route left Bembridge Station at 9.57 on Saturday night. During the week the only arrival at Bembridge has been an engine and truck of coal for local consumption. Since the weekend Bembridge and St Helens stations have been locked up and deserted. Even the taxi rank outside Bembridge Station has been discarded and an uncanny silence seems to hang over the terminus. At Bembridge, where trains have been running regularly since 1877, two railway coaches remain idly by the platform. It is estimated that about 60 work people and children use the services daily...

———————————————◆———————————————

The whitewashed remains of St Helens Old Church on the Duver act as a sea mark today and the former churchyard, long gone to grass, is now home to deckchairs and holidaymakers in high summer. As late as 1951, its original purpose was occasionally being revealed by tidal action...

March 3rd, 1951
ST HELEN'S OLD CHURCH ENDANGERED
HUMAN REMAINS UNEARTHED BY COAST EROSION.
A serious threat to the safety of St Helens Old Church tower, which stands almost on the foreshore below Nodes Battery, has arisen as a result of recent rough seas making a breach in the sea wall. For some time there has been a small hole, but during the last fortnight this has been considerably enlarged, and the sea has washed out a cavity behind it measuring about 30 feet by 12 feet, and about 12 feet deep. The land affected is just to the north of the tower, and that it formed part of the churchyard is proved by the fact that since the latest erosion, parts of human skeletons have been washed out onto the shore, and human remains can be seen about 2 feet below the surface of the ground. The presence of the remains was first noticed by children playing in the vicinity last week, who picked up a skull. On Wednesday a resident discovered a femur and foot and ankle bones. Little history of the old church is known, beyond the fact that owing to the inroads of the sea it gradually became untenable and the new Parish Church was built in the 18th century. Some of the remains in the old churchyard were taken up and reinterred in the present churchyard, but the old burial ground, although much grown over, is still acknowledged to be consecrated ground, and campers are prohibited from using it...

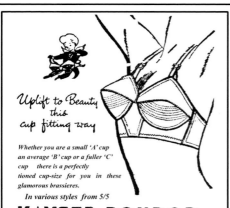

THE WEEK'S NEWS.

BRADING COTTAGES PRESERVED. – At a meeting of the County Planning Committee yesterday a recommendation for an order to be made restricting the demolition, alteration, or extension of 1 and 2 The Old Cottages, Wall Street, Brading, was adopted. The chairman said that this was the first case of preserving buildings of historical or architectural interest with which the committee had had to deal. The cottages, built in 1500, had been examined by the panel of architects, who have decided they were well worth preserving as they represented one of the few examples of timber-framed building remaining in the Island. The Order would not alter the financial position of the owner. (March 10)

According to an article in the "Daily Express" on Tuesday, which quoted a government spokesman, the Princess flying boats at present under construction by Messrs. Saunders-Roe at East Cowes will never earn a penny in fares. Designed originally for the South American run, and estimated to cost some £3 million, their cost is now calculated to be in the region of £9 million, and the Government has decided to give them, on completion, to the RAF. (March 10)

Advertisement. RESIDENT CARETAKERS – ASHEY SMALLPOX HOSPITAL. Applications are invited from married couples (no children) for the Caretakership of the Smallpox Hospital, near Ryde, Isle of Wight. Payment at the rate of £50 per annum for the joint appointment, with free accommodation. Full particulars together with form of application will be supplied on request to the undersigned. H. FORSHAW. Chief Administrative Officer. (March 10)

A RAT'S DOUBLE ESCAPE. – A daylight battle between a large rat and a barn owl was witnessed in the main road at Freshwater Bay during the week-end. As the rat crossed the road the owl swooped and attempted to carry it off, but the rat showed fight and the bird was forced to drop back to earth to continue the struggle. At this stage the contestants were interrupted by the arrival of a man and a dog, and the owl, releasing its grip, fluttered to a nearby fence to watch developments. Trapped in a corner formed by two walls, the rat, bleeding profusely, turned on the dog, which backed away in fear. Disgusted at the lack of spirit shown by his dog the owner pushed it out of the way, allowing the rat to escape.

———————————◆———————————

The price of petrol doubled between 1950 and 1955 and allowing for inflation, petrol was more expensive in real terms then than it is today. A Ryde baker took action...

March 17, 1951

RYDE BAKER REVERTS TO HORSE POWER
MOTOR RUNNING COSTS TOO HIGH.

The rising costs in the upkeep of motor vans has caused a Ryde bakery firm, Messrs. J.P. Clarke Ltd., to revert partially to horse traffic for deliveries within the borough. Two of four motor vans are being replaced by carts with old-style coachwork. If, as Mr. Raymond Clarke, a director anticipates, the price of petrol is further increased next month, two more carts will be obtained. He estimates that the cost of delivery will be halved. The decision to bring back the horse-drawn vehicle was made as a result of the doubling of costs in the last few months. Mr. Clarke told a "County Press" reporter that the margin of profit on bread allowed to bakers was so low that, in view of the fantastic cost of running motor vehicles, he felt sure that his firm's example would be followed by other bakers. It is interesting to note that deliveries have been completed an hour quicker than by the motor vans.

For a brief period it seemed the Isle of Wight might become part of the route of a national car rally...

April 7, 1951

ISLAND CAR RALLY.
ENCOURAGING SUCCESS OF FIRST VENTURE.
EXCITING TESTS AT SANDOWN AND VENTNOR.

Today the concluding events in connection with the first car rally ever to be held with the Isle of Wight as its objective take place at Cowes and Ryde. The rally attracted 86 competitors from all parts of the country and 74 completed the course and the tests for a challenge trophy presented by the "Daily Telegraph." The winner was Mr. E.S. Ridley of Bury St Edmunds, driving an MG T.C., who was taking part in a rally for the first time. The rally itself concluded at Sandown on Thursday, but hill climbing tests in association with it were held at Ventnor yesterday. As a result of the rally the Island has received an extremely large measure of national publicity through the Press, radio, and cinema. The event was sponsored by the "Daily Telegraph," which in particular among the London newspapers has devoted a large amount of space to the rally... The first competitors to arrive in the Island disembarked from the 9 a.m. passenger steamer at Cowes Pontoon and covered over 40 miles before reaching Sandown... Large numbers watched the cars pass along the route, notably at Ventnor, which the first arrivals reached by 10.30 a.m... Despite heavy rain, there was a fairly large attendance of spectators to watch the trial runs in the hill climb at the Cascade, Ventnor, yesterday morning, when times varying from 45 seconds to 60 seconds were recorded. The cars started from opposite Alma Road on the Esplanade and after taking the well-known triple bends with a one-in-four gradient, finished on a line outside Channel View Hotel. Some of the larger cars took the hill very carefully, but the sports models went up at fairly high speeds. The wet surface caused a number of competitors to skid perilously near the stone walls and protecting bales of straw, but there were no incidents.

Four Royal Navy submarines have been lost since the end of the war. The worst loss of life occurred when HMS Affray was lost, supposedly somewhere off the Isle of Wight...

April 21, 1951.
SUBMARINE LOST OFF THE ISLAND.
SEARCH CONTINUES. NO HOPE OF SURVIVORS.

One of the worst peacetime submarine disasters ever known, involving the loss of 75 men on board, occurred in the Channel some 30 miles south of the Needles this week. HMS Affray, one of the Navy's latest ocean-going submarines, failed to make the pre-arranged surfacing signal after a war patrol exercise, in the course of which she was due to dive off the Island at 9.15 p.m. on Monday and surface near Start Point between 8 a.m. and 9 a.m. on Tuesday. The Affray was reported missing by the Admiralty at about midday on Tuesday, and the codeword "Subsmiss," which puts search and rescue operations into immediate effect, had been sent to all Naval stations immediately the expected signal failed to come through... High hopes were entertained on Wednesday, when the Admiralty announced that at 1.45 a.m. the submarine Sea Devil had made contact with the Affray by supersonic telegraphy, which indicated that someone was alive in the control room of the sunken submarine. The position was given as about 30 miles south west of St Catherine's Point, and at dawn explosive sound signals were made over the spot where the submarine was believed to be lying. This would tell the men that ships were waiting to pick them up and that they could make use of their escape apparatus, but no survivors came to the surface. It became clear from later messages that the exact position of the Affray was still not known. A later Admiralty statement spoke of "much diminished hope." Throughout Thursday hopes dwindled following the Admiralty announcement that chances of any success were small. There were no further developments during the day and that evening the Admiralty issued the gravest statement of all, "There is now no reasonable hope of the rescue of survivors."... Naval experts have been puzzled by the absence of any clues as to the whereabouts of the submarine. She was fitted with a marker buoy which could be released from inside the hull, and other means which could be used were the discharge of smoke candles, and pumping out fuel oil... Her complement of 75 officers and men included 25 who were on a training course.*

RURAL NOTES

Lovers of the countryside will be interested to note the new and distinctive colouring of the signposts indicating footpath and bridle roads. The white lettering on a green background is the idea of the Ministry of Transport, and the new signs will make their appearance gradually as the old ones fall due for replacement or repainting. (April 21)

---

* After two months of searching, the Affray was discovered not off the Isle of Wight but close to Alderney in the Channel Isles. All hatches and torpedo ports were closed, the only damage being the 'snorter' mast which had been sheared off, possibly as the submarine crash-landed. The sinking is still unexplained. No attempt was made to recover the bodies and the wreck of the submarine was later declared a war grave.

Coast artillery practice with six-inch and three-pounder guns will be carried out at Nodes Battery, St Helens, on May 5th and 6th, between 7 a.m. and 6 p.m.

YARMOUTH - DUCK AHOY! – The harbourmaster (Mr. W.W. Doe) one day this week handled a craft entirely outside the range of any previous experience. While walking along the river bank during an exceptionally high tide, he saw what appeared to be a bundle of dried rushes being carried slowly upstream. As it came closer he saw that it was the nest of a wild duck, with the bird still sitting. The nest grounded close by, and the duck remained undisturbed as Mr. Doe made it secure and built a screen of rushes and grass to hide it from the view of passers-by. On visiting the nest Mr. Doe found the bird had tranquilly accepted her new quarters, and she hatched out her brood on Thursday.

SOMERTON AIRWAYS LTD IN VOLUNTARY LIQUIDATION. – The "London Gazette" announces that at an extraordinary general meeting of Somerton Airways (Cowes), Ltd., held on April 28, the following resolution was passed: "That the company be wound up voluntarily and that Mr. John Henry Ace, of 39 Osborne Court, Cowes, is hereby appointed liquidator for the purposes of such winding up. (May 12)

AN ENTERPRISING TRADER. – Mr. W. G. Sherratt, radio dealer, of High Street, claims to be the first tradesmen in the South of England to have radio-telephone contact between his shop and his repair and delivery vans. The van drivers and mechanics, if out in the district, can be given fresh instructions by radio-telephone in a matter of seconds and so extra journeys can be avoided. The equipment has other uses and Mr. Sherratt has offered it to the police, fire, and medical authorities in the event of an emergency.

<hr />

THE WEEK'S NEWS

MERSTONE - VENTNOR LINE CLOSING? – British Railways told the Council that because of the small volume of traffic handled on the line they were considering the withdrawal of passenger and freight services... Figures supplied by British Railways revealed that winter trains averaged eight passengers per train, and summer trains 20. About three wagons of coal a week were dealt with at Ventnor West and 134 wagons of sugar beet were loaded at stations on the branch line during the season. ..

CAR RALLY DEFICIT OUTWEIGHED BY PUBLICITY VALUE. – The first annual meeting of the I.W. Automobile Rally and Racing Association discussed the financial and publicity aspects of the recent Island car rally. It was unanimously felt that, although the event had incurred a deficit, the general gain in prestige and publicity for the Island far outweighed the loss. The Chairman ... thanked the "Daily Telegraph," who had sponsored the rally. The deficit, about £300, was small in proportion to the size of the project...

TOTLAND BAY PIER RESTORED AFTER 20 YEARS - FIRST PLEASURE STEAMER'S VISIT. – A former attraction as a holiday resort was restored to Totland Bay on Sunday when the pier was reopened and the first pleasure steamer to call for 20 years arrived from Bournemouth. She was the Red Funnel Company's P.S. Lorna Doone and brought nearly 300 visitors who enjoyed just over an hour ashore... Although the official opening of the pier will not take place until next year, when the superstructure is complete, the news of the Lorna Doone's arrival attracted large crowds of spectators to the beach, the Turf Walk, and the pier... Eventually it is hoped to introduce a regular service between Totland Bay and Bournemouth. (June 23)

At Freshwater bees have attacked and stung a penned-up cockerel to death.

———————————◆———————————

The cleanliness, or otherwise, of Britain's rivers was regulated by the Pollution of Rivers Act of 1876, an Act introduced at the height of Britain's industrial activity. Anxious not to trouble the country's manufacturers any more than was necessary, the act had carefully avoided any meaningful restraint on them. Indeed, so weak was the Act that for the last 75 years factories had been free to pump vast amounts of industrial waste into the river systems of Britain quite legally and it was a practice still freely indulged in on the Island. The much tougher Pollution of Rivers Act of 1951 was just a few months away. It would be a timely arrival...

June 23, 1951.

THE POLLUTION OF TIDAL WATERS
RIVER BOARD UNABLE TO TAKE ACTION.

Cases of pollution of tidal waters in the Island were referred to at the meeting of the River Board at County Hall, Newport. It was stated that until the new anti-pollution measures became law and defined the powers of river boards, no action could be taken. Mr. B.V. Harris referred to effluent from Newport Gasworks entering the River Medina. He said that on May 23rd, just before high water, there was a swirling mass of red and blue effluent on the water. When the tide was out fish were found dead on the mud banks. He had informed the Southern Sea Fisheries Board who investigated the matter. They were hoping to have dead fish sent for analysis but, in the meantime, asked if the board could take any action. Mr. J.B. Rayment said that he visited the Newport Town Quay on the previous day at low water, and he had seen tar seeping out of the quay walls. – The Chairman said that he was afraid the board could take no action until their position had been clarified by legislation being prepared by Parliament. – Sir John Thornycroft recalled that in the Yar it was a regular thing when the gasworks cleaned their tanks, for all the fish in the river to be killed. Their complaints never got them anywhere, because the chairman of the River Board at the time was also the chairman of the gas company. He wondered what would happen when the new gasworks was erected on the banks of the Medina at Kingston. – The Clerk (Mr. L.H. Baines) : I have been assured that the effluent from it will be purer than clean water.

Newsprint, the paper on which newspapers are printed, was both scarce and costly. The County Press were still limited to 8 pages per issue, causing the loss of valuable advertising space, and now the cost of newsprint was to rise yet again...

May 5, 1951.

PUBLISHERS' ANNOUNCEMENT.

On April 30th the government-controlled price of newsprint was raised by nearly £14 a ton. In 1939 the price was £11 a ton, today its new price is more than £60 a ton. A considerable wage increase is taking place in the newspaper industry and all other costs, including production and distribution, have increased. The County Press is therefore compelled with great regret to increase its price to 3d. a copy, to take effect on June 2nd. The amount of newsprint available for home consumption is strictly limited and stocks stand at a lower level than ever before... No surplus papers can be supplied to newsagents to cater for casual customers and it is therefore requested that firm orders shall be given by readers for a regular weekly copy...

---◆---

The preservation of Britain's ancient buildings was not taken seriously until thousands of them were seriously damaged or destroyed by enemy action during World War II. In the late 1940s architects across Britain were employed to draw up a list of buildings, damaged or otherwise, worthy of preservation, and eventually the process was broadened to become today's listed building scheme. Although still far from restored today, Appuldurcombe House became one of the first beneficiaries of the scheme...

June 30, 1951.

PRESERVATION OF APPULDURCOMBE HOUSE

Appuldurcombe House, near Godshill, is in the course of being handed over, for preservation as a building of historic interest, to the ancient monuments branch of the Ministry of Works. Negotiations are in an advanced stage between the Ministry and Mr. H.N. Butler of Appuldurcombe Farm, in whose ownership the mansion will remain. About 10 acres of land surrounding the house and the Ionic entrance gate to the park are included in the negotiations... At present the estate remains closed to the public while dismantling and renovation work is being carried out. This will take some months to accomplish, but when completed it is understood that the mansion and grounds will be open for public inspection.

ISLAND'S LARGEST PRIVATE HOUSE

Appuldurcombe when occupied was the largest private residence in the Island and contained 52 rooms, 365 Windows, and seven staircases – figures indicative of the number of weeks and days in the year, and days in the week. The architect is unknown. Apart from its occupation by troops in the two world wars, the last residents were the Solesmes Congregation of Benedictine monks, who, when they were expelled from France in 1901, leased the mansion until September, 1908, when they removed to Quarr. A photograph taken in 1930 shows the building in a reasonable state of preservation, but in the last 10 years it has fallen into decay. The deterioration became more rapid after 1943 when a sea mine exploded on the town, just above the house and every window was shattered. Recently the roof became unsound, and in order to prevent damage to the walls, has had to be removed. Workmen have been engaged on the house since February and it is now almost roofless. The floors and practically all staircases have been removed and this week the Adam ceiling in the drawing room adjoining the grand entrance hall was the last of the ornate pieces to be taken down. When the interior has been stripped work will begin on strengthening the shell of the house. While removing the interior fittings workmen came across a piece of timber on which was pencilled "James Dennett Moses, Wroxall, June 1, 1831, masoner, carpenter, and joiner. James King, Godshill. King fit but not made."

TOWN AND COUNTY NOTES.

LADY CARNARVON'S BANKRUPTCY. – Almina Lady Carnarvon[*] admitted unsecured liabilities of over £30,000 and agreed that her insolvency was caused by "extravagance and generosity."... She said that on the death of her husband, the fifth Earl, in 1923, she became entitled to an income of £6500 a year... She agreed that her telephone bill for each half-year had fluctuated between £90 and £150 and she thought that was justified. For one thing, her children were very scattered... Asked whether it would be possible for her to submit a list of people to whom she had made gifts she said there were so many that she could not. Whether it was a bag, or gloves, handkerchiefs, stockings, or soap, she could not possibly say... A list of presents would be quite impossible.

EMBANKMENT OPENED 70 YEARS AGO. – In August 1880 the Bembridge embankment, shutting out the sea from Brading, was officially opened. The occasion was marked by a round of festivities, one of the most important being a cricket match played on the reclaimed land just at the rear of the embankment, which had been started in 1877. In the evening the embankment was illuminated with coloured fairy lights, which hung up on the railings extending the whole length of the road from St Helens to Bembridge...

GENERAL ELECTION USER REGULATIONS. – Owners of private cars and motor-cycles are reminded that under the Representation of the People Act, 1949, it is illegal for a person, with a view to supporting or opposing any particular candidate, to let, lend, employ, hire, borrow, or use any motor vehicle for the conveyance of electors to and from the poll... (October 20)

Foxes and badgers are stealing or mutilating a large proportion of rabbits snared by trappers in the West Wight.

NO FRONT GARDENS FOR NEWPORT COUNCIL HOUSES. – In spite of a spirited protest by several members of Newport Town Council on Wednesday it was decided by 11 votes to 7 that council houses on the Pan Estate should not have front gardens, but that the areas should be grass seeded and kept cut by the council. (October 20)

---

* Widow of Lord Carnarvon, joint excavator of the tomb of Tutankhamun with Howard Carter in 1922. Carnarvon died eight weeks later when a mosquito bite on his cheek turned septic.

Shide station on the Newport to Sandown railway line in the early 1950s. Today the site is home to the National Tyres garage.   *[Author's Collection]*

Merstone station in the early 1950s. The platform can still be seen today, while the former trackbed is now part of the Shide to Sandown cycleway.   *[Author's Collection]*

Three Princess flying boats had been under construction for the last six years. Some of the original customers had bowed out, tired of waiting for engine design problems to be overcome and they were also no doubt very aware that with the recent arrival of the jet engine the flying boats were rapidly losing any technological edge they had once possessed...

November 3rd, 1951.

THE FIRST PRINCESS FLYING BOAT MOVED
FROM HANGAR AT EAST COWES

On Tuesday at midday, in the presence of numerous representatives of the Press, and watched by hundreds of men who have helped to build her, the first of the three huge Princess flying boats which have been under construction by Messrs. Saunders-Roe, Ltd., at East Cowes since 1946, was moved from the hangar in which she has been erected onto an enlarged and strengthened concrete apron. Here the outer sections of the wings and the top of the tail unit will be fitted, the engines mounted, and the fitting-out of the huge machine completed. It is hoped that she will be ready for her first trial flight in June next, provided there is no further delay in supplying the engines.... The moving of the enormous machine necessitated very careful planning. It had to be brought out at an angle, and then the outer edge of the starboard wing only cleared the hangar entrance by about 2 feet. In order to get the very high tail unit out it was necessary to raise the nose of the plane... even then, there was only a clearance of about 11 inches*... It will be remembered that when the flying boats were first ordered they were intended for service with BOAC, and later by British-South American Airways. Circumstances, however, have compelled a change in the plans for their civil use, and the latest announced intention is that the three machines are to be completed for use as troop carriers.

ISLAND NOTES

CONSERVATIVE VICTORY. – The result of the General Election in the Island was declared at 12.35 p.m. at the County Hall, Newport, as follows: Sir Peter Macdonald (C.) 33,501. Mr. S.G. Conbeer (Lab.) 20,712. Conservative Majority 12,789. This was Sir Peter's seventh consecutive success. (October 20)

One woman discovered after surrendering her paper that she had not voted for her candidate of choice, having acted on the assumption that the man who headed the poll last time would automatically top the voting form.

A voter from hospital arrived at the booth at Nine Acres Junior School, Newport, in dressing gown and pyjamas.

NOTES BY VECTENSIS. – One of the most humorous examples of election repartee which I have seen was the following, published in the "News Chronicle" : Candidate: "Are you going to take this lying down?" Heckler: "No, the reporters are doing that."

* See photograph, page 25.

It is 80 years ago since Virginian cigarettes were first sold in this country, but cigarette smoking was actually introduced by veterans returning from the Crimean War of 1854-56. The early cigarettes were clumsily made, and consisted of a loose roll of tobacco wrapped up in almost any kind of paper that would burn slowly. It is interesting to recall that some of the early brands of Virginian cigarettes have retained their popularity, including Wills Gold Flake, which were sold between 1888 and 1915 for 3d.

A recent decision by Newport Town Council that council houses under construction on the Pan Estate were not to have front gardens had annoyed the prospective tenants waiting to move in and they wrote to the County Press complaining. Their protests did not go down well with those still living in Army huts ...

November 3rd, 1951

COUNCIL HOUSE FRONT GARDENS AT NEWPORT

In reply to the grumblers from Robin Hood Street in your last issue, are these people aware that there are many families still living in Army huts with no gardens at all; who have been there for years and are forced to eat, sleep, and work in one draughty room, with no gas, no water tap, no sink indoors, no privacy, no comfort, and only a small kitchen grate for cooking, washing, and warmth, which smokes whenever the door is shut? Any offers to change places would be gratefully accepted by these families, and if the council decided to grass the front garden they would mow it themselves and be truly thankful.

"ONE OF THE PATIENT FAMILIES WAITING FOR A HOME."

The following week, one of the chastised letter writers took the criticism on the chin while another correspondent spelt out the conditions in the Army huts that many hundreds of families were still living in...

November 17th, 1951

PAN ESTATE FRONT GARDENS

When you accepted for publication our previous letters, we felt justified in showing our resentment at the apparent intentions of the Housing Committee; it was not then, and is not now, our desire to enter into any controversy over the matter... We offer our sympathies with regards to the conditions and hardships under which the writer is living, but would remind them that the greater percentage of the present council house tenants have experienced conditions not alien to his own... "ROBIN HOOD" and A.E. BURTON.

THE HOUSING TRAGEDY

I have deep sympathy with the "Patient Waiters for a Home," and can verify and enlarge on the discomforts and squalor of the "Huttites" as I have heard them disparagingly called. Last winter it came to my notice that a girl of seven, just discharged from hospital after a throat operation, was lying in bed and crying with earache in one of these draughty huts. I was unwell and asked my husband to go and see what could be done. He found ... the hut full of smoke, with rain leaking through the roof in several places and trickling across the floor... Can nothing be done for these unfortunate families who are left year after year in such conditions? How can these innocent little ones be trained to be clean and respectable citizens? The lack of any comfort, convenience, or privacy makes it almost impossible, and a foul mark of discontent and unfairness is left in the minds of the children... "AN ORDINARY WOMAN."

TOWN AND COUNTY NOTES

Newport Town Council on Wednesday considered a letter from the Newport Rotary Club asking to be allowed to place their tree of goodwill on the pavement outside the Guildhall at the junction of Quay Street and High Street. Permission was refused on the grounds of possible obstruction to traffic and danger to the public... Mr. H.E. Harvey said if the council were to grant the request what would be their argument if other organisations made requests? The Boy Scouts, for instance, might want to put up a totem pole in the middle of the market...

A tin of Army issue stew, brought home by a Freshwater soldier on leave in 1915, was opened on Wednesday and found to be in perfect condition.

WELL-KNOWN BRICKMAKER'S DEATH. – A member of a well-known Island family of brickmakers, Mr. Francis Pritchett, died on Thursday aged 78. The first Pritchett brickmaker, and his son George, came to the Island in 1798. They worked at making tiles for the first Parkhurst Barracks. The son built up an extensive business with kilns at Berelay (sic) and Ningwood, where his white facing bricks were in great demand for use in erecting some of the early buildings at Brighton. George's elder son, Edmund, assisted in the Ningwood business, later moving to Shambler's Brickyard near Cowes, and opening two yards at Gurnard. His elder son William, became manager of the Ward estate agricultural pipe works at Hillis, Northwood, in 1856... Mr. Pritchett took over the Rookley and Northwood brickworks, until 11 years ago, when they passed into the control of the Island Bricks Co Ltd.

BBC television for the South of England was now a certainty, using a mast situated on the downs at Rowridge. Lord Mottistone took no pleasure in the prospect of a tall television mast on the Island, declaring that "some of these masts were almost obscene in their hideousness"...

December 15th, 1951
ISLAND TELEVISION STATION PROJECT.
'MONSTROSITY" ALLEGATION

The proposed erection by the BBC of a television transmitter, with a 750ft. steel mast, on the down at Rowridge, Carisbrooke, led to a lively discussion at a meeting of the Planning Committee at County Hall yesterday. The Plans Sub-committee had already informed the BBC that they had no objection to the proposal, subject to three considerations. Lord Mottistone said he took very strong objection to the proposed mast. Did the members realise what 750 feet implied? Salisbury Cathedral was 404 feet high, and the mast would be 350 feet higher. Nothing like that should be considered in the Isle of Wight.... Some of these masts were almost obscene in their hideousness, and it was disgraceful that such a monstrosity should be placed in such a small and still beautiful Island.

UNSIGHTLY H-AERIALS

... The Council had been informed by the BBC that, save in exceptional circumstances, simple dipole aerials, either indoors or below roof level, would be sufficient, and at a time when the installation of television sets was on the increase, the saving of perhaps hundreds of thousands of unsightly H-aerials would offset the loss of amenity which the sub-committee fully realised would take place if the station were erected... Mr. S.L. Glossop said he was unable to see how the erection of the mast would do irreparable harm to the Island amenities. He viewed it as something which should be accepted in the name of progress... The report was adopted.

1952

Seaview Pier was a survivor. It had narrowly escaped demolition by its previous owner, Mr Figgins, who became frustrated at the amount of red tape involved in its refurbishment, leading him to sell it on to the owner of the nearby Pier Hotel. After local campaigning the pier was listed in October 1950 and its future seemed assured until on Boxing Day evening 1951 it was severely damaged during a gale and about 100 foot of the pier was washed away leaving the beach strewn with pieces of decking. The damage was so serious that repair was not an option and even supporters of the pier agreed that demolition was now the only way forward. Two nights later, nature stepped in and did the job for them...

January 5th, 1952

SEAVIEW PIER DESTROYED

Hopes that it might be possible to restore in some measure the picturesque chain pier at Seaview faded when about 100ft. of the deck was washed away on Wednesday week, but few imagined that its total destruction would follow in so short a period. The pier had been unsafe since the war and had not been open to the public for many years. The only people who used it were the inward Trinity House pilots putting off to the cutters, and the anglers who did so at their own risk... The Esplanade adjoining the Pier Hotel possibly received the worst buffeting of any part of the coast between Seaview and Ryde and near the hotel the water was waist deep in places. At midnight it was as if a hurricane was raging and, although in the darkness nothing could be seen of the shank of the pier, it was obvious that extensive destruction was taking place as the tremendous waves swept masses of timber onto the Esplanade. At the height of the storm both the toll kiosks at the pier gates were lifted bodily and dashed onto the promenade. The iron turnstiles were also flung across the Esplanade. The ground floor of the cafe opposite the pier was flooded. Mr. Douglas Shiner, the caretaker and only occupant of the hotel, and Mr. R.L. Lovat Crosley, the cafe proprietor, worked throughout the night in salving material. Mr. Shiner had frequently to prevent floating timber from smashing the lower windows of the hotel. At daybreak the Esplanade presented a scene of desolation. The road surface was severely damaged and there were piles of shingle and sand, and the beach was strewn with timber. Only the pier-head and about 100ft. of the 900ft. Promenade deck remained. Along the coast as far as Ryde there was much timber washing about, and subsequently the police kept watch to see that it was not removed by unauthorised persons. A certain number had, however, taken a good deal before police aid was sought... The pier was offered for sale at an auction of the Seagrove Estate in November, 1947, and was bought by a contractor at Emsworth. He sold it to the present owners, the Seaview Chain Pier Co., in the autumn of 1948...

———————————◆———————————

In 1890 someone put over 100 bottles of beer in a store at Ryde and for reasons unknown never returned to retrieve them. For the next 60 years they lay gathering dust until they were rediscovered in 1952 ...

January 12th, 1952.

CACHE OF BEER FOUND AT RYDE
62 YEARS OLD AND STILL DRINKABLE

A dusty pint bottle of Anglo-Bavarian dinner ale displayed in the window of the "County Press" head offices at Newport has been attracting considerable interest this week. The bottle is one of a cache of about 10 dozen discovered in a cellar in High Street, Ryde, when Mr. G. Rea, a greengrocer, took over the premises formerly belonging to Henry and L. Adams and Co., as a store and garage. Mr. Rea presented several of the bottles to Mr. R. Adams of 10 Monkton Street, Ryde, the grandson of the original brewer, who then took a sample to the man who bottled it in 1890, Mr. S. Kemp, of 40 Monkton Street. Mr. Kemp, now aged 84, began work for the brewers in 1886, and remained in their employ for 52 years. He was able to identify the bottles by their distinctive non-screw tops. The hoard was part of the line then selling at 2s.6d. a dozen pints. A sample of the 62-year-old beer has been tasted, and the verdict is: "Drinkable, but only just."

———————————◆———————————

THE WEEK'S NEWS

A Totland Bay resident used one week's ration of cooking fat to cleanse the feathers of a guillemot found smothered in oil. The bird was later released from the pier.

MANHOLE EXPLOSION AT NEWPORT - SHOPPER'S NARROW ESCAPE FROM INJURY.* – Mrs Eileen Isherwood, of 24 School Lane, Newport, undoubtedly had her life saved by a passerby, who shouted to her as she was about to step onto the manhole cover in the pavement outside Messrs. W.B. Mew Langton's off-licence in the High Street, Newport, on Monday. After she heard a shout and saw the man pointing she looked down and saw puffs of smoke rising from around the cover of an electricity inspection chamber. She ran for the shelter of the passage alongside the Bugle Hotel, and was on the corner when there was a terrific explosion, which was heard all over the town. The two cwt cover was hurled into the air to a height of 100 feet, and crashed into the middle of the road, breaking into pieces. Although there were many people and cars about, no one was hurt... The explosion is believed to have been caused by an accumulation of gas...

A barn owl, disturbed in one of the buildings at Brambles Chine Holiday Camp, flew through a window, making a hole in the glass about 10 inches in diameter. It continued its flight, apparently uninjured.

———————◆———————

King George VI, a lifelong heavy smoker, had suffered complications following lung cancer and unexpectedly died in his sleep at Sandringham after spending the previous day happily shooting hares. He had retired in good health that night but early the following morning a servant found him dead in bed. The official announcement of his death at 10.45 that morning came as a surprise to everyone, including his daughter Princess Elizabeth, aged 25, who was on a foreign trip and officially became Queen whilst asleep in a treehouse in a Kenya game park...

Feb 9th, 1952
DEATH OF H.M. KING GEORGE VI
SHOCK OF BROADCAST ANNOUNCEMENT
PRINCESS ELIZABETH ACCEDES TO THE THRONE
The brief broadcast announcement on Wednesday morning, which conveyed to the nation and the News of the King's sudden but peaceful end, was received in the Island in stunned incredulous silence... The Island's deep sympathy goes out to the Royal Family in our sorrow, with fervent prayers for the new Queen, who assumes the heavy cares of state under such tragic circumstances... The accession of Queen Elizabeth II was proclaimed in the Island yesterday. At Newport the proclamation was read from the balcony of the Guildhall by the Mayor.

———————◆———————

The Council announced the details of their 20 year plan for improvements to Island towns and villages. Cowes residents, as they read through the plans for Cowes, might like to tick off the proposals that actually came into being...

---

*A similar explosion occurred in 1914 when a manhole cover in St James's Square was hurled into the air, falling on a soldier and killing him. See volume 2, page 170.

February 16th, 1952.
ISLAND DEVELOPMENT PLAN - COUNCIL APPROVE 20 YEAR PROGRAMME.
COWES TOWN PROPOSALS

The plan for Cowes was based on the assumption that the population in 1971 would be about 16,800. It was proposed to use the following as major traffic routes: Cross Street, Shooters Hill, Carvel Lane, Terminus Road, Park Road, Union Road, and Market Hill; these roads would have to be widened where necessary. It was also intended to provide a link road between Cross Street and Carvel Lane... As a long-term proposal there was the Medina Bridge and its approach roads... Small shopping centres would be provided near Bellevue Road. Industrial development areas would be at Cross Street and Denmark Road. Residential development was planned for Northwood Park and Love Lane... The grounds of Stanhope Lodge would be developed as a public open space and the need for small playgrounds would be provided for in the layout of new housing estates. The car park at the eastern end of Park Road would become a bus station, and there was a need for car parks near the High Street...

TOWN AND COUNTY NOTES

Practice on the 6-inch guns at Fort Culver, Sandown, will take place from Tuesday to Saturday inclusive, between 10.00 a.m. and 5 p.m.

THE PRINCESS FLYING BOATS. WORK ON THE LAST TWO PLANES SUSPENDED . – It was announced in the House of Commons on Monday that work on the completion of the second and third Princess flying boats being built at East Cowes by Messrs. Saunders-Roe is to be discontinued for the time being. The Minister of Supply, Duncan Sandys, said the temporary curtailment of the Princess programme would result in saving over £2,000,000 in the coming financial year... The Minister added, "There is, of course, no intention of abandoning these two important development projects, on which much money has already been spent."(March 22)

It was not until midday on Tuesday that workmen completed the digging of a path through snowdrifts which had blocked Brummel Lane, Shorwell, for 10 days. (April 12)

Half an hour after locking a Newport cinema on Sunday night, the commissionaire was roused at his home by a stranger, who asked him to unlock it again, as he thought one of his children might have been shut in. The commissionaire and his visitor opened the cinema and discovered the child fast asleep in a seat.

RODENT DESTRUCTION. – Interesting facts are revealed in the annual report of the I.W. Rodent Destruction Joint Committee. During the year, 40,000 rats were estimated to have been killed. Expenditure during this period was £4387 16s. 6d., or about two shillings per rat estimated destroyed. Of 6416 properties inspected 1312 were treated in 16,570 visits. The report states that rat trouble in sewers has not been entirely eliminated, but the position is described as being under control.

SOMERTON AIRFIELD CLOSED. – At the meeting of the Cowes Urban District Council on Tuesday it was reported that a communication had been received from the Ministry of Civil Aviation stating that Somerton Aerodrome had been closed until further notice, and that the aerodrome licence had been withdrawn. (April 19)

* * *

It was now generally accepted that that the Merstone to Ventnor West railway line was not long for this world and railway enthusiasts from the mainland took their last opportunity to visit the line...

May 24th, 1952

"RAIL FANS" TOUR ISLAND SYSTEM

On Sunday a Whitwell resident was basking in the sunshine in a hammock in his garden when the quiet of the afternoon was disturbed by the sound of a train on the Ventnor West line. He was so startled that he fell out of his hammock - and no wonder, for this was the first Sunday train on the branch for some years. The occasion was the Railway Correspondence and Travel Society's first visit to the Island. Some 124 members and friends left Ryde Pier Head at 11.22 a.m. in two coaches, glistening in the new red livery of British Railways - one the Island's ex L.B. & S.C.R. saloon - hauled by the locomotive "Ryde," bearing "R.C.T.S." head and tail boards. The first stop was at Newport, where the motive power depot and paint shop were inspected, also the site of the former Freshwater, Yarmouth, and Newport Railway terminus and an old F.Y. & N.R. boundary plate near St Cross Mill Bridge. A return trip to Cowes included some of the fastest running on the tour, and a trip was then made to Freshwater and back, and, after refreshments at Newport Station, the visitors rejoined the special, now headed by "Bonchurch," bound for Merstone and Ventnor West. The sudden view of the Channel through the luxuriant foliage of the Undercliff on emergence from St Lawrence tunnel was much admired. The many photographers in the party had an ideal day for snapping items of railway interest, one particularly keen enthusiast was seen attempting to photograph the inscription embossed on a rail chair on a Merstone siding! After the return to Merstone the train continued along the Yar Valley to Sandown. A prolonged stop was made at Brading, as the party travelled in two groups on the branch line train to Bembridge. The special was rejoined for the journey to Ryde St John's Road, where the motive power depot and works were inspected and the last journey was then continued to the Pier Head in time to catch the 7.35 p.m. boat... Local railway officers accompanied the party and spent a busy

day answering questions. The crowded trains, both public and special, on the ex I.W.R. mainline on a May Sunday showed the visitors that railways still play a vital part in Island life - despite rumours of closure. All of the 58 miles of line in the Island were covered except the six mile Sandown to Ventnor section.

ISLAND NOTES

LITTLE CANADA HOLIDAY VILLAGE REOPENS. – Guests of the Polytechnic Travel Association at Little Canada Holiday Village, Wootton, on Saturday, when the 1952 season opened, were officers of the Royal Canadian Air Force, a representative of the Canadian Pacific Railway (who have supplied many views of Canadian Mountain areas for decoration of chalets and communal rooms in the village to heighten the backwoods effect), and local residents who in different ways will be serving the holiday community throughout the season. The village will be half full next week, and then for the remainder of the season until September, all accommodation is fully booked.

FOOT AND MOUTH DISEASE SPREADS TO ISLAND. OVER 60 CATTLE SLAUGHTERED. – The first outbreak of foot and mouth disease in the Island for eight years was confirmed on Monday among cattle at Vittlefield, on the main Yarmouth Road. The whole Island was at once declared an infected area and strict control of the movement of all cloven-hoofed animals, and of poultry and dogs kept within five miles of the seat of infection, automatically came into force. Yesterday a further outbreak was confirmed at Forest Farm, half a mile from Vittlefield... 66 cattle and six pigs have been slaughtered at the infected premises.

DRILLING FOR OIL AT MERSTONE TO COMMENCE SHORTLY. – Preliminary site works commenced this week near Perreton Farm, Merstone, where the Anglo-Iranian Oil Co. are to drill for oil, and drilling will commence shortly. The company state "we wish most emphatically to assure all your readers that they will not be overwhelmed by the sort of scene that has been all too prominent in any American film dealing with oil fields. Those vast areas bristling with unsightly derricks, those impressive but very wasteful gushers, with Mr. Clark Gable standing below getting a free oil bath, are scenes which have been familiar in America, but will not be seen in this country.... a small pump tucked away in a corner of a field will be all that is left to show that an oil field is in existence.

Mr Holland, a Freshwater correspondent, wrote to the Editor proposing a ban on American comics, which he felt were corrupting the minds of British youth. Obviously well-read in the matter, he informed readers that sadistic sex was being peddled in the guise of jungle romance involving "telescopic-breasted Amazons" and "heroines in panties"...

May 31st, 1952
FILTHY LITERATURE
It is to be hoped that there will be some positive action designed to put a stop to this serious threat against the minds of young (and other) readers. Garishly printed in lurid colours, humourless and almost jokeless, saturating their weekly pages with pictorial beatings, stranglings, shootings, and what have you, elevating the tough gangster and the thug, glossing crime with only a perfunctory nod at moralities they deliberately insinuate an ethos of violence. They cynically engage the teenagers, especially girls, by introducing a sadistic sexual suggestivity in the guise of jungle romance – telescopic-breasted Amazons with ropes and whip; heroines in panties rescued from torture. Nor is it sufficiently recognised that these American comics, so avidly read by youngsters and adolescents (I have seen National Service men wallowing in them), are continually seeping into receptive minds antisocial standards of conduct. The law and its officers are invariably depicted as either helpless or venal, thus glorifying the superman who defies them. Such few printed words as there are express either a simian howl of pain or have an infantile incoherence. Oh for the vital writings of Kipling or H.G. Wells or even the harmless violence of Tarzan... The most important reading is that read earliest in life. Can we do nothing? ... Not every juvenile reader becomes a delinquent, but can we deny responsibility while we tolerate this continued infection of poisonous views? ... While I realise banning such papers will not remove the source of interest, it is surely necessary as a first step.

GEORGE HOLLAND. Bay Tree Cottage, Freshwater.

◆

British Railways had announced its intention to close the Merstone to Ventnor railway line* in June of the previous year and now the time had come and the official closure announcement was made. It was a railway line that couldn't even generate enough income to pay the wages of the 18 staff and opposition to the closure was minimal, the Council asking only that a suitable alternative bus service be put in place...

June 14th, 1952
THE MERSTONE - VENTNOR RAILWAY LINE
PERMANENT WITHDRAWAL OF SERVICE PROPOSED
At their monthly meeting Ventnor Council had before them a letter from British Railways reading as follows: "An exhaustive investigation into the economic circumstances of the Merstone – Ventnor West branch line has been made, and after full consideration it is felt that there are no grounds for maintaining the passenger and freight service on the branch..." The attached statements detailed the trains provided, eight in each direction, and pointed out that a census of passengers during a typical summer week showed that from Merstone to Ventnor West the maximum number on any one day was 122 on the 5.27 p.m. ... The minimum number on any day was one, on the 1.25 p.m.... For a typical winter week the maximum number on any one day was 34 on the 7.35 a.m.. There had been no passengers at all on the 11.27 a.m. and 7.27 p.m. and only two on four other trains....

* See photograph page 65.

In a recent column 'Vectensis' had told the tale of a hot and thirsty harvest worker who eventually told the farmer, "This be a terbul hot job and the beer's run out. If my brother was yer he'd ask for some more - but I ain't got the neck to," - a statement that caused the farmer to smile before supplying more refreshment. A request for similar stories brought the following recollections...

June 21st, 1952

AN ISLANDER' S NOTES
By VECTENSIS

Writing with reference to my story last week about thirsty harvest workers, Mr. Arthur Williams, of Gatcombe, writes that he believes that the last man to brew real farmhouse beer in the Island was the late Mr. Henry Orchard, of Chale. He says he had some there in 1906 and "it was jolly good stuff." Mr. Williams tells a story of three men who started to mow a field of wheat, but visited a nine-gallon cask so frequently that they were soon incapable of wielding a scythe. Their punishment was that they had to finish the job the next day on water. This brought the comment from another worker: "Beer talks about work, but cold water has to do it." Mr. Williams also mentions that Mr. A. Henton of Loverstone Farm, Chillerton, can remember helping to brew farmhouse beer. It was kept in a large tub in the courtyard. The tub had four taps at different levels – No. 1 was called "Admiral," No. 2 "Knock me down," No. 3 "Six o'clock," and No. 4 "What the little pigs wrassel for." The first was for dealers who called, to get them into good humour for a deal. Once the men in the harvest field were given the wrong mixture and they were all good for nothing by teatime. All callers helped themselves, even tramps.

The cliffs at Blackgang were on the move again prompting recollections of past landslides...

June 28th, 1952

AN ISLANDER'S NOTES
By VECTENSIS

Mr. G. F. Mew, who has voluminous records of happenings in the Blackgang area sends a quote from "The Yearbook of Facts" for 1854 which reads: "The Blackgang cliff in the Isle of Wight has been blown up, and the process was an interesting one. Eight holes were bored and filled with about 2 cwt. of powder, seven of which were fired and caused a vast quantity to fall, but the most prominent part and the most mighty still remained. This piece, in which was bored the eighth hole, was rent away from the body of the cliff at the top about five yards. Mr. Dennis placed his life in the most imminent danger by putting an iron bar across the gap and crawling on it to set fire to the charge. In about two minutes a very loud report warned the bystanders, of whom there were about 150 present, that it would fall, and it certainly was a grand sight, for it fell with a tremendous crash. One piece weighed upwards of 350 tons. Several other pieces of from 50 to 150 tons also fell, and this tremendous weight on land previously saturated with water, so shook it that about 250 yards of the high road is entirely gone, and the land for some distance round is completely rent in pieces." Mr. Mew is of the opinion that these blasting operations caused the former well-known landmark at Windy Corner – a huge block of pointed rock known as "Big Rock" which was a familiar sight to all who travelled on the Undercliff Road. It survived the landslide of 1928, which occurred just to the east of it, but by a strange coincidence it was demolished during the last war by American soldiers who experimented on it with high explosives, much to the disgust of local residents, who viewed it as a notable and singular feature of the wild landscape...

—————————◆—————————

Life was becoming more homogenised and more 'modern', and obituaries for 'local characters' were now few and far between. One of the last of the line to receive one was the part-time smuggler Frederick Bastiani, son of full time smuggler, Joe Bastiani*...

July 26th, 1952
LAST OF ISLAND SMUGGLERS DIES AT AGE OF 97
The death occurred on Saturday at 91 Pelham Road, Cowes, of the last of the Isle of Wight smugglers, Mr. Frederick Bastiani, aged 97. He was born in the old wooden watch-house on Atherfield cliffs on October 26th, 1854, and was the third son of the notorious "Back of the Wight" smuggler "Joe" Bastiani. At the age of five he was sent to the village school at Shorwell, controlled in those days by the village "Dame." After a few days, however, his father said that if he could walk four miles to school and four back every day he was man enough to go to work, and go to work he did. He was employed in scaring birds from the cornfields of his uncle's farm with a wooden clapper. At seven he went on his first "run" to Barfleur with his father and nine-year-old brother. In the ensuing years he took part in no fewer than 60 "runs" to the French coastal ports. During this time Mr. Bastiani's father had a joint interest in the ex-pilot cutter Sarah, and it was in this vessel that his last run was made. After the cargo of tubs had been sunk off the Saltmead Ledge at Newtown, and the Sarah had been brought to anchor in the river, the preventive men came and posted a confiscation notice on her side and the crew had to disperse. Mr. Bastiani, then 17, joined a collier brig at Cowes and in her made several voyages to Sunderland. Later he signed on in a large barque, and in her made many voyages to distant parts of the world. Returning, he married and settled at Niton, where in addition to his fishing activities he established a nursery at Head Down. In the early part of the century he was a familiar figure at seaside resorts with a basket of lobsters on one arm and a basket of choice flowers on the other. In later years he cultivated allotments at Pan, Newport.

—————————◆—————————

THE WEEK'S NEWS
PRISON ENQUIRY CALLED FOR - "ALARMING EVIDENCE" FROM PARKHURST. – A House of Commons Select Committee calls for an enquiry into British prisons, particularly with regard to staff shortages, overcrowding, and ill-discipline, on which "alarming" evidence had been submitted... During

---

* See photograph page 65.

their investigation the committee visited Parkhurst and Camp Hill... Their report states "The working week at Parkhurst is, on average, 17 hours. Prisoners spend as much time in association, smoking, playing darts, listening to the wireless, and reading newspapers as they spend at work."

TEA OFF RATION. – The Minister of Food announced on Thursday that rationing and price control of tea will end on Sunday.... He wished he could say meat was to be de-rationed and the trade handed back to private enterprise but he could not do so... Stocks had been built up, and he was confident that there was enough tea in the shops to meet all demands. There was no need to fear that the price of tea would rise... On Monday morning people would be able to go to the nearest shop and buy as much tea as they liked for the first time since July, 1940. (October 4)

The law in Eire forbidding football pools and lotteries is to be enforced rigorously from now on, a Department of Justice spokesman said.

There were 12 million wireless receiving licences in force at the end of August, including 1,500,000 for television and 158,000 for receivers in cars.

———————————◆———————————

After six years Saunders-Roe finally unveiled the first Princess flying boat. It took to the water and made the first of what would be 46 test flights, eventually running up 100 hours of flying time which, in the event, were to be the sum total of its flying career...
August 23rd, 1952
"PRINCESS" FLYING BOAT AIRBORNE
Thousands of holidaymakers, Air Ministry officials, directors of Messrs. Saunders-Roe, and all the staff employed in the vast works, gathered at vantage points around Cowes Harbour on Tuesday morning to see the launching of the first of the "Princess" flying boats but they were disappointed. Because of the strong north easterly wind, estimated at from 30 to 35 miles an hour, conditions were considered to be too dangerous to risk possible damage... Bad weather again delayed the launching on Wednesday morning, but by midnight on the same day the conditions were favourable, and the launching was successfully accomplished. The Princess was airborne yesterday shortly after 12.30 p.m., and thousands of residents and holidaymakers had a marvellous view of her as she made surprise sweeps over Newport, first at about 5000 feet and then at a much lower height... As the huge machine flew over Newport on her second circuit, just before one o'clock, huge crowds of holiday-makers, and office and shop workers, enjoying their luncheon break in the sunshine, watched her. One summed up the general impression in the words "She is a lovely Princess, dressed in silver."
THE "PRINCESS" FLYING BOATS
In spite of repeated criticism of the building of the huge "Princess" flying boats on the grounds of cost and utility, those who designed the aircraft and the men who have fashioned the first machine, which made her maiden flight

yesterday, may well be proud of an achievement described this week by the air correspondent of the "Daily Graphic" as a triumph of aeronautical achievement." It is a pity, therefore, that the future of these aircraft is so uncertain. They were originally designed to carry over 100 passengers in luxury across the Atlantic at 370 miles an hour, but now it seems likely that they may be used as troop carriers by RAF Transport Command. There is a sharp division of opinion among the experts as to the comparative commercial value of passenger-carrying flying boats and land planes. Those who favour the latter have had their opinion endorsed by BOAC who have ceased to use flying boats...

_____◆_____

With barely a word of protest from Islanders and County Press alike, the Merstone to Ventnor West railway line quietly passed into history...

September 20th, 1952

FAREWELL TO THE MERSTONE - VENTNOR RAILWAY
CROWDED TRAIN FOR LAST JOURNEY

When the 7.57 p.m. Merstone train pulled out on Saturday from Ventnor West Station, the hand bell rung by an enthusiast on the platform sounded the death-knell of a line which for over half a century has carried passengers through some of the most beautiful Island scenery, and which has been regarded with affection by Islanders everywhere.

In the official phrase of the Railway Executive, the closure, which was in practice effective from Saturday, was due to "the policy of closing unremunerative branch lines where adequate alternative services exist," but no "alternative service" can provide the beautiful view of the sea which burst upon the traveller as the little train emerged from the tunnel connecting the Whitwell and St. Lawrence sections, nor equal the pleasure, and even fascination, of travelling to Ventnor by the other railway line. At the moment no information is available as to what will happen to the permanent way, but we understand that the workers involved, about a dozen, have been absorbed by transfer to other jobs.

TRAIN BESIEGED ON FINAL TRIP

Residents and railway enthusiasts from all parts of the Island, and even further afield, made up the large body of people who awaited the two-coach train at Merstone Junction as it came in to make ready for the last round trip. It was drawn by No. 27, the engine named after the station, and manned by Driver J. Sewell, of Wootton, Fireman L. Harris, of Newport, and Guard R. Seaman, also of Newport. Small white boards on the front and rear of the engine bore the inscription "British Railways. Farewell to Ventnor West, 1897 - 1952." Camera shutters clicked busily in the interval before the "Wight Express" was taken to a siding to allow the Newport and Sandown trains to cross - a procedure very familiar to travellers on the line, and now taking place for almost the last time. In the fading light the branch line train came back to the platform, filled even to the guard's compartment and, with a shrill whistle, pulled out of the station. Girl Guides in camp were among those who stood watching to cheer and wave as the train went by, and there were many more at each station. Godshill, Whitwell, the tunnel - and again that glorious view of the sea, now sombre in the fading light of a perfect September evening - followed rapidly by the halt at St Lawrence and the glide through the leafy Undercliff to the terminus.

A NOISY GREETING

At Ventnor West intending passengers and sightseers began to assemble nearly an hour before the last train was due. There had been such a rush for tickets, the majority of which were kept as souvenirs, that the printed supply was exhausted, and the booking clerk (Mr. A. Widger) was kept busy writing further tickets. There were requests for all classes of tickets, and some souvenir hunters obtained those printed when the line was under the control of the former Southern Railway... As the train arrived in the gathering dusk a mighty cheer went up, streamers were thrown at, in and over the station signs, and fireworks were set off. While the engine was shunted and took on water Ventnor Jazz Band marched on the spare track and platform. A BBC television cameraman recorded the scene, with the aid of magnesium flares and flashlight photographs were taken of the train and its crew. It was doubtful if there would be enough room for those who wished to board the train, but all were somehow squeezed aboard. Michael, Guard Seaman's seven-year-old son, waved the green flag and, to the sound of more cheers, the playing of "Auld Lang Syne", taken up by those on the train, clanging bells, whistles, and a series of crashing fog-signal detonators placed on the line, the train steamed out a few minutes after 8 p.m. Crowds waited to give it a farewell cheer at St Lawrence, Whitwell, and Godshill, and cottagers stood at their doors to wave a last goodbye. At Whitwell Mr. A. Western, who lives in the Station House, was waiting with cups of tea for the train crew and other officials on board the engine, and at Godshill it was discovered that someone had pulled the communication cord when the train was in the station. When the train arrived at Merstone, to the accompaniment of a veritable fusillade of detonators, crowds of passengers went up to the engine to say farewell to the men aboard and before boarding other trains to travel to Newport or go back to Ventnor, via Sandown, they watched as the train was shunted into a siding on the final few hundred yards of her journey...

UNRIVALLED SCENERY

The closure has aroused widespread discussion through the correspondence columns of the "County Press" and other Island newspapers, and the decision has been greatly deplored as likely to have an adverse effect on the Island's popularity as a holiday resort, and as depriving visitors of the enjoyment of unique views of one of the finest stretches of coastline and countryside... Many suggestions were advanced for making the line a paying proposition, including the provision of light railcars or purchase by private enterprise. The fact unfortunately remains that public use of the line has progressively dwindled over a period of several years, until it has now become impossible effectively to resist the argument that no undertaking can continue to run such a service at a loss. A census of passenger traffic showed that the average number of passengers travelling from Merstone to Ventnor West on a typical summer

A scene on the Merstone to Ventnor West railway line shortly before the branch closed in September 1952. A train bound for St Lawrence has just left Whitwell Station, seen in the background, and is crossing the bridge over Nettlecombe Lane.   [Author's Collection]

TRUE TO TRADITION

Mr. Frederick Bastiani, the last of the Island smugglers, who died at Cowes last week, at the age of 97. He formerly lived at Niton and Newport. (See page 61)

Mr. Percy Mew, left, of New Fairlee Farm, doyen of Island sportsmen, in his 85th year, maintains the yeoman tradition of riding to town on horseback. The picture shows him arriving at Newport Market, but he also rides to town on most of his business visits. His horses are so well trained that they wait patiently at the pavement edge while he is making calls, unperturbed by the noises of the town and "No Parking" notices! (Dec 13)   *[Photo : John Owen]* weekday was 46, maximum, and five, minimum... The winter average figure in either direction fell to 24, maximum, and one, minimum. On some trains in the winter there were no passengers at all. The Railway Executive stated that the corresponding bus services carried an average of 450 passengers per day...

(Editorial) Confident prophecies of future heavy traffic due to progress and development in the Ventnor area, which were made at the opening of the Merstone - St Lawrence branch line in 1897 were predestined to be unfulfilled... The chief cause of the lack of passenger traffic on the line has been the tremendous progress made in the last half-century by the internal combustion engine. It is well-known that one can cover any comparable distance in the Island by car in roughly half the time taken to make the journey by train, with the additional convenience and saving of time due to door-to-door transport.

◆

ISLAND NOTES

FAIRLEE HOUSE* - NEWPORT'S "WHITE ELEPHANT". – The main discussion at the monthly meeting of the Newport Town Council on Wednesday was on a recommendation from the Finance Committee that Fairlee House should be demolished. The Mayor presided, and the committee report stated that as no offers to purchase the house had been received, they had resolved to recommend that it be demolished. After a long discussion it was decided to refer the recommendation back, with the suggestion that the house might be useful as the Island Civil Defence headquarters.

OIL DRILLING MAY START ON WEDNESDAY. – Wednesday is the target date for the commencement of drilling for oil on a site at Perreton Farm, Arreton... The site has for some weeks been marked by the now familiar 130ft. lattice steel tower, an essential to the drilling operations, which was erected earlier in the summer, but further work has been held up until recently by delays in the arrival of ancillary plant. In the last week much of this has been delivered and many will have seen heavy loads of blue-painted machinery en route from the ferry at Yarmouth.

ISLAND RAILWAYS "BOMBSHELL" - ONLY RYDE-VENTNOR LINE TO SURVIVE. REMAINDER TO CLOSE WITHIN FIVE YEARS. – Following a statement at a meeting of the Chamber of Commerce on Wednesday that the question of closing the Newport-Sandown and Freshwater lines was under consideration, a further and more alarming announcement was made by the chairman at Thursday's meeting of the County Planning committee. It was that the Railway Executive proposed to close the Newport-Sandown and Freshwater lines within a year and the Ryde-Cowes line within five years leaving only the Ryde-Ventnor line in use at the expiration of that period. In a statement the Clerk of the County Council (Mr. L.H. Baines) said it had come as a shock to him to learn that before negotiations were concluded a decision had been reached behind the backs of those concerned. (November 22)

* See photograph page 79.

In the years following the end of the war, and perhaps as a reaction to it, Britain began to develop a sense of national identity for the first time. The notion that there were cultural traditions and an architectural heritage worth preserving slowly began to gain ground...

October 25th, 1952

BEMBRIDGE WINDMILL
AGAIN IN NEED OF REPAIR

...To Islanders anxious for the preservation of such an interesting old structure, Bembridge windmill has an increasing fascination as the years go by. In 1935 about £100 was raised to restore the vanes and for certain interior work, but the ravages of the weather have again had their effect and the mill is once more in need of repair. Although no further appeal has been made, or even suggested, it would be a pity if the mill were allowed to fall into ruin. There are many who would like to see repair work carried out. The mill is still privately owned... No records exist of the history of the mill, but this is not surprising, as in bygone days a mill was as much a part of village life as a blacksmith's shop, just serving the community year after year, and consequently ignored by the local historian... It is generally thought to have been built early in the 18th century from stone brought from Swanage... The walls are 18 in. thick and on the south side have been faced in order to give greater protection against the prevailing winds. The entire machinery is of wood and remains practically intact... Before the First World War the mill came into the possession of the late Farmer Alfred Morris, of Stanwell, who on his death in 1937 bequeathed it to his niece, Mrs. R. Smith, who still lives at the Mill Farm... The only part of the machinery missing are the millstones, which were sold to the late Mrs. St. George, who had them placed at The Priory, Nettlestone... Although about 15 years ago the mill caused some consternation by suddenly starting on its own account, the last time it was worked was 37 years ago by Mr. Ernest Orchard, of High Street, Bembridge, a brother-in-law of Farmer Morris and a professional miller who had been employed at the late Mr. L.J. Souter's Mill at Wootton Bridge. Apparently Farmer Morris was "a little bit scared" of the mill and had no wish for its working. Mr. Orchard, however, influenced him and used to come over from Wootton to superintend matters, although he could never persuade the owner to remain in the building while the mill was running. Mr. Orchard has ground about 15 to 20 sacks of wheat and barley at a time and says that once the mill was in motion it could be left, as whatever the strength of the wind the speed of running was automatically controlled. He relates that a miller's life was not all honey, and if after a calm day the wind got up in the night the miller had to get up as well and set to work. Mr. Orchard recalls that he frequently endeavoured to persuade Farmer Morris to allow the mill to be open for inspection by the public, but the owner had some phobia about the place and seemed to think that everyone else had, so it never came about...

1953

NEWS IN BRIEF

A STRANGE CATCH. – On Thursday last, at Seagrove Bay, I pegged out a line on the sands of 18 hooks. My catch was six small ling, one bass of 3 lbs., and a "shag" (I do not know its correct name), but am told it is one of the most destructive of seabirds. It was hooked on the foot.

E. MAJOR. Anchor Gate, Seagrove Bay, Seaview.

VANISHING CATS. – Some weeks ago I asked in your columns if foxes ate cats. "Countryman" replied assuring me that they did. But he also said cats were in great demand to help the fur trade. Since writing, several more cats have vanished from Whitwell... It may interest your readers to know that in one London factory alone 250,000 cats and 100,000 dogs are skinned annually. Hundreds of these were someone's pets. And this is Christian England!

INNEL JOLLIFFE. The Mill House, Whitwell.

Hearing the sound of breaking glass, a Freshwater Bay householder rushed upstairs to find that a pheasant had crashed through a bedroom window pane. The bird, which had taken refuge on top of a wardrobe, escaped, apparently uninjured, through the hole in the glass.

An RAF .38 revolver in a service holster with lanyard, and loaded with one round of ammunition was hooked on his line by a fisherman on Ryde Pier last weekend. He took his catch to the police.

———————◆———————

For the Princess flying boats it was the end. After seven years of development, there were still two insurmountable problems. Firstly, the powerful engines required for the huge sea-planes had failed to materialise. Secondly, and more devastatingly, in the intervening years the jet engine had been developed...

February 14th, 1953

PRINCESS FLYING BOATS
SECOND AND THIRD BEING COCOONED

The second and third of the three 140 ton 10-engined Princess flying boats built by Messrs. Saunders-Roe are being cocooned and taken to the flying boat station at Calshot to await completion of the engines. The first cocooned Princess is now ready for dispatch to Calshot and will probably be towed there within the next week. On Tuesday representatives of the Press and photographers were invited to the works to inspect the plastic spraying work carried out on these huge aircraft to ensure their preservation... The cocooning of each of the Princesses will make the largest "package" in the world. Some eight tons of desiccant was used on each flying boat to dry the air inside the "package" to prevent corrosion. Before the plastic was sprayed on, a sealing compound was brushed over the outside of the mainplanes and the other sharp projections were covered with a plastic sheet to ensure adequate strength, thus avoiding any breakage when the sprayed coats shrink into position. The approximate weight of plastic sprayed in position is nine tons. Three coats of plastic have been applied, giving a thickness of 40 thousandths of an inch. A bitumen coat was then applied to all surfaces, and the area along the chine reinforced with a band of hessian to safeguard against abrasion during the towing. Another coat of bitumen was then applied to the hull and all upper surfaces, giving an overall thickness of approximately 100 thousandths of an inch. A final aluminium spray was then applied... 18 hygrometers have been installed, so that the relative humidity inside can be ascertained at a moment's notice.

———————————◆———————————

The end was also in sight for more of the Island's railway lines. In common with the recently closed Merstone-Ventnor branch, the financial arguments for the closure of the remaining lines were irrefutable. Letters appeared in the County Press protesting about the closures but no correspondents were able to offer any practical solutions. The Railway Executive spelt out their closure plans and in an editorial the County Press conceded the strength of their argument...

February 28th, 1953

MORE RAILWAY CLOSURES PROPOSED
ANNUAL LOSS EXCEEDS QUARTER OF A MILLION

The Railway Executive have submitted proposals that the Brading-Bembridge line will close on June 8th and that the Newport-Sandown and Newport-Freshwater lines together with Ashey, Wootton, and Whippingham stations, on the Ryde line, will close on September 21st... an accompanying memorandum states that the approximate annual net loss on Island railways is £271,200, of which £90,000 is expected to be saved if the proposals are accepted...

LOSSES ON ALL LINES

The memorandum states: An intensive review has revealed that the whole of the lines are worked at a considerable loss. The annual deficit of £270,000 is made up as follows: Ryde-Ventnor £84,000; Ryde-Newport-Cowes £80,000; Newport-Sandown £35,000; Newport-Freshwater £46,000; Brading-Bembridge £25,000... In support of their case the Executive published details of a census of rail traffic compiled during July 1952 for summer working and October 1952 for winter working. This shows that the number of passengers travelling on any one train during the summer period were: Newport-Sandown, maximum 383, minimum 14; winter, max 96, min 6. Newport-Freshwater, summer, max 256, min 1; winter, max 67, min nil. Brading-Bembridge, summer, max 210, min 1; winter max 56, min nil.

Editorial same issue:

THE RAILWAY PROBLEM

The announcement of line closures by British Railways this week was not surprising, in view of the previous indication of such intention, but the figures of losses and of passenger traffic published in support of the proposals are surprising. They clearly show that if financial considerations alone are to be the criterion, the Island must lose all its railways five years hence, unless there is some drastic change of circumstances. The Railway Executive estimate the annual loss on the railways at £270,000, and the largest deficit, £84,000 a year is on the Ryde-Ventnor line, in spite of the huge number of visitors carried on that route in the summer. As the present proposed closures are estimated to result in a saving of only £90,000 a year, it would seem inevitable that complete elimination of the Island Railways is a possibility, if not a probability...

ISLAND NOTES

FIRE EXPLOSION AT CALBOURNE INN - CUSTOMER "SHOT" IN THIGH. – A customer was wounded in the right thigh and a window was broken when an explosion occurred in the bar fireplace at the Sun Inn on Tuesday evening. The injured man sustained a puncture wound caused by a flying splinter of metal, and the hole in the bar window resembles that caused by a small calibre rifle bullet. The coal on the fire is believed to have contained a detonator.

Pier porters at Yarmouth on Sunday watched a seagull attack something in a rock pool and finally pull a fish on to dry land. They drove off the bird and recovered a bass weighing 1½ pound.

OAK, NOT ASH – In the report of the wedding last week of Mr. John Tilbury and Miss Patricia Wells, we stated that the bridegroom was presented with an ashtray by his fellow members of J.S. White's fire brigade. It was an oak tray.

RYDE AIRPORT SOLD. – At an auction sale at the Wheatsheaf Hotel, Newport, on Tuesday, a purchaser whose name was not disclosed bought Ryde Airport for £5925. The solicitor acting for the purchaser refused to give the new owner's name, but said he was a Cornwall man. (March 28)

RYDE AIRPORT TO BE RE-OPENED. – Ryde airport, which was recently sold by auction to a purchaser whose name was not disclosed, has been acquired by East Wight Air Charter, Ltd., the firm who operate Bembridge Airport. The Aerodrome will be re-opened but no major developments such as regular air services are likely to operate from there this season. It is the company's intention to make the airport available for use by private owners and for joy flights, and to re-open the pavilion and office. (April 25)

The 1970's television series, "The Duchess of Duke Street" was an Edwardian drama set in the fictitious Bentinck Hotel, featuring its owner and manageress, Louisa Trotter. Her character was based on Rosa Lewis, who in real life owned the Cavendish Hotel in London and a home in Cowes. Edward VII was a lifelong patron and admired both her work and her personality, and society hostesses did well to employ her whenever he was a guest. She created stunning dishes for royal functions, including many at Cowes in the Season. On her death, her will included "a strange request"...

March 28th, 1953

A STRANGE REQUEST

A bequest of £50 to the local Salvation Army with the wish that they "should play God save the King" on August 5th every year, was included in the will of Mrs. Rosa Lewis, of the Cavendish Hotel, Jermyn Street, London, and later of Castle Rock, Castle Hill, Cowes, who died on November 28th, at the age of 85. She left £122,924 gross. Mrs. Lewis, who also left £50 to Holy Trinity Church, opened her hotel nearly half a century ago and entertained members of the Royal family and many other distinguished people. She began her career in domestic service, where her talent for cookery came to the notice of King Edward VII, when, as Prince of Wales, he was entertained by Lord Ribblesdale. When interviewed regarding the bequest, Bandmaster F. Day told our local representative that he did not know whether it would be possible for the band to always carry out a request on the stipulated day. Mrs. Lewis resided at Castle Rock during the summer months for many years and she used to do a lot of entertaining there during Regatta Week. The house and grounds is now the local headquarters of the Royal Corinthian Yacht Club.

———————————◆———————————

Mr Heal, the one-time Calbourne blacksmith, had just died aged 89. The Island was still a small place in the 1950's with many Islanders being well known to each other and as was the County Press way, Mr Heal received the customary obituary...

April 25th, 1953

VILLAGE BLACKSMITH AND METHODIST
DEATH OF MR. F.D. HEAL OF NEWPORT

The death of Mr. Frederick Daniel Heal, aged 89, of Menheniot, Barton Road, Newport, brings to a close a life spent in the service of his fellows. Mr. Heal had a family association of over 200 years with the village smithies of Calbourne and Locks Green in succession to his father, who had been the blacksmith at Calbourne, where the smithy was in the family for four generations. Shortly after his marriage, Mr. Heal took over the smithy which had been conducted for three generations by members of the Arnold family, of which Mrs Heal is a member... Mr. Heal and his wife are affectionately remembered by many who served during the 1914-18 war and who were ordered to the Newtown rifle ranges for firing practice. Anxious to provide a little comfort, Mr. and Mrs. Heal invited the men to take cups of tea at their home adjoining the ranges, and they were soon providing what amounted to a regular canteen for the troops, a service which they dispensed with generous hospitality in spite of their many other duties in the smithy and on their small dairy holding. For four years after his retirement in 1933, Mr. Heal lived at Freshwater, but had since resided at

Newport where his son, Mr. C. Heal, has established a reputation as a gunsmith... In June 1952, on the occasion of their diamond wedding anniversary, Mr. Heal told our representative that he had never smoked, nor tasted intoxicants, and had never shaved. He had vivid memories of notable Island events, including the great snowfall of 1881, during which he was the first person to get through from Calbourne to Newport on horseback and to bring back much needed supplies of bread and flour. He was a keen follower of cricket and athletics and, as a young man, a good left-handed batsman for the Westover team.

———————————◆———————————

For good or bad, the Island was not destined to be part of Britain's oil industry. For the past few months the County Press had published regular reports on the progress of the drilling at Arreton but now the end had come. After drilling down over 5000 feet the only liquid encountered so far was sea water...

April 25th, 1953

MERSTONE OIL SEARCH ENDED

The 130 ft. latticework steel tower on the site of oil drilling operations at Merstone Cross, which has been a landmark in the Arreton valley since operations commenced in September, is shortly to disappear. It was stated yesterday that the search for oil has been fruitless and further work has been abandoned. On Sunday, when drilling was suspended, a depth of 5161 feet had been reached by which time the borehole had passed through the strata in which oil was most likely to be encountered, and had reached salt water deposits which made further useful discoveries improbable. During this week technicians of the D'Arcy Exploration Co. carried out further tests which confirmed the conclusions reached by engineers and scientists on the site and the decision to abandon the project was reached. We reported recently that traces of oil were being encountered, but as the engineer in charge put it, "We have had a smell of oil but it looks as if it has gone elsewhere." Further drilling in the Island is unlikely* as the Arreton site gave the most favourable indications when an underground survey was carried out in 1950 by a seismic reflection survey party of the Anglo-Iranian Oil Company. Work has proceeded in round-the-clock shifts since September, and the brilliantly illuminated tower has been visible for miles at night.

———————————◆———————————

NEWS IN BRIEF

At Norton Green, Freshwater, a hen is acting as a foster mother to 23 chicken.

When a Naval MTB arrived at Ventnor Pier about midday on Monday it was the first craft to tie up for landing purposes since 1939.

Robins are raising a family in the pocket of an old overcoat left hanging on the wall of the shed on a Freshwater farm.

---

* Further drilling took place at Arreton in 1975, with similar results.

East Cowes once had a castle*. An imposing sight, visible for miles, it stood on what is now the open piece of ground just above the junction of Hefford and Hendy Roads. Still basically sound but unoccupied when the war started, the property suffered structural damage at the hands of soldiers billeted there, a common fate for many houses requisitioned during the war. It was handed back to the owners "a disintegrating shell." The 1950's saw it fall further into disrepair...

May 2nd, 1953

EAST COWES CASTLE
STATELY HOME FALLS INTO RUIN

Many visitors to the Island, learning from their guidebooks of the existence of an East Cowes Castle and viewing from a distance the desolated outline which dominates the landscape on the rising ground towards Osborne, have been surprised to learn how recent a structure the building is. Residents, too, who know more about its history, have come to regard it as one of the essential features of the district, and, in the last few years when the castle began to fall into decay, considerable concern has been felt at the probability that East Cowes might soon lose its familiar landmark altogether. In spite of its superficially mediaeval outline, East Cowes Castle is little more than 150 years old, having been built in 1798 by John Nash, later to achieve lasting fame as the outstanding architect of the Regency period. The house ... contained more than 40 rooms, including a picture gallery, two libraries, and a billiards room, and its outward appearance showed all the complexities of outline which the then Prince Regent favoured in his Brighton Palace. Extremely well-regarded at the time, East Cowes Castle earned the description of "elegant" in the guide books of the early 19th century, but a a few decades later, the Victorian reaction had set in and a guidebook of 1865 describes it as a "tawdry specimen." The 1860 Venables Guide to the Isle of Wight dismisses it contemptuously in four lines as "a piece of gingerbread Gothic."

REQUISITIONED BY THE ARMY

After Nash's death, the castle passed through various hands before coming into the ownership, in 1934, of the East Cowes Estate Company, the principal directors of which were Mr. and Mrs. Arthur Lowein. For a short period the castle became a tea garden, but on the outbreak of the war it was requisitioned by the Army. During the war years it suffered badly from bomb blast,† efficient maintenance was impossible, and, after the Army left, the building fell into severe disrepair. Thieves broke in and stole roofing, cut the floors and tore down some of the bookcases, and the structure was hit by decay. A proposal to have it protected as an historic building was rejected. Then the owners, now the Cowes Estates, Ltd., surveyed the property which was by that time overgrown with weeds and almost a wilderness, and it was decided to attempt to revive the area as a fruit farm under the title of Castle Growers, Ltd... The fruit farmers brought a bulldozer and a team of tractors to the task of clearing the land of its rank growth of weeds. Dangerous parts of the castle, including the billiards room and the large library, had to be demolished, but the company now hope to retain the safe part of the building as an impressive ruin. Some of it will still be able to be utilised, and the picture gallery and cellars are to be used as

---

* See photograph page 77.

† Former estate workers, speaking after the war, maintained the damage was caused solely by billeted soldiers.

packing rooms and stores for the fruit. Under the management of Mr. J. Perry, the estate is now planted for greenhouse and cloche grown strawberries, blackberries, raspberries, and blackcurrants, and plans for next year include the planting of an apple orchard.

———————————◆———————————

Built by Cowes Council in 1901, Victoria Pier at Cowes* had had its heyday and its profit making days were over. Like East Cowes Castle it was requisitioned for military use during the war and had been handed back in a damaged state at the end of the war and now required substantial repairs. During the past few years the town's councillors had regularly debated whether or not to renovate the pier but had so far decided not to spend public money on it, believing that the pier would never become a commercial proposition. And there the matter rested. The pier stood unused, its pavilion was demolished and as the years passed the pier slipped into a terminal decline...

June 20th, 1953

VICTORIA PIER, COWES

Sir, I should appreciate space in your widely read paper to register a strong protest to Cowes Council at the present deplorable condition of the Victoria Pier. Quite apart from its utter uselessness in its existing dangerous state, the pier is the first object to strike the eye of the visitor to the town by sea, and the picture it presents is one of depressing stagnation and decay – hardly an attractive advertisement to a town which has been described as one of the gateways to the Island and the world's premier yachting centre. Furthermore, such a description is a farce when one pauses to consider the totally inadequate landing facilities offered to yachtsmen using the harbour... For many years the old Marine Hotel presented a very dismal picture of neglect and it was left to private enterprise to reconstruct it into what is now quite an attractive block of flats. If Cowes is to maintain its prestige and increase its present popularity as a yachting centre it is incumbent upon the Council to set an example and restore the pier to a useful and profitable amenity.

EDWARD G. ELLIS. Pavilion Hotel, Cowes.

———————————◆———————————

On the eastern side of the mouth of Newtown creek is the area known as Elmsworth. Here, at Brickfields Farm, the Prangnell family had lived in virtual isolation for nearly 100 years, manufacturing bricks in the family brickyard. Their house still stands but today is uninhabited, and the impressive kiln, now in the care of the National Trust, is slowly falling down. Production of bricks in any great quantity at the works ceased just before the First World War but knowing no other way of life the Prangnells stayed on at Elmsworth, moving into dairy farming. In 1953 a County Press reporter visited the reclusive family...

May 16, 1953

THE PRANGNELLS OF NEWTOWN

Mr. Bill Prangnell with his sister, Miss Annie Prangnell, live in their farmhouse at Newtown, where apart from a wireless set, life goes on much as

See photograph page 25.

Wootton station, on the Newport to Ryde railway line, nestling under the roadbridge carrying Station Road. The station was closed to passengers in September 1953.   [Author's Collection]

East Cowes Castle in its heyday. The Vereker family sold the castle in 1933 and it stood empty until the war when it was requisitioned by the Army. It was damaged by troops stationed there and rapidly deteriorated during the 1950's. Demolition began in 1960 and the castle and grounds made way for a housing estate. (See page 75)   [County Records Office]

it did 100 years ago. Their farm can only be found after difficulty, for no road leads to it – not even a track. The farmer's only means of transport is a boat. His only water supply is a pond. That farmer, according to Aubrey de Selincourt's latest book, "The Channel Shore" which gave the first hint of this isolated residence, "is the most contented of men, without envy for what others enjoy."

Intrigued by the hint of mystery, a "County Press" reporter decided to locate the happy farmer, and it turned out to be one of his most remarkable quests. He found that his steps had taken him back for over a century into the rural life of the Island...

BRICKWORKS HISTORY

Enquiries revealed that the brickworks were founded on this remote site early in the 19th century by a Mr. Henry Prangnell, who, with his two brothers became famous for their speciality white bricks, but also produced red bricks, fancy bricks, and tiles, all of which had to be transported across to Newtown by barge. Alfred Prangnell became the expert of the family and eventually won the Island brickmaking championship.[*] A grandson, Tom, eventually operated the business but since his death the family have turned to farming, concentrating on cattle, and because of the lack of transport for milk, Brickfields Farm was one of the few farms allowed to continue producing butter throughout the war years.

This information whetted my appetite for the search. A map indicated the position of the brickworks, but two afternoons were spent in a vain search.... Eventually I drove to Porchfield and then set off across country, which got rougher and wilder with every step, and over which no real track or path existed... and after 45 minutes walking I sighted the first building, a long, low red-tiled drying shed... As I drew nearer a man passed into the building, and then I had my first view of the entrance to the farmhouse itself - a shady pathway leading through a tangled orchard of plum trees. Walking towards the building, I was greeted pleasantly by Miss Annie Prangnell, who lives there with her sister, Miss Mary Prangnell, and brothers Bill and Ned, all lifelong teetotallers and non-smokers. As we chatted, Bill returned from a job at Porchfield and came forward immediately to extend a welcoming hand clasp to a complete stranger.

CRAFTSMANSHIP

Looking at him, I could understand how he came to own the description "the most contented of men." His bright blue eyes twinkled with delight as he proudly showed me round the house, pointing out where the old craftsmen, his forefathers, had decorated the handmade wall bricks apparently quite haphazardly and according to the whim of the moment, but nonetheless beautifully. A door key motif predominated but there were also elaborate designs in relief interspersed with the heads of animals, fruits, and complete scenes, the whole surmounted by an artist's dream of a round twisted brick chimney.

COMPARATIVE VALUES

Neither he nor his sister appeared to mind the lack of such modern services as electricity, gas, water, or main drainage, although they admitted that they would not like to have to manage without their radio set. The only water available comes from a pond more than 100 yards away, and every drop has to

---

* See 'Yesterday's Papers ,Volume 1', pages 46 and 51.

Mr. Bill Prangnell with his sister, Miss Annie Prangnell, at their farmhouse at Newtown, where apart from a wireless set, life goes on much as it did 100 years ago. (See page 78)

Katie, the veteran Newport van-horse. (See page 81)

Fairlee House, near Newport, a Georgian residence on the banks of the River Medina, which is shortly to be opened as a school for boys training for entrance examinations to the nautical establishments H.M.S. Conway and H.M.S. Worcester. (See page 66)

be strained and boiled before use. For lighting they have oil lamps. When I jokingly remarked that it must be pleasant to have no electricity bills, Miss Prangnell replied smilingly, "Yes, but the income tax man knows where to find us!"

SHARED DUTIES

While Bill rows a mile and a half up the creek to leave any farm produce for collection at the bridge, or to pick up any heavy supplies for the farm, Miss Annie takes charge of shopping. She trudges across that baffling stretch of countryside in all weathers to collect the family mail and, on Saturdays, her copy of the "County Press" from the post office at Porchfield. Bill is a first-class waterman, who knows every inch of the winding creek, and he's also a great authority on the raising of oysters, an industry in which he has taken an active part throughout his life. He told me that brickmaking had been abandoned by the family for more than 40 years but as we parted we arranged a further meeting to discuss oysters the next time there is an "R" in the month!

ISLAND NOTES

FIGHT TO SAVE THE ISLAND RAILWAYS. – At the final day's hearing of the objections by the County Council, Chamber of Commerce, and 40 other associations to the Railway Executive's proposal to close three Island branch lines... Mr. Melford Stephenson, QC said: "The issue is now clearer than it has ever been since the enquiry began. You have been presented by the Railway Executive with a set of figures that are false ... The figures have now been demonstrated beyond any doubt to be quite wrong. If the same form of accountancy as has been applied to the Island were used for the whole of British Railways, their 1951 profit of £34 million would be turned into a loss of £40 million."(June 20)

REVOLUTIONARY NEW BUSES FOR THE ISLAND – A new type of double-deck bus has recently been on trial on routes of the Southern Vectis Omnibus Company. Known as a "Lodekka," the bus seats 58 people. There is a novel "transverse seat" across the front of the bus with backs to the driver - which has been a cause of complaint by travellers, who generally like to see where they are going.

DECISION TO CLOSE FRESHWATER AND BEMBRIDGE RAILWAYS. – British Railways have announced their decision to close, on September 21st, the Brading-Bembridge and Newport-Freshwater lines and Whippingham and Wootton stations on the Newport-Ryde line. (August 15)

PARKHURST CONFLICT FLOGGED. – For attacking a prison officer on November 5th with a shovel, a convict at Parkhurst Prison was sentenced by a board of visiting magistrates to six strokes of the cat. (November 21)

THE BLEAKDOWN ADDER. – We have received a number of communications with reference to the item last week stating that an adder 35 inches in length was run over by a motorist on the Bleakdown Road... Mr. Fred Cole, of Blackgang, who has caught over 200 adders and in pre-war days captured them alive and sent them to Germany, where the poison from their fangs was extracted for medicinal purposes, informs us that he has never caught one larger than 29 inches.

That last item provoked several letters, including one from the very motorist who had run over the snake. Writing from London, he explained that he had photographed the snake and was now waiting for the film to be developed, when he would send a copy to the County Press. Unfortunately, the picture never materialised. Meanwhile, another correspondent to the letters page reflected on the one that got away...

July 18th, 1953

GREAT SNAKES!

Sir, I have been very interested in the accounts about the large adder killed at Bleakdown. My opinion is that there are some abnormal sizes of these reptiles. About 50 years ago I was working in Northcourt Gardens, Shorwell and during a walk in the grounds I killed two adders and six grass snakes. The larger of the adders was 34 inches long. On another occasion I was clearing away some manure from a cucumber frame, when I came upon a nest of grass snakes. There were 165 in all, about 9 inches long. Previous to this, when working at Haslett Farm, on going to fetch the cows one day at about 5.30 a.m., I heard a loud hissing and saw a huge snake lying over a bramble hedge. I should say it was about 6 to 7 feet long. The farmer, Mr. Attrill, told me to take a gun with me and shoot it if I saw it again. I took the gun on several occasions, but I never saw it again.

J.H. RALPH. 4, Egypt Cottages, Baring Road, Cowes.

In the space of twenty years working horses had virtually disappeared and by the 1950's a working horse on the streets was something of a novelty for local children...

August 1st, 1953

NEWPORT'S LAST COAL VAN HORSE
RETIREMENT OF "KATIE"

For 14 years "Katie" the black mare used by Messrs. Wood and Jolliffe, Ltd., for coal deliveries has been a familiar and welcome sight in the streets of Newport,* but now the firm have reluctantly decided to place the horse in retirement. The decision was made because of the unsuitability of modern roads for horses, the age of "Katie," and the fact that delivery by horse-drawn vehicles has been largely superseded by mechanical transport. "Katie" will go to the RSPCA home at Ningwood Manor on Tuesday, where she will spend the remainder of her days. Mr. Charlie Gamlin, of 36 Melbourne Street, Newport, who has looked after the horse since it came to the firm in 1939 said he and

* See photgraph page 79.

many of the residents would miss "Katie," who had become almost an institution in the town. Children, particularly, were thrilled by the sight of the horse, and they and their parents generally reserved some delicacy for it.... During the years Mr. Gamlin has developed a close understanding with it and often she seems to interpret his wishes without any words being spoken, sometimes moving to the next customer's house while Mr. Gamlin serves another... When she goes to Ningwood the friendship between them will not be severed, as Mr. Gamlin intends visiting her every week... On her 21st birthday, in May, 1950, "Katie" wore a special coming-of-age brass, fashioned as a key.

———————————◆———————————

It wasn't just the working horse that had disappeared. As Alderman King reflected in an after-dinner talk in 1953, he would never again see 3000 lambs being driven down Newport High Street as he had in his childhood...

September 5th, 1953

NEWPORT IN THE NINETIES

Ald. E. King, C.C., gave an entertaining talk to members of Newport Rotary Club at a luncheon on Wednesday at Messrs. Week's Regency Ballroom... He said that when he first came to the town in 1895 Queen Victoria was often to be seen riding through the streets in her carriage. The population of the borough was about half of what it is today... Most of the shop windows were then bay windows, such as could still be seen at God's Providence House. Where the Rotary Club was meeting used to be a candle factory behind a grocer's shop, with a bookmaker's next door... He recalled that it was a common sight, 60 years ago, to see between 2000 and 3000 lambs being driven down the High Street enroute for the London markets. His father was a farmer. He sold his eggs for 5d. a dozen and butter for 10d. a pound. The shopkeepers took a profit of a penny a dozen on eggs and 2d. on a pound of butter, and were well pleased. In the old market place he had seen as many as 200 calves, from 40 to 50 beasts, and the whole of the rest of the floor space of the market filled with pigs. The South African War brought considerable development to the town, particularly on the Mount Pleasant estate. He recalled that he walked four miles from Skinners Farm to town, along the lane now known as Medina Avenue, and through narrow passages which were Church Litten and Town Lane. The Grammar School and Library sites at Node Hill were Nursery Gardens, and the Trafalgar Estate site was fields owned by Dashwood's Brewery. Development was going on apace and he was keeping three men hard at work doing nothing else but making Venetian blinds. Nearly every house built then had them...

———————————◆———————————

In one of the many efforts to cut down imports during the war, the Government banned the consumption of white bread in 1940 and in its place introduced the "National Loaf," a close relative of today's brown bread. Containing additives such as calcium, in theory it was healthier than white bread but its coarseness and off-white colour did not endear it to everyone. It took until 1953 for the white loaf to return ...

September 5th, 1953
RETURN OF THE WHITE LOAF

Making a reappearance on shop counters after 13 years, the white loaf is proving popular, if only as a curiosity, and demand is exceeding expectations in some instances. Bakers at Newport report that they are selling all they bake, despite the higher price. The National subsidised loaf costs 4½d., while the white loaf costs 6d. More milling processes are involved in milling white flour and the texture of the bread is much finer. Some bakers doubt whether the demand will prove constant in view of the popularity of the improved National loaf but others think the demand will last and that people are genuinely appreciative of the return of the white loaf.

———————————————◆———————————————

The debate about the impending closure of the Freshwater and Bembridge railway lines had filled up many column inches in the County Press over the past months. British Railways had been shown to have been less than truthful when stating the profit and loss figures, and residents and overners alike had written to the County Press declaring their opposition to the closures. Unfortunately they were unable to provide little more than over-romanticised arguments and the majority view continued to remain that the closures were inevitable ...

September 19th, 1953
RAILWAY CLOSURES TOMORROW

Tomorrow will be a sad day in the annals of Island railways for it will mark the end of rail travel in the whole of the western half of the Wight, and, some say, the beginning of the end of all Island rail transport. The last train on the Freshwater-Newport line will leave Freshwater at 9.34 p.m., and on the Brading-Bembridge line the final passenger train from Brading will commence the 12 minute journey at 10 p.m... We understand that so far as the Freshwater line is concerned dismantling will commence on Monday with the removal of the stop-block, or safety buffers, at Freshwater, without which the Board of Trade will not permit passenger trains to be run...

———————————————◆———————————————

The following day the Bembridge and Freshwater lines passed into history. Reports of the closures took up the best part of two pages, and excluding general election results and the Queen's coronation, it was the largest amount of space given to any subject since the war. What follows is a precis of those reports...

September 26th, 1953
ISLAND RAILWAY AXE FALLS
PACKED TRAINS MAKE EVENTFUL LAST JOURNEYS
MEMORABLE SCENES ON BEMBRIDGE AND FRESHWATER LINES

The protracted and hard-fought battle for the future of the Brading-Bembridge and Freshwater-Newport railway lines ended on Sunday with a

See photograph page 87.

defeat for the forces who have opposed the move to close the lines. The passage of the final trains over the routes on Sunday evening was accompanied by remarkable scenes which only served to hide the real regret felt at the passing of two lines whose history is closely bound up with the rise of the Island to the position of a premier south coast holiday resort.

FAREWELL ON THE BEMBRIDGE LINE

Most of a crowd of nearly 300 passengers who made the last return journey between Bembridge and Brading on Sunday evening did so in the spirit of saying "au revoir" rather than a sad farewell. This was largely on account of the fact that a rumour that the dismantling of the track would start on the following day had proved to be incorrect. Throughout the day the number travelling was far in excess of normal. The affection with which local residents regarded their railway was in evidence throughout the day during which, many purchased tickets as souvenirs.

THE LAST TRAIN

Half an hour or more before the train made her last return journey from Bembridge at 9.41p.m., the platform was filled with passengers whose hilarity was tinged with regret. The number of tickets issued for the last train at Bembridge was 189, but practically double this number of passengers must have travelled as many had taken the precaution to book earlier in the day in case they should be left behind. Apart from the passengers there was a large crowd waving and cheering as the train steamed out of the station. It had not travelled 200 yards before the not unexpected happened - someone pulled the communication cord and the train came to a standstill. Driver and guard dismounted to put things right and the train started off once more. The temptation to pull the communication cord was irresistible to the "Bembridgers" fighting against the loss of their railway, and once again the train came to a standstill. Roars of laughter could be heard from one end of the train to the other but the driver and guard took it all in good part as they dismounted once more. The remainder of the mile long journey to St Helens was completed without further incident and at this station a tremendous cheer was raised by the crowd that filled the platform. More passengers were squeezed in and to the shriek of the engine's whistle the train pulled out. It had not travelled very far before the communication cord was pulled again. At Brading station both the up and down line trains between Ryde and Ventnor were waiting. Cheers and waves from the passengers in the other trains and from a crowd on the platform greeted her. While the engine changed ends of the train the majority of passengers alighted but practically all were on board again for the return journey. The departure from Brading for the last time, far from being a sad occasion, had all the air of a day's outing and a moment or so later the train was at a standstill - the cord had been pulled for the fourth time. When next the train got on the move there were loud explosions from fog detonators.

COMMUNICATION CORD DISCONNECTED

Once again the communication cord was pulled, but by this time even the good-humoured railway officials had had enough, as such actions by the practical jokers had reduced the steam pressure on the engine and had they continued there would have been a long delay in getting to Bembridge. The guard was therefore given permission to disconnect the communication cord system, and the train left Brading about 10 minutes after schedule. Detonators had been placed on the line as far as the cement mills level-crossing where the lights of the train could last be seen from Brading. There was one final hurrah on arrival at Bembridge but it was a more subdued crowd that left the train, and joyous occasion gave way to expressions of regret. Most of the travellers having said farewell to the train, lingered to watch the engine pull the now darkened carriages out of the station to the sound of a couple of blasts on the whistle and under the light of a harvest moon. A few minutes later the porter-in-charge had locked up the station for the last time and was away to his home by motorcycle. Outside the station there were still some train passengers - St Helens residents who had completed the last journey and were waiting to get back by bus!

REMARKABLE SCENES AT FRESHWATER

There were amazing scenes at Freshwater railway station on Sunday evening when hundreds of people gathered on the platform to give a rousing send-off to the last train for Newport. The gloomy atmosphere of the station was in marked contrast to the gaiety of the public, as the only illumination came from a single oil lamp in the hand of a railwayman and in the jostling throng it was almost impossible for friends planning to make the journey into Newport to avoid becoming separated. Some people bought return tickets in order to preserve the return halves as souvenirs of the occasion, but many others did not bother about tickets at all, simply crowding into every carriage and even packing every inch of the luggage van. The train, which left about three minutes late, arrived at Newport dead on time, but to the disappointment of the waiting crowd did not stop at Carisbrooke, where its passing detonated a crashing series of fog signals - practically the only ones encountered in the whole run. The first stop was at Yarmouth where a large crowd cheered. Here, quite a number of additional passengers packed themselves aboard and added to the general uproar with whistles, bells and a hunting horn, the proceedings being filmed in colour by Mr. F.G. Pritchard Flanders, who will have a valuable memento of the historic occasion if the lighting proved adequate. Even at the little farm crossings along the route groups of people had gathered to wave lamps in farewell, and in each case the driver replied with a series of resounding blasts on the whistle. A small crowd had assembled at Newport, where the spectators included Mr. H.W. Miller, of Florida Terrace, Newport. As a boy Mr. Miller travelled in a decorated coach which ran from Newport to Freshwater to celebrate the joining up of the rails at Carisbrooke a year before the line was actually opened to the public!

FAREWELL TO WHIPPINGHAM AND WOOTTON STATIONS

In the excitement attending the running of the last trains on the Bembridge and Freshwater railway lines the closing of the Whippingham and Wootton stations on the Ryde line passed almost unnoticed. The final train on Sunday called at the stations without ceremony, although many enthusiasts bought tickets as souvenirs...

In 1948 the UK gas industry was nationalised and on the Island at that time there were gasworks at Ryde, Shanklin, Newport and Cowes where gas was produced by the time-honoured method of heating coal and collecting the gas which was driven off. Over 1000 tons of coal a week was consumed and the gas, known as 'town gas', was stored in massive holders located in various towns across the Island. The gasholders, painted green and resembling giant tin cans, became part of the local landscape, the last one at Kingston Works only being dismantled in 2005. During the 1950's two of the gasholders caught fire. The first was at Newport...

October 17th, 1953

NEWPORT GASHOLDER EXPLODES
FIVE MINUTE SPECTACLE OF SEARING FLAMES

The main gasholder at Newport Gasworks exploded at 4.15 a.m. on Tuesday, yet the first intimations that many residents of the town had of the incident was when police patrol cars fitted with loudspeakers, went around the area asking them to check gas taps of lights normally left burning all night, and warning that there would be a reduced pressure during the morning. For some residents however, particularly those whose homes overlook the gasworks, it was a terrifying experience. Hundreds of people witnessed the five minute spectacle of searing flames, looking like a volcano in eruption... Houses were shaken but undamaged by the force of the explosion, and fortunately there were no personal injuries, although pieces of debris fell into gardens and on open ground... The Fire Brigade were quickly on the scene, and hoses were run out, but after five minutes the flames died away.

Just after 4 a.m. Police Constable R. Phipps, on night duty at the police station, went to the stokehole to see to the boilers. He heard a loud hissing and rumbling, and ran outside. He realised at once that the noise was coming from the gasholder, which lies 40 yards away... He ran back and alerted the fire brigade, and on the way saw a blinding sheet of flame as the gasholder exploded. Outlined in the flame he saw the metal sheeting of the roof of the gasholder lift and fold over like a piece of cloth. The hissing and rumbling had turned into a tremendous roar and the flames went high into the air. In about five minutes they died down, leaving the smoking ruins of the gas holder with the top open like an old tin can*... Mr. A. Leal, of Elm Grove, whose bedroom windows look out across the town, said that the sound woke him, and the glare in the sky made him get out of bed. The pillar of flame, from such a distance, looked like "a giant Roman candle."... Mrs. G. Brimson, of 7 Fairlee Road, was another resident who was brought from deep sleep to wakefulness in a split second. She said, "I heard a rumble and thought it was thunder. Then the room was lit by a vivid flash, and I thought an atom bomb had been dropped."

An official of the Southern Gas Board said on Tuesday morning that it was not yet possible to say what had caused the explosion... The gasholder which exploded contained about a quarter of a million cubic feet of gas... The Fire Brigade explanation of how the explosion occurred is that a weakness in the envelope developed and the gas pressure forced open a portion of the roof, the tearing of the metal causing a spark which ignited the gas as it mixed with the air.

---

* See photograph opposite.

Mr. H.G. Occomore, of Broadfield, Bembridge, aged 83 (centre), who travelled on the first train from St. Helens in June, 1881, and was a passenger on the last train on Sunday. (See page 83)   *[Photo: Paterson]*

The shattered top of the main gas holder of the Newport Gas Works after the explosion on Tuesday morning. There were no personal injuries and surprisingly little damage to surrounding property. (See page 86)

Donald McGill was the creator of the quintessential British seaside postcard. Buxom ladies at the bar of the Cock Inn and "Just married and it sticks out for a mile," both came from his pen. Taste, like beauty, is in the eye of the beholder, so while many found the cards harmless, others wanted them banned. In the early 1950's councils across England studied McGill's postcards to satisfy themselves that the shops in their area selling the cards did not fall foul of the Obscene Publications Act of 1857. On the Island, local police prosecuted four shopkeepers following one complaint...

October 31st, 1953

RYDE MAGISTRATES ORDER 814 POSTCARDS TO BE DESTROYED
PROCEEDINGS UNDER OBSCENE PUBLICATIONS ACT
CONFISCATED FROM FOUR SHOPS

Ryde magistrates on Monday ordered 814 picture postcards of 67 types, which had been confiscated by the police from four shops in the town, to be destroyed as obscene.... Four shopkeepers, Gordon McFarlane, of 3 Melville Street, James Harry Purkis, of 177 High Street, Alfred Vernon, of Ryde Pierhead shop and Gordon Skinner, of 20 The Esplanade were summoned under the Obscene Publications Act of 1857... Opening the case against McFarlane, Det. Con. W. Goodall said that in consequence of a complaint he visited defendant's shop... and seized 12 postcards... He produced the cards. Cross-examined, witness said that he considered the actual pictures together with the caption underneath made the cards obscene. There was a double meaning.

"DEGREES OF DECENCY"

Making his submission for all the defendants, Mister Eldridge said it was a very difficult matter to decide what was obscene. The degrees of decency varied with the age in which we live. They had all been down on the esplanade and seen persons of both sexes bathing, men in brief trunks, and ladies in two-piece costumes. Some years ago these people would undoubtedly have been prosecuted for offending against public morals.... He submitted that these cards were not obscene. They came into different categories. The first was that age-old musical jest of overdeveloped ladies and small insignificant gentlemen. The next category showed men drinking too much, or slipping on banana skins. They might not be in good taste but they were not obscene. Then there were the pictures with a double meaning. Many things have a double meaning but unless it was blatant, it took a person willing to read indecency into something to follow the indecent meaning... In the case of Vernon, evidence was given by the director of the firm producing all the cards which defendants sold. He said that the cards were all designed by Donald McGill, who had been drawing for 50 years.* One particular card which the police were claiming was obscene had been passed by the Government board of censorship in the Isle of Man, Blackpool and Grimsby... Of the total of 1659 postcards submitted from defendants' shops the Chairman said the bench ordered 814 to be destroyed. Of those remaining, they would pass without comment, while others were remarkably vulgar, and it would be better for Ryde and the reputation of the town if they were not exhibited for sale.

---

* The following year McGill, then aged 80, was prosecuted for breaching the 1857 Act and was found guilty and fined £50. In an odd coincidence the copyright for McGill's postcards is today owned by Greaves and Thomas, globe makers of Union Street, Ryde.

1954

As East and West Cowes residents can confirm, the beach at East Cowes produces unpleasant smells from time to time, particularly in high summer. It is not a modern phenomenon. The smell had occupied the minds and nostrils of local residents as far back as the late 19th century and continues to do so to this day. To add insult to injury, East Cowes residents also had to endure a drinking supply contaminated by seawater...

February 27th, 1954

THE EAST COWES BEACH

Regarding the beach at East Cowes, Dr. Mills, Island Medical Officer of Health, says in his annual report that it presents a sorry spectacle at low water with large areas of decaying seaweed emitting a very foul, nauseating odour lying exposed. The sight of holidaymakers, adults and children, wading through this stinking material in order to bathe raises some alarm. The stench from the beach when low water is combined with hot weather beggars description, and when the wind is from the east, West Cowes also suffers from the smell. Unpleasant and revolting though the smell is, there is no evidence that disease has been caused by it, but serious consequences would be expected to ensue following the swallowing of the water from this beach while bathing. A full-scale bacteriological investigation of conditions on the beach has been undertaken...

EAST COWES WATER

Dealing with the East Cowes water, which was renowned for its unpalatability, Dr. Mills states that its taste is so objectionable that some of the residents are unable to drink it raw and relied to a great extent upon mineral waters bought from shops. In some cases water has to be carried from better quality supplies outside the district. Tea brewed from the East Cowes water is unpleasant and to many people, undrinkable. The residents of East Cowes bear a great burden in this water supply. Not only is the flavour unpleasant, but the extreme hardness produces rapid furring of pipes and utensils, clogging of valves, and corrosion and damage to certain metal containers... It appears that the quality of the water is deteriorating. A recent analysis showed that organically, the water was satisfactory and there was no evidence of excessive animal or vegetable pollution. The sample was free from metallic contamination. The taste was brackish and the water would be regarded as unpalatable by the majority of consumers. This was due to a very high content of soluble solids and approximately 4 per cent sea water... It is clear, therefore, that an improved supply is a matter for greater priority to alleviate the long-suffering residents of the town.

NEWS IN BRIEF

ISLAND VETERAN CAR FOR EXPORT. – Owned jointly by Mr. George Marvin of Gurnard (a grandson of the original owner), and Mr. R Porter, of Cowes, what is believed to be the oldest running motor-car in the Island, a 22 hp Mors 1908 with the registration number DL 557, has been sold to Mr. H.L.

Cook of Akron, Ohio... During the first world war the car was laid up by its owner because of petrol restrictions and it was not moved out of the garage again until last year. It was then restored to its original condition and reappeared on Island roads again. The hood and upholstery are in perfect condition and the body still has the original paintwork... The car's estimated top speed is 50 miles an hour. It does 18 miles to the gallon and has covered only 6000 miles.

RAILWAY LIFTED. – Dismantling of the track of the Ventnor West-Merstone railway is proceeding and little more than the Godshill-Merstone section still remains. (March 6)

MOTHER OF 28 CHILDREN PRIZEWINNER AT HOBOES' PARTY. – Mrs. Louisa Jane Broomfield, of 79 High Street, Newport, won a prize for the mother of the largest family at the Hoboes old folks' party on Tuesday at the Regency Restaurant, Newport. Mrs. Broomfield, who is 93, claimed to have had 28 children. She told the "County Press" that she married at the age of 20, when her husband was 23, and they lived at Paradise Row, Newport. She was born in Pyle Street, and was one of 13 children. Her husband, a general labourer who died 20 years ago, came from a family of 12. Her children included two sets of twins but unfortunately many of them died when very young. A spry and active little woman, Mrs. Broomfield does all her own cooking.

RABBIT DISEASE IN THE ISLAND. – An outbreak of myxomatosis[*] - a deadly disease affecting rabbits - has been confirmed by the county pest officer after examining rabbits found dead in the Barton Manor and Kings Quay area. This disease spreads rapidly and exterminates practically all rabbits within the affected area... (March 27)

--------◆--------

The war had left some dangerous legacies. On land there were still unexploded bombs to contend with, while at sea, mines were still turning up from time to time...

March 13, 1954

DRIFTING MINES IN CHANNEL

Shipping in, or approaching, the English Channel, including the liners Queen Elizabeth and United States, was warned by Niton Radio Station on Tuesday to keep a watch for two mines reported drifting in the Channel. When the liner Orion docked at Tilbury from Australia, her officers reported the sighting of a mine about five miles off the Needles. It was described as very old and covered with barnacles. Other reports were received... An Admiralty spokesman told a newspaper reporter that it was not regarded as a matter of any special concern. If mines were seen by naval vessels they were sunk by rifle fire. Expert opinion is that there is no great danger from such floating mines, as they are usually rendered inoperative in breaking free from their moorings.

[*] Myxomatosis, a contagious virus, was illegally introduced into the UK in 1953 and killed 95% of the rabbit population. A third of rabbits now survive the disease and in 2005 the UK Land Registry reported that the rabbit population was increasing threefold every two years.

By the 1950's working-class housing had changed beyond all recognition. The era of tin baths and outside lavatories was fast disappearing and "all mod cons" had become the norm. It didn't suit everyone...

March 27th, 1954

HOME COMFORTS

The familiar ruin of a cottage alongside the Calbourne-Brighstone Road is still occupied. Mr. Alfred Summerfield, 76-year-old former gamekeeper to the first Sir Charles Seely, Bt., prefers to live in the ruins of his old home* rather than share the comforts of a cottage with his family in Calbourne. For companions he has nine cats and two goats and is perfectly happy and content. Apart from its more than adequate "ventilation" the cottage has no modern services, and Mr. Summerfield has to carry his supplies of drinking water from a house more than half a mile away, though the main pipe-line to the new reservoir runs within a few yards of the building. He uses oil burners for cooking and illumination and enjoys listening to the radio programmes on his battery-operated set. A native of Surrey, he served in the South African War with the Yeomanry and held three mainland appointments as gamekeeper on famous shoots before coming to the Island in 1907. He moved into his present home after the first world war, in which he served with the Hampshire Regiment.

NEWS IN BRIEF

SQUIRREL IN THE STREET. – For some weeks, a red squirrel has been seen from time to time at different business premises in High Street and Pier Street, Ventnor, and when it was spotted on the shop blind outside Thurgood Sisters, on Monday, a determined effort was made to catch it and when its flight was cut off in Pier Street it shot into Jury's Stores. It bit the finger of one of the chasers before being caught and later released at St Lawrence.

PIGEON SHOOT TOTAL. – The pigeon shoots arranged in conjunction with the NFU and the County Landowners' Association accounted for 7335 pigeons between September 1st, 1953, and April 1st, 1954.

PLAGUE CAN WIPE OUT ISLAND'S RABBITS. – The rabbit plague, myxomatosis, which has broken out in the Cowes and Wootton areas, is likely to wipe out all rabbits on the Island, a Ministry of Agriculture official stated this week. Conditions are now almost perfect for the rapid spread of germs and many thousands of rabbits have already died. The official added that experts believed that no effective measures to contain the attack would be possible... The Ministry official was asked: "Since rabbits are agriculture's biggest and costliest pest, why not allow myxomatosis to wipe them out?" He replied that fur and show-rabbit breeding was now a sizeable industry, and might be seriously hit... (April 3)

---

* See photograph page 97.

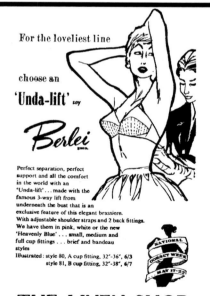

Against the odds, Calbourne Mill outlasted every other mill on the Island and was still trading well into the 1970s. This was mainly due to the far-sighted decision in 1894 to install a state-of-the-art roller mill plant, usually found in much larger mills. Steel rollers driven by gas engines were highly efficient and the traditional method of grinding wheat between stones couldn't begin to compete, and so it was that following the end of the first world war, while the other Island mills closed one by one, Calbourne remained competitive and continued milling. In 1954 it stood alone...

April 10th, 1954.

FLOUR GRINDING CEASES AT CALBOURNE
END OF AN ISLAND INDUSTRY

When the steel rollers stopped at Calbourne Mill last week, flour milling came to an end as an industry in the Island. But that does not mean that the picturesque building on the Caul Bourne will become derelict; far from it, as the provender mill continues in full production of cattle food. For this, however, the grain is crushed between huge millstones just as it was centuries ago... Calbourne Mill has been in the ownership of the Weeks family since 1878 and there was a bakery attached to the mill up to half a century ago.... Stones were used to grind the wheat until 1894, when the rollers were installed to give a production rate of one and a half sacks an hour. Motive power comes from the Winkle Street stream, which springs up in nearby Westover Park. This stream is completely overlooked as an industrial asset by the thousands of visitors who flock to Winkle Street each summer... At one time, however, it turned the wheels of three mills in the course of its short journey to join the sea in Newtown Creek... Mr. R. Weeks, who showed a "County Press" representative over the mill, recalled that until comparatively recently five mills were producing flour in the Island. He added that he had known for years that for economic reasons the day must come when the operation would have to cease, but he was glad to have realised his hope that the family would be the last flour millers in the Island.

◆

Spring or 'mineral' water has always had a cachet attached to it. The Island possessed two popular and successful 'Chalybeate' springs in the 19th century, producing endless supplies of water rich with salts of iron, which were said to possess health giving properties. One was at Shanklin and the other at Blackgang...

April 24th, 1954

BLACKGANG'S CHALYBEATE SPRING
By VECTENSIS

A century and a quarter ago, water from rocks at Blackgang was being supplied to Londoners by a famous firm of chemists, with the recommendation that it was "the most powerful tonic known." I am reminded of this fact by a reader who has shown me an advertisement card of Messrs. Savory & Moore Ltd., recently exhibited in their London premises. On the card is an advertisement from the "Morning Herald" in 1829 reading as follows: "Isle of Wight Chalybeate Spring - The medicinal properties of the aluminous chalybeate water from the sand rock in the Isle of Wight (the most powerful tonic known) are now so well recognised as to require no further comment on its merits"... This "life-giving stream" still runs from the rocks in the grounds of Mr. R.P. Young's residence, Sandrock Spring,* on the clifftop at Blackgang, but has long since lost its commercial value, although at one time it was obviously the source of considerable profit to the then owner... The iron content in the little streams which trickled down the cliffs is evident by the discolouration of parts of the foot of the cliffs. Quite near, on the opposite side of the road, is a shrine-like memorial to Shakespeare with a similar spring emerging from it, with a pipe through the wall from which passers-by could drink... This spring, too, is said to have tonic properties, but last week-end, when I passed by, the little wall fountain was dry.

◆

No sooner had Calbourne Mill stopped producing wheat flour than Yafford Mill announced that it was to start production. Up until then, Yafford had been producing animal feed and as Mr. Salter the miller explained, the mill had never produced wheat flour in all the 51 years he had been associated with it but had, in fact, produced barley flour. Mr. Salter continued to operate the mill until the early 1970s...

April 24th, 1954

YAFFORD MILL TO GRIND FLOUR AGAIN
AFTER MORE THAN 50 YEARS

A few weeks ago we announced that with the closing down of the roller milling section at Calbourne Mill, flour grinding had ceased in the Island. To-day we are pleased to announce that the closure signalised not the end of flour milling, but merely the close of an era in the history of this ancient local industry. At the picturesque Yafford Mill new flour dressing equipment has been installed and grinding will commence as soon as the necessary chutes can be fitted. Stoneground flour has always been acclaimed as the finest available, and at Yafford the wheat will be crushed between stones that were in use more than half a century ago.

The jovial Miller, Mr. A.C. Salter, who started work at Yafford as a boy 51 years ago, recalls talk of the mill being used to produce wheat flour, but states that none has been ground there in his time. In the First World War the stones that are now to grind the wheat were brought into use to produce barley flour. In recent years, however, they have stood idle, and Mr. Salter is just completing the laborious and exacting task of re-dressing them for their new role. This calls for the cutting of fine lines into the surface of the stones - lines so fine that it is laid down that they should number 16 to the inch. The mill is driven by a waterwheel deriving its power from the stream which rises at Northcourt... From the mill the stream meanders down to Brighstone Mill and so on to the sea at Grange...

Mr. Salter's most alarming experience, and one which might easily have cost the life of a man of less sturdy build, occurred some years ago. In those days it

---

* The house, still in the ownership of the Young family, slipped over the cliff edge in 1979. The Shakespeare memorial can still be seen by those determined enough to ignore the warning signs and scramble down onto the landslipped road (which is technically private property.) All traces of the spring mouth disappeared in a landfall of 1958.

was his confident habit to switch off that part of the machinery no longer required by pushing the driving belt off the moving wheel by hand. On this occasion the belt became twisted in some manner, whipped round his left leg, and hoisted him to the ceiling where, with the belt rapidly tightening, he was crushed against the edge of a revolving iron wheel. He remembers thinking, "Well, this is it!" and the next thing he knew the mill was silent, apart from the tinkle of the water splashing over the stationary outside wheel. Apparently his weight and the pressure of his leg against the machinery had stopped the drive. Alone in the mill, he was still in an awkward situation as he hung suspended from the twisted belting, with the machinery straining to resume its turning once the pressure was eased. Groping with one free hand, he managed to get his pen knife from his waistcoat pocket and, opening it with his teeth, he cut through the belt. Freed of its toils, he fell heavily to the floor, the waterwheel commenced turning, and immediately the miller became the target for a shower of iron-hard fragments of wood. These came from the splintered wooden teeth of the giant crown wheel, 13 of which had been smashed by the braking effect of his body and the tangled belting. Mr. Salter replaced those teeth very carefully, and to-day he is equally careful never to lapse into his former casual method of switching off... Formerly owned by the late Mr. Jim Jolliffe, the mill was bought about seven years ago by Mr. J.P.S. Clarke, of Bowcombe.

———————————◆———————————

With the Merstone to Ventnor West Railway line a thing of the past, the level crossings and overbridges along the route were quickly dismantled...

May 22nd, 1954

DISMANTLING A RAILWAY

Our photograph shows the removal on Tuesday of one of the two main girders of the railway bridge spanning Nettlecombe Lane, Whitwell, in the course of the dismantling of the Merstone-Ventnor West Railway by Messrs. Thomas Ward, Ltd, of Sheffield. Only one other road bridge, that at Godshill, now remains to be removed to complete the job of demolition of the track and ancillary equipment which was started in November by a gang of seven men with the assistance of a British Road Services seven-ton lorry and a mobile crane from the Newport depot. Work commenced at the Ventnor West end, and one of the most interesting parts of the job was in the half-mile tunnel between St Lawrence and Whitwell, which was worked through by the lorry and the crane taking up the track as they went, by the light of Tilley lamps in a darkness which, as one man remarked, could be felt. The metals removed from the track will mostly be put into service elsewhere, and the steel from the bridges will be used as scrap.

———————————◆———————————

TOWN AND COUNTY NOTES

PRISONERS AWARDED THE "CAT". – Punishment with the "cat" was awarded at Parkhurst Prison, on Monday to two prisoners who were concerned in an incident following a football final on Easter Monday. A statement by the

In the summer of 1954, after years of development problems, the last of the three Princess flying boats was filled with eight tons of dessicant and cocooned on a slipway at Medina Road, Cowes. An optimistic Saunders-Roe spokesman told the County Press "We are convinced that the flying boat has a big future." 13 years later the planes were sold for scrap.   *[Photo, Marie Coundley]*

This cottage alongside the Calbourne-Brighstone road is still occupied by Mr. Alfred Summerfield, aged 76. (See page 92)

Home Office reported: "The awards of 12 strokes with the cat to the prisoner Fred Simm and six strokes with the cat to the prisoner Michael Hogan, were carried out this morning."

NUNWELL CANNON RECOVERED. – Persistent enquiries by the Island police have resulted in the recovery of the ancient bronze cannon which was stolen from Nunwell House, the residence of Brig. Gen. and Mrs. C. Aspinall Oglander, in January. It disappeared just prior to the snowfall of that period and for some three months nothing was heard of it. Recently it was found at the premises of a London metal dealer and returned to Nunwell. The gun has been in the possession of the Oglander family since the days of Edward VI.

DEMOLISHED RAILWAY BRIDGES "UNSIGHTLY." – Complaints that the demolished railway bridges on the former Ventnor West to Merstone line had been hastily removed and left in an unsightly and untidy condition were made by the Ventnor Chamber of Trade... Mr. P. Netherton said the remains of the bridges presented "a ghastly sight" and he complained of the removal of two footbridges in Pelham Woods. The Chairman said it seemed that the job had been hurriedly done so that no one else could come along with any proposals to reopen the line.

LAST "PRINCESS" TO BE COCOONED. – The last of the three Cowes-built Saunders-Roe Princess flying-boats is to be "cocooned" shortly and the future of the planes - the biggest built in Britain - is uncertain. The whole project is likely to be shelved for about two years until more suitable engines are available. The bill for the "Princesses" had amounted to over £10 million by June 1950... A spokesman of Saunders-Roe told the Press yesterday: "We are convinced that the flying boat has a big future..."

———————◆———————

To destroy a cargo vessel which had played a part in the Battle of Trafalgar would be unthinkable today. The Bee, owned by the Newport firm of Shepard Brothers was just such a vessel and when its useful service life came to an end in 1927, it was unceremoniously grounded in the waters of the Medina to become a breakwater at Werrar brickworks, adjacent to Stag Lane. In 1954, after 27 years in the mud, the hull still remained virtually intact and at that point the boat could still have been saved. The hull has since disappeared and all that can be seen today are the remnants of her ribs protruding from the mud...*

July 10th, 1954

THE BEE

The hulk lying on the Medina mud at Werrar once held the distinction of being the oldest British trading vessel afloat. She was placed in position 27 years ago to form a breakwater, and retains her shape, although other and younger vessels have gone to pieces in a much shorter period alongside her. She was the Bee, built in 1801 at Hansen's Shipyard, Cowes, as a ketch-rigged cargo vessel. Manned by a crew of three she was in regular service for Messrs. Shepard Bros.,

---

* See Yesterday's Papers, Volume 3, page 115.

Newport 1954.

At the top of the picture are the viaducts bringing the Ryde and Sandown railway lines into Newport station, and behind them is the tower of Newport gasworks. At the bottom is South Street, prior to the arrival of shops and bus station in 1962.   *[Author's Collection]* of Newport for 124 years, trading between the Island and Southampton. She was replaced by a motor ship in 1925, and has been in her present position since 1927. Through Mr. A.W. Bishop, of Newport, whose firm, maintained the Bee from 1883 to 1925, the National Maritime Museum, Greenwich, have taken an interest in her, and are sending experts to record her lines for posterity. The Bee was a victualling ship for the fleet at Spithead before the Battle of Trafalgar.

━━━━━━━━━━◆━━━━━━━━━━

The County Press was never backward in coming forward in its editorials. It made no secret of its Conservative allegiance and many editorials had all the flavour of a party political broadcast. This one, marking the end of rationing, is a typical example...
July 10th, 1954

THE END OF RATIONING

At long last we have said a hearty goodbye to ration books, following the decontrol of meat this week. It is 14 years since they were necessarily inflicted upon us. We have borne them during the war, and far too long since, with a patience which is a tribute to the qualities of our race. But in our relief at their passing let us not forget that if the Socialists had had their way we should still have ration books. Moreover, there would appear to be a danger of their return if the Socialists are given the opportunity of carrying out their announced policy. Under the present Conservative Government one control after another has been lifted, in accordance with their policy of setting the people free. They have given us freedom to shop where we wish, plenty instead of scarcity, and above all, stabilised the cost of living, while recently the wages index has passed the cost of living index, a healthy sign in relation to future food prices...

━━━━━━━━━━◆━━━━━━━━━━

NEWS IN BRIEF

Visitors to Foreland, Bembridge, have been surprised and charmed to see a large number of budgerigars on the trees and telephone wires with the sparrows and other birds... This colony of homing budgerigars has been formed by Lady Godfrey-Fausset, who has a sizeable aviary in her garden... The birds were liberated for the first time last week and caused no little excitement in the neighbourhood, and perhaps a little understandable anxiety on the part of the owner... They show little inclination to fly very far away and although at liberty for several hours each day... they slowly return to the aviary in the evening.

The schoolboy who rendered valuable assistance when the bus overturned near Carisbrooke last week was Roger Scott, of Freshwater, who is a pupil at Newport Grammar School. He happened to have a bottle of smelling salts in his pocket at the time.

Guests in hotels near the Eastern Gardens, Sandown, were awakened by an unexpected "entertainment" soon after 6.30 on Sunday morning when a party of young campers forced open the piano which is used by the ladies orchestra in the bandstand and started to play and sing "Knees Up Mother Brown." The police were called but the entertainers had moved on.

THE CALBOURNE HERMIT. – Sir, on Sunday evening, in a deluge of rain, I visited the old man who lives in the ruined cottage at Gotten Leaze, Calbourne. It is almost unbelievable that a man of nearly 80 should be allowed to live in such conditions. He is a veteran of the first world war. He did not grumble at his lot, but was very concerned at the fact that his old goat, which supplied him with milk, was blind. He said how terrible it was for his only friend to live in perpetual darkness. ARTHUR WILLIAMS. The Orchard, Gatcombe. (July 31)

A Totland Bay fisherman who found a large conger eel in a lobster pot killed the fish by chopping off its head. After cutting up the body for bait he picked up the eel's head just as the powerful jaws closed, inflicting a nasty gash on his hand.

◆

Different times have different priorities. A part of Ventnor's coaching history had recently been revealed when a horse-drawn coach built in 1880 came to light after being in store at Ventnor for over 30 years. Today it would be restored and preserved for posterity but this was the 1950's. Would there be a happy ending?...

July 31st, 1954

VENTNOR COACHING DAYS
PASSING OF THE LAST FOUR-IN-HAND

A link with coaching days in the Undercliff was recently severed when the last of the late Mr. Henry Brown's fleet of four-horse coaches was sold for breaking up. After the sale of Mr. Brown's property at the Pier Street Mews the coach came into the possession of Mrs. Saperstein, who has had it stored in the Clock House, Park Avenue, formerly the stables of Steephill Castle... The coach, The Magnet, was the most famous of Mr. Brown's fleet. It was built in 1880 and, although the timber had become decayed, the axles when dismantled were as bright as on the day the coach first ran. The coachwork by the former Ventnor firm of Messrs. Martin, of Albert Street, was finished in yellow and scarlet, and the lower portion in blue. There was room inside for four passengers. Mrs. Saperstein has preserved the steps used by passengers to reach their seats on the top of the coach, and one of the wheels is to be placed in the Commercial Hotel tap converted as a hanging stand for lights... Mr. Brown's establishment was in lower Pier Street, and at the top end opposite the town clock was another coaching-master, Mr. Jackman, whose coaches were painted in yellow and navy blue and there were also Milligan's coaches... The coaches ran until a year or so after the first world war and were then superseded by motor coaches. The late Mr. "Drummer" Drake was for many years driver of The Magnet. "Billy" Wateridge was another familiar figure of the coaching days. In his declining years he touted for Jackman's tours and, standing at the top of Pier Street, was known to thousands of visitors.

The previous article prompted a letter from a former Cowes resident with memories of coaching days in the town...

August 14th, 1954

COACHING DAYS AT COWES

Mr. J.W. Irwin of Weymouth writes: "The passing of the last four-in-hand, described last week, takes my mind back to 1899 when I was about 15 years old and working as stable boy or ostler for Mr. George Smith at the Fountain Mews posting yard at Carvel Lane, Cowes. Mr. Smith also rented some stables at Market Hill, where coaches from all parts of the Island used to put up during the summer. It was my job to look after the stables, collect the money from the drivers, and clean up the stables after they had gone. I have had as many as 30 horses there at once to look after. Sometimes I had to ride on the first step of the coach down to the Marine Hotel and collect the money from the passengers, which was one shilling. I used to wash out the horses' heels and brush the sweat off them, in the hope that I might get twopence from the guards. I knew all the drivers and guards. One of the smartest drivers was Curley Rayner, from Ventnor. I knew Mr. Henry Brown, also the two Mearmans from Sandown (very smart turnouts). Some of the guards were expert horn blowers. I knew Mr. Payne; he was the champion, I think. It was a grand sight to see a four-in-hand go through Cowes High Street and up to the Market Hill stables. I have seen them go up Carvel Lane and into the Fountain Mews very nearly touching the sun blinds outside the shops. I cannot remember all the names of the coaches, but there was the "Tally Ho," "Old Times," "Royal Blue," and "Magnet" (in those days the Royal Mail van used to run from Cowes to East Cowes, Osborne, and Ryde, and arrive back at East Cowes in time for the first bridge over at about 5.45 a.m.). The horses were kept at the Anchor Yard. In those days I used to work from 6 a.m. to 7 or 8 at night, seven days a week, for 3/6d. I might get a few coppers as tips if I were lucky."

Mr. Irwin adds: "I can also remember seeing the soldiers marching through Cowes High Street from Parkhurst, on their way to South Africa, in the Boer War. Some of the soldiers handed me a bottle to go in a pub and get some beer for them, and when I came out with the beer they had moved on a bit, so I didn't know which one to give it to. Some of the officers were taking it away from the men and tipping it in the gutter. This was before breakfast. The pubs were open at 6 a.m. then."

THE WEEK'S NEWS

THE ROWRIDGE TV STATION. TESTS COMMENCE ON MONDAY. – The BBC announces that it is hoped to start regular test transmissions from the new television station at Rowridge on Monday. The transmissions will continue until Rowridge is brought into full programme service on November 12th. They will give the radio trade an opportunity to install and adjust television receivers and aerials. The test transmissions will consist of either a trade test demonstration film or a locally originated pattern accompanied on sound by music or tone. (October 16)

STEER GOES MAD. NEWPORT MARKET INCIDENT. – One of three steers from Mr. R.B. Cheverton's farm at Little East Standen caused excitement at Newport Market on Tuesday. As it was being unloaded from a lorry it jumped the five feet high wall between the market and the football field. For some time the animal evaded recapture ... a cow was taken to the field in the hope that the steer would go to it, but that proved unsuccessful. In the meantime the steer, which was badly gashed in the side, was cornered in a ditch and roped... and slowly the maddened animal was tethered sufficiently close for Mr. Biles' slaughterhouse staff to shoot it.

VEHICLE REGISTRATIONS. – Many Islanders have noted with interest the appearance of the motor vehicle registration "LDL" in the last few days. Enquiries at the County Hall showed that the last 12 months to the end of July have accounted for exactly 999 vehicles lettered "KDL." There are indications that at the present rate more than 1000 vehicles may be registered in the calendar year 1954. This compares with 816 vehicles registered during 1953.

◆

For those living in the London area, television was almost old hat. War years excepted, BBC television had been on the air for nearly 20 years and for millions it had already become a part of everyday life. On the Island there were several hundred determined viewers who had been receiving patchy, weather-related reception from the London transmitter at Alexandra Palace and as a result there had always been advertisements in the County Press over the years from retailers selling televisions. Since the late 1940s, in what was perhaps a reflection of healthier economic times, the advertisements began to grow in number and in the last two or three years they had begun to appear on the front page.

In late 1953 the BBC announced the opening of the Rowridge transmitter to serve the south of England and in the months prior to the opening, the number of advertisements for televisions soared and became a regular feature in the advertising columns. There was intense interest in the arrival of television and to celebrate the start of service, a 12 page supplement accompanied that week's issue, an event without parallel; even Queen Victoria's death was not accorded a 12 page supplement...

November 12th, 1954

ROWRIDGE TELEVISION STATION OPENED

The BBC's Rowridge transmitter came into service yesterday. It will eventually bring television to a further 2 million viewers over a large area of the South of England. The station, erected on an isolated site at Rowridge Down was built by the Westridge Construction Co., of Ryde, who, in spite of being hindered by bad weather, finished the buildings and the foundations for the 250 foot temporary mast within the contract period, and within the contract price of £40,000.... The station is some three miles from the nearest water mains and all the water to the site has to be carried in tankers. These fill a 2000 gallon underground tank... The transmissions from Alexandra Palace are received at Alton in Hampshire at a Post Office repeater station, from where they are re-transmitted to Rowridge by microwave link equipment. At present this is a one-

way link, but it is proposed to make it two-way and then it will be a simple matter to televise Island events. We understand that the BBC intend to make full use of this local publicity facility.

THIRTY TWO YEARS OF BROADCASTING.
Local Pioneer of Television Looks Back

W.G. Sherratt writes: "Yesterday, November 12th, was without doubt the most exciting day in the Island's connection with broadcast entertainment since its inception on November 14th, 1922 when the first regular radio broadcasting began under the call sign 2LO from Marconi House, London... The first television signals were received in the Island in 1932, although the BBC had been experimenting as far back as 1926. These first signals were broadcast by the Baird Company on the medium wave band... These broadcasts were extremely crude, artists having to have their faces painted white and their lips and eyebrows black!... The present high-definition television service from Alexandra Palace was started in 1936, and after a break during the war, was restarted in 1946. Island viewers may remember the first demonstrations in a specially picked house on the Newport-Cowes Road in July 1938, when the first public demonstration was given to a small audience... Until 1952 the London transmitter was the only one received in the Island, and this very poorly, unless one lived on a hill facing London and near the sea. Then in 1952 the Wenvoe Station opened in South Wales and Island viewers in the West Wight had their chance of trying their luck with this new transmitter. But, like London, it was extremely variable and the weather played a tremendous part in this long distance type of reception... There was, for instance, that amazing fortnight in February, 1953 when the signals from Wenvoe were extremely strong in all parts of the Island and reception was perfect...

What will reception be like now? 85% of the Island should have really wonderful results. With a perfect picture there will soon be viewers criticising the programmes and the presentation, not to mention the actors and actresses...

———————————◆———————————

The marshes of Newtown nature reserve which are now home to curlews and oystercatchers were once home to grazing cattle. Until 1954 the mudflats were fields, reclaimed from the sea, forming part of Marsh Farm but in November of that year the Island suffered severe gales and at the height of the storms the seawalls which had kept the Solent at bay for over 200 years were breached, and millions of gallons of seawater flooded back onto the pasture land. In all, 134 acres were lost to the sea, probably for ever, and with no commercial use in prospect the land was eventually donated to the National Trust. For an event that had far reaching effects and radically changed a substantial part of the Island, it received scant coverage at the time...

December 4th, 1954

GALES BRING SEVERE FLOODS TO THE ISLAND.
FARM INUNDATED AT NEWTOWN.

...Farmers generally have been badly hit, but perhaps none suffered more severely than Mr. K. A. Spearing, of Marsh Farm, Newtown. For nearly 3 years he has been building a wall to keep out the sea and had completed all but a stretch of 250 yards when the gale caused his land, 134 acres in all, to become flooded to a depth of from one to five feet. Normally, Mr. Spearing grazes dairy cattle. Luckily, the farm buildings are on slightly higher ground and have escaped the worst of the flooding, but it will be a long time before the rest of his land is sweet again.

◆

The following week, even more land was swallowed up by the sea...
December 11th, 1954
ATHERFIELD CLIFF FALL - TWO ACRES DISAPPEAR
Coastguard P. Petty, who was on duty in the look-out station at Atherfield in the early hours of Thursday morning, had an unenviable experience when a landslide resulted in some two acres of land slipping into the sea. It was between 7 a.m. and 8 a.m. that he heard a heavy rumbling, felt the ground shaking, and then saw everything slide away. In front of the look-out a crack opened up 25 yards from the cliff edge and the whole area beyond it fell away, leaving the look-out only 13 ft. from the edge of a 130 ft. drop. The ground in the area was so badly cracked and the general situation so unsafe, that after examining the look-out site the District Officer of Coastguards, A.E. Booth, ordered it to be abandoned. The equipment was removed, and watch will now be maintained from the duty room in the Coastguard Cottages...

1955

Proving the adage that there is nothing new under the face of the sun, the Island's cinemas at Newport and Ryde introduced stereo sound to their audiences...
January 8th, 1955
CINEMASCOPE AND STEREOPHONIC SOUND
ISLAND PREMIERE OF THE LATEST FILM INVENTIONS
At the Commodore, Ryde, on Monday an audience of over 1000 saw the first presentation in the Island of the latest development by the film industry, when the 20th Century Fox first Cinemascope production with stereophonic sound, "The Robe," was shown.[*] The first part of the programme was shown on the old screen, but when the new concave screen, which extends the whole width of the proscenium, was revealed it immediately showed the limits of the old system... The viewer has the feeling of actually being present in the action, but, of course, it is the stereophonic sound which completes this sense of realism. When a character is speaking the voice comes from whichever part of the screen he happens to be and as he moves across the screen the sound of his voice travels with him as in real life... Cinemascope, with its revolutionary new lenses, achieves the illusion of depth but it is the stereophonic sound through the 14 strategically placed loudspeakers which completes the lifelike quality of the pictures. "The Robe" will receive its premiere at the Medina, Newport, on Monday in similar projection and sound effects.

---

[*] A biblical epic starring Richard Burton and Victor Mature.

By now, myxomatosis had killed off nearly all the Island's rabbit population and this had led to hungry foxes supplementing their diet elsewhere...

February 19th, 1955

FOX RAIDS AT WOOTTON
MOONLIGHT ATTACKS CAUSE HEAVY DAMAGE

Foxes have been intensifying their raids on poultry in and around Wootton and Woodside during the last few weeks and with the breeding season near, farmers regard the outlook for the next three months as alarming. Mr. R.A. Philips, of Wootton Farm, Church Lane, has lost just over 100 laying pullets since Christmas, representing 40 per cent of the total. Foxes have also killed 40 out of 45 ducklings at the farm, and Mr. Philips estimates the value of the birds destroyed at about £140. Attacks have also been reported in other parts of Wootton, and Mr. R.T. Breese, of Woodside Farm, lost a four weeks old piglet, which was killed in the sty at night. The other piglets were unharmed, but the sow showed signs of a fight, with scratches about the head. Mr. Phillips told a "County Press" reporter this week that it seemed that the raids on his farm were concentrated on the few nights before the full moon. On one such occasion recently foxes crept right up to the house at four in the morning and killed 14 pullets housed immediately in front of the bedroom window. Mr. Phillips, awakened by their cries, rushed for his shotgun, but by the time he got it the attackers had left, leaving him a sorry mess to clear up. After another attack Mr. Phillips discovered a dozen birds dead or dying in a barn, some with their backs broken and others with their heads bitten off. Mr. Phillips said the position had got steadily worse since the end of last summer. Rabbits had almost disappeared from his land and the fox was not the only creature to feel the pinch. Stoats were desperate for food and recently climbed a roof to kill nine of his pigeons while they were roosting. The following day he left a trap and caught one...

------------------◆------------------

ISLAND NOTES

MAMMOTH'S TOOTH FOUND AT COWES. – After the recent gales Mr. Robert Stones, of 27 Albert Street, Cowes found a remarkably preserved mammoth's tooth in the mud near Messrs. Groves and Gutteridge's slipway at Cowes. Mr. A. Grapes, curator of the Geological Museum at Sandown, says it is the finest specimen he has seen. It is at least 750,000 years old. It is 13 inches long, about 15 inches in circumference, and weighs 9½lbs.

SUCCESSFUL FOX SHOOT AT EAST COWES. ISLAND FARMERS UNITE – Over 20 farmers from all parts of the Island met at Dallimore Cottage, Barton Manor, East Cowes, on Thursday morning to take part in the first of the fox shoots organised by the county pest officer in conjunction with the I.W. Hunt... Local farmers provided beaters who preceded the shoot with dogs. They worked from King's Quay to Norris Castle, and in about six hours killed seven foxes. (March 5)

FOXES KILL SEAGULLS AND A GOOSE. – Myxomatosis has practically wiped out the rabbit population on the downs in the West Wight and during the recent spell of hard weather foxes have been feeding on seagulls roosting near the cliff edge overlooking the Needles. Torn off wings of half a dozen or more of their victims have been found on several mornings by shepherds who are anxious for the safety of lambs due to be born in the next few days... (March 12.)

FINDS AT YARMOUTH POST OFFICE. – Structural alterations at Yarmouth Post Office have brought to light a number of interesting items dating back nearly a century. A copy of the newspaper "The Leader," dated 1864, was found, and in a cavity the workmen found a pair of postman's boots wrapped in a newspaper while under the floor a letter bearing a King George V penny stamp and addressed to a Chale resident was discovered. It had been lying there for about 30 years. The doors of the cupboard which once contained the Morse telegraph apparatus bear a note of sending 45,000 words by Press telegram, in addition to 600 private messages, following the sinking of HMS Gladiator in 1908. Pinned to the door, and still legible, is a printed instruction to telegraphists sent out from the GPO in London in 1870, and scribbled in pencil on the woodwork are reminders of personal anniversaries...

◆

Escapes from Island prisons were still fairly frequent and a source of embarrassment for the authorities, a situation not helped when the hiding place of the latest escaped prisoner was discovered...

March 19th, 1955
PRISONER HID IN GOVERNOR'S HOUSE
CAMP HILL MAN'S TWO-DAY FREEDOM

After a prolonged and thorough search of the countryside between Parkhurst and the north coast of the Island on Tuesday, Wednesday, and Thursday for an escaped prisoner from Camp Hill, police and prison officers found him hiding in the governor's house. Patrick Callaghan, aged 23, who is serving a four-year sentence... attended a class in the gymnasium and at 8.10 p.m. he was missed... Following his disappearance no trace was reported for nearly 2 days. No food or clothing was missed. Without any clue as to where to look the police and prison parties were faced with the task of scouring a wide area. To help them the Southampton police lent Quaker, the Alsatian who took part in the hunt for the two prisoners who were at large from Camp Hill for 18 days before recapture on Christmas Eve. The search continued without result until Thursday evening, when the Camp Hill governor (Cmdr S.W. Lushington, R. N., retd.) returned to his house outside the main prison grounds and discovered a pair of plimsolls and a rope on his doorstep. He called the police, and the prison patrols and a search party, with Quaker, were rushed to the house. A close search was just about to begin in the garden, when one of the prison officers glanced through a window into the house and saw Callaghan creeping across the hall. He heard the commotion and had evidently gathered that his hiding place was liable to be disclosed. He surrendered philosophically to

Quaker and the search party. He seems to have spent most of his 48 hours of freedom in the loft.

———————————◆———————————

Charcoal was once in great demand, especially by blacksmiths who used it in their forges until coke took over in the early 20th century. In the 1950's the demand for charcoal arose once more and led to a temporary revival of charcoal burning...

April 16th, 1955

AN ANCIENT CRAFT REVIVED.
CHARCOAL BURNING AT BOULDNOR

The ancient craft of charcoal burning has been revived on the Island following the felling of timber on Forestry Commission land at Bouldnor*. Messrs. Valentine Wood, Ltd., of Reading, have taken over the cut timber on some 80 acres of land at Bouldnor, and have set up saw benches on the site. In the past only the main lengths of timber have been made use of by such contractors, all the smaller branches and mis-shapen pieces being disposed of cheaply as firewood. Messrs. Valentine Wood, however, have set up a battery of four modern kilns to turn the former waste into charcoal. The kilns, standing about eight feet in height and of similar diameter, are made of metal, and are in two circular parts, one fitting on top of the other, to facilitate loading and unloading. Each unit takes about one ton of wood, and produces about 24 bags of charcoal weighing 7cwt. every two days. The small amount of unconverted timber which is left is used as tinder in the firing of the next unit.

THE PROCESS

In the first instance the metal container is packed tightly with the branches, which are heaped several inches above the upper edge, with a lid resting on top. Leading into the container at ground level are four equidistant fireboxes, to which a chimney is fitted during the early stages of the operation. To start the unit an old piece of sacking is soaked with paraffin and ignited. The flaming mass is then pushed into the aperture left by the removal of one of the fireboxes, which is replaced immediately it is seen that the fire is well alight. Between each firebox there are two ventilation pipes leading into the container, also at ground level, and the rate of combustion is controlled by blocking these as necessary with sand and clay.

Firing usually takes place in the afternoon, and 24 hours later, when the expert can tell by the changing colour of the smoke that the contents are "cooked" the chimneys are removed, the fireboxes and ventilation pipes sealed with sand, and a similar treatment is applied to the lid, which by that time rests snugly on top of the container as a result of the shrinkage of the contents. Sand is applied wherever a trickle of smoke can be seen escaping, and the unit is then allowed to cool down. The following morning the charcoal is removed, sifted, and bagged, the unit reloaded, and firing takes place the same afternoon to continue the cycle of production. The work is so arranged that two of the units produce their quota of charcoal every morning. Basically the method is the same as the old one, where the wood was stacked into a pile with an air vent in the centre, ignited, and combustion controlled by covering the heap with

---

* See photograph page 117.

moist soil and turves, but it is infinitely speedier and far less wasteful. Most of the charcoal goes to the chemical industry, but a certain amount is used as fuel for cooking purposes in high-class restaurants and luxury liners. Most of the timber at Bouldnor is oak, with a light sprinkling of ash, and it is proving excellent for converting to charcoal.

TOWN AND COUNTY NOTES

ESCAPED PRISONER RANG THE BELL. – At 5.15 p.m. on Wednesday, 27 hours after a prisoner had escaped from Camp Hill Corrective Training Prison, Parkhurst, there was a ring on the main gate bell. The prison officer on duty found the runaway waiting to ask permission to be allowed back inside. The man was Frank William Harrison, aged 23, of Coventry, who was serving a three-year sentence imposed in August last year for shop-breaking and larceny. He escaped at 2.40 p.m. on Tuesday, when a rainstorm swept across the Island. Harrison was working in the gardens with other prisoners and when officers urged the men to take shelter he ran in the opposite direction and scrambled over the wall at a point where the ground rises.

WELL TRAVELLED FAMILY. – A cat is raising a family of kittens in a wooden container fixed to the rear of a Brighstone farmer's car. She travels everywhere in the vehicle, slipping out for food as the opportunity occurs.

CARRIED QUEEN VICTORIA'S TELEGRAMS. – Mr. Harry Pike, aged 82, and his wife, Mrs. Ellen Pike, who was 80 on Monday, celebrated their diamond wedding anniversary with a quiet tea at their home, 1 Victoria Cottages, Lower Whippingham Road, Whippingham, on Wednesday. Mr. Pike's first job, at the age of 13, was as a telegraph boy to Queen Victoria at Osborne House. Many of the telegrams he carried dealt with important matters of State, and at one time he remembers the Queen shouting at him for allowing a door to bang. Mr. Pike recalls that the Queen was very concerned with the welfare of her employees, and that later, when he was apprenticed to the Royal painter, she prevented him from carrying a ladder, saying there were horses and carts for that sort of work. Mr. Pike ... had latterly been employed as groundsman at the East Cowes Vics' football field... In his younger days he was a keen member of the I.W. Volunteers, and rode a "penny-farthing" bicycle. Mr. Pike believes that Mr. Harry Lever, aged 84, of 71 Adelaide Grove, is the only other surviving employee of Queen Victoria in the Island. (May 21)

The future of Cowes Pier had been discussed at great length over the years and had occupied a great deal of space in the County Press. In short, the businessmen of Cowes felt that Cowes Council should spend ratepayers' money on restoration of the pier whilst the ratepayers of Cowes, on whom the expense would fall, by and large disagreed. A decision had finally been reached and seemingly the end had come....

June 25th, 1955
COWES PIER TO BE DEMOLISHED
APPROXIMATE COST OF BETWEEN £3500 AND £5000

Cowes Victoria Pier, which has been the subject of heated controversy in the council chamber for several years, is to be demolished. This decision was reached at a meeting of Cowes Council at Northwood House on Tuesday. It reverses a previous decision to re-build, which was reached by the casting vote of the chairman. The Works Committee, who had reconsidered the future of the pier, suggested that an approach should be made to the Admiralty to see whether the demolition could be carried out as part of training in that type of work. Mr. F. Smart said ... it was an eyesore, and had been for a good many years... Mr. S. L. Glossop, C.C., said he was very pleased to see that at last common sense had prevailed. — The recommendation was approved.

◆

The Island was still home to thousands of soldiers, with Albany barracks and the forts and batteries scattered around the Island fully manned and operational. The sound of cannon fire was by no means unusual since all the establishments carried out regular gunnery practice and Islanders in many towns were quite used to it, the times of practice being regularly advertised in the County Press but in 1955 there were protests from the townspeople of Sandown. The gunnery practice was being carried out at the height of the tourist season, causing the closure of local paths and clifftop walks; it was not a popular move as these two letters to the Editor make clear...

July 23rd, 1955
GUNNERY TRAINING AT SANDOWN

Sir, According to an announcement in your current issue, Sandown Bay, at the very height of its season, is again to be the scene of that abominable military outrage called gunnery training, which has now been inflicted on it for no less than 91 years! The accumulation of steel on the floor of the bay over that period, amounting now to thousands of tons, is slowly disintegrating into a mass of black oxides and silicates of iron, steadily transforming our golden sands into what a recent visitor described as "a most uninviting mess." The Director-General of Military Training assures me that this training is absolutely essential but when I enquire how it proposes to defend our coast against a hail of guided missiles I am met with the customary War Office attitude of silence. Access to the leading attraction of Culver cliffs, whether by cliff path, beach walk, or by boat, is restricted out of all reason throughout the height of our too-short season. Over 1000 journeys per day are being made through our already overcrowded streets by every description of military truck. Smoke, I see, is to be used in addition to night firing. What an inducement to visitors! ... How long is it to be before this foul and festering sore in the midst of some of nature's loveliest scenes is to be permitted to continue? Surely this utterly useless and arrogant extravagance of spending millions in such a senseless and unfair manner can be brought to an abrupt conclusion before we are all bankrupt?
A.T. GRAPES. 71 Station Avenue, Sandown.

Sir, In connection with the promised renewal of gunnery activity in Sandown Bay, may I draw attention to the colossal cost involved by the unnecessary duplication of noisy target-towing high-speed launches and patrol boats. These latter would appear to have abrogated to themselves the right to interfere with the normal activities of local watermen and fishermen engaged in earning an already hard enough living. When one is precluded from working pots and nets in one of the most fertile parts of our Channel, for fear of losing expensive fishing gear one begins to question the meaning of the word "freedom."... I am absolutely nonplussed to think that such important artillery practice should be carried out in our beautiful bay involving so many runs that only a few shots can be fired at the fast-moving targets on each one. If this were practised in a more remote part of the country the excessive costs could be reduced to a minimum, to say nothing of ridding this bay of these noisy, obnoxious-smelling disturbers of the peace. One ponders whether Bournemouth, Eastbourne, or Torquay would tolerate such a nuisance in the height of their summer season...
IVAN. D. HOOPER. Shanklin.

———————————◆———————————

In Freshwater the circus came to town. Not everyone was pleased to see them...
August 20th, 1955
CIRCUS ANIMALS
Sir, I have just returned from a visit to the circus at Freshwater, where I saw a collection of wild animals in very small cages. The polar bears were in acute discomfort, their cage facing the blazing sun, three lions together in a miserably small cage, a bear pacing to and fro, and a gazelle in a tiny cage. I am not attacking the people who look after the animals, I am sure most of them do their best for them, but I do attack the cruel practice of carrying round wild animals in small cages, their only release being death. The law is lagging behind public opinion in this matter.
SYBIL WILLIAMS. Blackbridge House, Freshwater Bay.

———————————◆———————————

The death throes of East Cowes Castle were a long drawn-out affair. For ten years now, it had been slowly falling to pieces, a victim of decay and vandalism. Its undignified end provoked a lyrical lament...
August 27th, 1955
EAST COWES CASTLE
by RICHARD JOHNS
Round the boundaries of the castle the fences are broken and the shrubbery beaten and torn. Weeds grow high towards the walls which wear a melancholy, defeated air. This was once a castle fit for a fairy tale, with beetling grey walls and high turrets, buttresses, gargoyles, courtyards, and stables, with a commanding view of rolling fields and the distant harbour... East Cowes Castle was built in 1809 by a man who had nothing to defend and nothing to attack, by one who was already a famous architect, for his own residence. John Nash

Isle of Wight County Press
AND SOUTH OF ENGLAND REPORTER

TELEPHONE — NEWPORT 2241 & 2297
WITH WHICH IS INCORPORATED " THE ISLE OF WIGHT EXPRESS "

No. 3695, Vol. LXXI.   **SATURDAY SEPTEMBER 17, 1955**   16 Pages—PRICE 3d. (Postage 2d.)

HATS!
HATS!
HATS!

THEY HAVE JUST ARRIVED IN THEIR HUNDREDS — SO MANY SHADES TO TONE WITH THE NEW AUTUMN **COATS !**
COATS !
COATS !

Dabell's
NEWPORT 2122

THE FINEST VIEWING NOW...
and all set for **commercial T/V!**

This new Ekcovision 14" aluminised tube table model incorporates what we consider to be the most efficient system of multi-channel tuning to receive both the existing B.B.C. stations and the new alternative programmes when they become available. Come and see this outstanding multi-channel receiver which incorporates all the advantages of Ekco quality and engineering' plus single-switch TURRET TUNING.
66 Gns. (tax paid)

Sherratts OF NEWPORT
YOU'RE SURE WITH SHERRATTS
SHOWROOMS: 81, 82, 83 HIGH STREET
PHONE 2506
your **EKCOVISION** *Dealer*

WE ARE CLEARING ODDMENTS
GODWINS The Island Clothiers
WE HAVE SOME ASTOUNDING BARGAINS IN
MEN'S SUITS
MEN'S OVERCOATS
MEN'S RAINWEAR
MEN'S TROUSERS
HOSIERY, SOCKS, WINCEYATERS.

If you are in want of Clothing, pay us a friendly visit next week. You are always AT YOUR SERVICE

GODWINS The Island Clothiers
NEWPORT, EAST & WEST COWES, FRESHWATER.
SERVICE WITH A SMILE

What the eye doesn't see...

is what goes on behind the screen of your TV set. Our job is to know; our maintenance and repair service is always at your disposal. Mind you, you won't often be needing our service if you choose a Ferranti. Look to ourselves, and let us show you what we mean.

YOUNGS
NEWPORT RYDE COWES
Clearly FERRANTI for sight and sound

A precious Trio

GOLD   PALLADIUM   PLATINUM

BERNARD MITCHELL LTD.
60 UNION STREET, RYDE.

Personally Conducted
FUNERALS & CREMATIONS
Island or Mainland, by
A. E. WYATT
Proprietor, MOORMAN & SON.
85/87 Upper St. James's Street, Newport. Phone 2612.

STONEHAM MEMORIAL
135 Milliford Road, East Cowes
MEMORIALS ERECTED
In any County or Cemetery without extra charge

ARTISTIC MEMORIALS
In British Stones and Granites
Domestic and Ecclesiastic Fonts
F. COOPER
St. JAMES'S ST., NEWPORT.

SCHOOLWEAR
for the NEW TERM
"WHITCHERS FOR VALUE"
We also stocks the "Old Boys"
134 HIGH STREET, NEWPORT.

ISLE OF WIGHT HONEY
The I.W.B.K.A. recommend 4/- per lb. as a minimum retail price for this product.

COMMODORE
RYDE ★ Tel. 2616
The Island's Leading Cinemas

MONDAY SEPTEMBER 19th, for 6 DAYS; Doors open 7 p.m.
CINEMASCOPE
20th Century Fox present
SPENCER TRACY
ROBERT · JEAN · RICHARD · KATY
WAGNER · PETERS · WIDMARK · JURADO
Broken Lance
Also
PRINCES OF THE NILE

SUNDAY SEPT. 18th, for ONE DAY ONLY; Doors 5 p.m.
Robert Mitchum in MACAO
Also
Maxwell Reed in THERE IS ANOTHER SUN

MEW'S
BREWERS, WINE, SPIRIT & TOBACCO MERCHANTS
MINERAL WATER MANUFACTURERS

Have you tried our **EXTRA LARGE FAMILY SIZE** mineral waters ?
LEMONADE, LIMEADE
ORANGEADE, "FIZ"
CHERRYADE
You may have a mixed crate of the above flavours if you wish
6/- PER CRATE

W. B. MEW, LANGTON & CO. LTD.

THEATRE ROYAL
MONDAY SEPT. 19th—ALL THE WEEK—At 2,8, 5,40, 8.25
A motion picture of compelling power of ecstasy and rawness!
ELIA KAZAN'S
EXPLOSIVE PRODUCTION OF
JOHN STEINBECK'S
EAST of EDEN
CINEMASCOPE — WARNER COLOR
JULIE HARRIS · JAMES DEAN · RAYMOND MASSEY and cast

Scala
RYDE
MONDAY SEPT. 19th—ALL THE WEEK—At 3.5, 6.0, 8.55
A PICTURE YOU WILL WANT TO SEE AGAIN AND AGAIN
MARTY
ERNEST BORGNINE · BETSY BLAIR
Screenplay by PADDY CHAYEFSKY
Directed by DELBERT MANN · Produced by HAROLD HECHT

GRAND
NEWPORT
MONDAY SEPT. 19th—ALL THE WEEK—At 2.50, 5.35, 8.20
A new DAY dawns! CINEMASCOPE
DORIS DAY · JAMES CAGNEY
Love Me Or Leave Me
15 SONGS

YOU MUST TRY

THE ALL-ISLAND CREAMERY BUTTER
in the Green Wrapper
ASK YOUR GROCER FOR IT
Sole Makers:
ISLE OF WIGHT CREAMERIES, LTD.
MILL STREET, NEWPORT
Telephone : 2284

MEDINA
NEWPORT ★ Tel. 2691

MONDAY SEPTEMBER 19th, for 6 DAYS; Doors open 7 p.m.
PRE-LONDON RELEASE
At 1.79, 5.30, 8.48
ALASTAIR · BILL
SIM · TRAVERS
Geordie
Also JOHN BENTLY, HY HAZELL
STOLEN ASSIGNMENT
COMPLETE CHANGE OF PROGRAMME EVERY SUNDAY
Doors open 5 p.m.

THESE NAMES MAKE NEWS

Not for many years has there been so wide a style choice among Autumn Coats, Suits and Dresses, and after several visits to some of the most famous Fashion Houses in the country, we are now receiving the latest Fashion values from

GRAYSON · DERETA · RENSOR · SAMBO
HORROCKSES · LINZI · REMBRANDT
NORMAN LINTON · MORNESSA · BLANES
HEBE SPORTS · VALERIE BLOUSES
PRINGLE and TANYA KNITWEAR smart rainwear by ALLIGATOR, QUELRAYN and TELEMAC etc.

See our very beautiful fur trimmed Coats and Suits at very reasonable prices

MARDERS
OF NEWPORT
HIGH ST. NEWPORT
UNION ST. RYDE
HIGH ST. SANDOWN

CYCLES
Over 100 in stock
PHILLIPS
ARMSTRONG
WEARWELL
HOPPER
NORMAN
HERCULES
DUNELT
VINDEC
COVENTRY-EAGLE

All available from £1 deposit
PARKES CASTLE GARAGE
JOHN ST. RYDE 2752
The Cycle Specialist

RUNYARDS offer
this fine tough shoe

the ideal all-weather walking shoe for school and holidays
OXFORD BROGUE
In imitation brogue aspect, with plantation-finished crepe rubber soles.
C and E fittings.

RUNYARDS—FRESHWATER   Phone 303

NOW YOU CAN OWN A SMITHS DE LUXE WATCH FROM £1 down!
AND EASY MONTHLY PAYMENTS
SMITHS DE LUXE
BENZIE COWES

wished to build himself a home which would be different, but it is to be feared that if his ghost walks the ruins to-day it must be a very dismal ghost indeed to see what has become of its home in so short a time... This castle's dark days came with the death of Lord Gort. Neglect, already begun, became total, and it is to be regretted that advantage was taken of its vacancy to strip it of many fittings, even to the point of semi-demolition. Recently the grounds have been used as a small fruit farm and some of the outhouses pressed into use again, but now even that is for sale again... Nowadays one can look from the gaping windows down over the busy river and the shipyards and aircraft works from which the town derives so much of its prosperity, and it is easy to regret the passing of the colour and pageantry, but hard to deny that progress has also brought a great deal of good to we common mortals. However we feel, the days of the castle are numbered; pigeons clatter from the tumbling ivy, and a gargoyle leans grotesquely out from the wall, battered and humiliated, punctured in a dozen places by some idle rod. Where the roofs have fallen in brickwork strews the inner floors, and only here and there is there shelter from the sky, and in such spots hay is stacked beneath moulded ceilings which were once the architect's delight. Creepers grow in profusion and trail among the ruins as nature reasserts herself after so temporary defeat at the hands of men. So passes an age. The good and the bad in it have gone, and the castle remains as a poor monument, tired and aloof, and awaiting its own passing.

NEWS IN BRIEF

PROPOSAL TO CLOSE NEWPORT-SANDOWN RAILWAY. – On Saturday, unheralded by any similar notification to Island authorities, British Railways announced through a special correspondent of "The Times" that they have decided to close the branch line from Newport to Sandown. If their decision is approved the closure will come into effect next February... This announcement, coming at the height of the best summer season the Island has enjoyed since the war, has not caught the authorities completely unprepared, for it was known that two years' reprieve, granted in 1953, would end in September (August 20)

SLUM CLEARANCE AT NEWPORT. – In Newport 100 houses, 54 in clearance areas, and 46 sited separately, have been scheduled as slum property, to be demolished in the next five years...

WARTIME DEFENDER OF COWES. – On Saturday, the day before she was due to complete her short courtesy visit to Portsmouth, Cowes councillors visited the Polish destroyer Blyskawica in Portsmouth harbour... The visit recalls how in 1942, when she was being refitted, her fierce anti-aircraft fire saved Messrs. J.S. White and Co.'s works from being bombed out of existence, and a heavier death toll in the town of Cowes on the night of May 4th-5th. The ship put up such a fierce barrage that although some 200 tons of bombs were dropped, the majority fell harmlessly in the sea...

**AN ANCIENT CRAFT
REVIVED.**
CHARCOAL BURNING AT
BOULDNOR

Charcoal burning, the modern way, on Forestry Commission woodland at Bouldnor, near Yarmouth.
(See page 110)

Headstones removed from the old churchyard at Church Litten, Newport, which is being laid out by the Town Council as a garden of rest. Some are to be used for making paths. (See page 118)

COMMERCIAL TELEVISION RECEPTION IN THE ISLAND. – Mr. A. Williams, of Parkhurst, writes that on Tuesday, when the Independent Television Authority put out their first full strength test card signal from London he was able to get a fairly good signal. He has a home-made aerial and thinks that an even better signal might be obtained when certain adjustments have been made. (September 17)

Today's Church Litten park is what is left of the graveyard attached to St Thomas's Church. By the 1950's it was no longer in use and it was decided, not without some local opposition, to remove the hundreds of headstones to make way for a recreational garden. The work was about to begin ...

October 15th, 1955

GARDEN OF REST FOR NEWPORT
ADAPTATION OF OLD BURIAL GROUND

Another page in the history of Newport is being written by the hand of the landscape gardener. The 17th-century burial ground at Church Litten is to be converted for use as a garden of rest conveniently situated in the centre of the town. In place of vaults and tombstones will be greensward, shrubbery, footpaths, and a rose garden. The dignity of the garden will be in keeping with its former setting and notable memorials are to be preserved. Newport Town Council have acquired the land, with the adjoining site of Bradley Lodge, demolished in an air raid on April 7th, 1943... With the commendable object of using the two and two thirds acres of land to the best advantage, the council has commissioned an eminent landscape architect, Mr. H. Milner-White... The immediate plan is to convert about nine-tenths of the total area to greensward, interspersed by attractive meandering footpaths... Demolition work, and tree felling, has been going on for some time and the ground is now ready for cultivation... It is hoped to open the gardens to the public in late 1956, but so much depends on availability of funds, as already costs have exceeded estimates. Filling in vaults, in many places where only single graves were anticipated, has added to the expense, and felling trees has made inroads into the budget... The remaining one-tenth of the site, at the Church Litten end, will be untouched until a further considerable sum is available. The plan is to make of this section a rose pergola, and to include a lily pond and a shelter. Tombstones will be broken up to provide paved walks; at the moment they are stacked at this end of the site, and are likely to remain so for some while... The council are respecting the wishes of the ecclesiastical authorities and also those of many residents by preserving certain memorials. The monument to Valentine Gray, the young chimney sweep who suffered an untimely death in 1822, is to be resited in the rose garden section. A dozen or so other headstones bearing examples of quality carving and lettering, or with similarly notable features, will be preserved around the walls of the garden...

See photograph page 117.

Prompted by a reader's query, Vectensis provided an account of the reclamation of Brading harbour...

October 22nd, 1955

AN ISLANDER'S NOTES
by VECTENSIS

A reader asks me when the sea was shut out from Brading Harbour by the building of the Bembridge embankment. The reclamation scheme was started in 1877 and completed in 1880. Mr. W. Burden, the well-known gardener at Bembridge, who is 89, grows his magnificent apples, which are so often an admired feature of horticultural shows, on land where, as a young man, he gathered cockles. The reclaimed soil has certain properties which give the fruit a more pronounced colour. Before the reclamation, the sea swept up to Brading Quay, where ships loaded and unloaded merchandise. The harbour was famous for mullet, bass, and sea trout, and there was, too, a famous oyster bed between St Helens and Brading. A few elderly East Wight residents can still recall being taken out in rowing boats in Brading Haven... The sea was finally shut out in February, 1880, and 740 acres of land reclaimed... The embankment was built from thousands of tons of chalk, rubble, and clay from Bembridge Down and Portsdown Hill, and when first made was wide enough only for a footpath. Then came a critical period, for the sea broke through close to where the Bembridge railway station was eventually built, and for a few weeks it became a battle between the sea and man's ingenuity. Thousands of tons of chalk, debris, and tree trunks were thrown into the breach. The flood, often 6 feet deep, swept it all away, including a steam pile-driver, which still lies buried underneath the roadway. This stage was not without tragedy, for a horse and cart were swallowed up and the carter drowned... In the end the battle against the sea was won by driving a row of piles and constructing a fresh embankment inside the breach. When the embankment was safe and the roadway was built along it the promoters immediately started on the building of the railway from Brading to Bembridge...

———————————◆———————————

In the late 19th and early 20th century the Island boasted a large number of breweries and mineral water manufacturers. Prominent among them was Gould, Hibberd and Randall whose mineral water factory was located on the site of today's Marks & Spencer store. In the 1950's conglomerates and multinationals had still to make their presence felt but in 1966 Gould, Hibberd and Randall were taken over by the Beecham Group who were themselves eventually taken over by Glaxo SmithKline. Local production and bottling came to an end in the early 1980s but for the moment business was booming...

October 22nd, 1955

SUMMER SUNSHINE AND SOFT DRINKS
"OPERATION THIRST-QUENCHER" MEETS RECORD DEMAND

During the glorious summer just passed, a record number of Island holidaymakers returned to the mainland refreshed for the battle of winter fitness. They were also refreshed in a more mundane sense of the word, for the intense sunshine gave them a healthy thirst, which, thanks to the efforts of the brewers and soft drink manufacturers, was satisfactorily slaked. One of the Island firms which rallied their forces was Messrs. Gould, Hibberd, and Randall, Ltd., soft drinks producers, of Newport.* This company is old established and steeped in Island associations... Since the turn of the century the company remember only five summers to approach 1955 – 1911, 1921, 1935, 1947, and 1949. Mr. L. J. Harvey, (general manager) told the County Press, "We satisfied demands for most of our popular lines. We worked six and a half days a week and our output exceeded 1 million bottles."... One factor over which the firm had no control might conceivably have sabotaged a prompt delivery service - the supply of bottles. Occasionally bottle stocks fall dangerously low, many consumers apparently assuming that payment of 2d. deposit entitles them to the bottle. In fact a bottle costs 5d. and each one not returned represents a loss of 3d. to the drinks producer... The million-plus thirsts were quenched in fairly equal measure by mineral waters and fruit squashes... The term "mineral" is a common misnomer. A more correct description would be "aerated, flavoured drinks" because it is the pumping of carbon dioxide into the water which gives its sparkle.... Although the factory at Church Litten is 24 years old, it is claimed to be one of the finest of its size in the country. The principal machines are a gas pump, a labelling machine, a bottle-washer, and a three-operational machine which applies syrup to the bottle, fills it with aerated water, and crown-seals. Including all cleansing processes, a bottle of soft drink requires half a gallon of water... In 1863, the present chairman's grandfather, Mr. Charles Hibberd, opened a factory in High Street, Ventnor, with stables nearby. Horses were used for haulage - notably a constantly-admired pair of greys - and also for operating a bottling power-unit. The animals pulled a stake, rotating on a central pivot, to operate the gas pump... Mr. F. Randall came from Southampton to Ryde in 1887 and purchased a mineral water manufacturing business in Church Lane, which under his direction soon flourished... In 1921 Gould and Co. and Hibberd and Co. amalgamated and the following year at Mr. Hibberd's instigation, Mr. Randall was brought in. The three factories continued to operate under individual management until the Church Litten factory was built in 1931.

NEWS IN BRIEF

CARISBROOKE FARMER INSTALLS MILK PARLOUR. – A boon to dairy farmers, a milking parlour with equipment incorporating the latest American ideas, has been installed at Great Park Farm, Carisbrooke, owned by Mr. W.A. Curtis. It is the first of its kind in the Island, and there are relatively few on the mainland... For milking under this arrangement, the cow walks up a ramp onto

---

* The 'donkey in the well' moulding on the side of Marks & Spencer's store was recovered from the Gould, Hibberd and Randall factory front when the building was demolished in the early 1980s. It had originally started life as the trademark of Goulds Mineral Waters and was set into the wall of their factory in St Thomas's Square, the building now known as Charter House. The moulding, made by Alfred Pritchett, a local brickmaker, was removed in 1931 to become part of the frontage of Gould, Hibberd and Randall's new factory.

a platform and stands beside one of the four installations. Being on a level with the milker's elbow, stooping is eliminated. In the words of Mr. Curtis, "The equipment takes the backache out of milking."

SURPRISE FOR TOTLAND BAY ANGLERS. – Anglers fishing from the pier at Totland on Sunday evening were surprised when a motoryacht tied up alongside and a voice asked: "Is this Newhaven?" They informed the three occupants, two men and a young woman, that they were still a long way from Newhaven, and directed them to the Coastguard Station.

FIRE AT COWES GASWORKS. – Firemen from Newport dashed to Cowes on Monday morning to assist local firemen in dealing with an outbreak at the Cowes Gasworks, where one of the large holders was on fire. Workmen were engaged on repairs to the top-side of the holder and while a hole was being drilled a spark ignited the gas, flames about 8 ft. high coming from the holder. A gas official told a reporter that there was never any danger of an explosion.

A burst water main just above Clatterford Cross on Saturday practically emptied the reservoir, and the low-level area of Newport was without water until Sunday morning while repairs were effected.

BIG BIRD CARRIES OFF HARE - WAS IT A BUZZARD? – A few days ago an employee of Mr. H. Morris, of Froglands Farm, Carisbrooke, while working in a field near Dark Lane, saw a large bird rise from the ground with a leveret struggling in its talons. It alighted in the next field and presumably tore its victim to pieces, as the leveret's screams quickly ceased. The bird was probably a buzzard, as they are occasionally seen in the Island during the autumn and winter.

1956

No doubt those living in Lake today would welcome a return to the traffic levels of the 1950's but everything is relative. In a letter to the editor in 1956, a Mr. Rees, who had grown up in Lake in the days when a horse was the fastest thing on the road, reflected that the 1950's had brought what he termed "a constant stream of charabancs and cars which every second speed along the highway to-day." Quite what Mr. Rees would have made of the traffic that passes along Lake High Street today is anyone's guess...

January 14th, 1956

OLD LAKE
[by F.A. REES]

A few months ago I passed through Lake, now a suburb of Sandown, and my thoughts went back many years. When I was a boy Lake was a country village, separated from its two larger neighbours, and as I thought of it as it was and as it is now I experienced a feeling of disappointment.

In those not so distant, but at times to me, far-off days, there arises in my mind a picture of a lovely old village, quiet and peaceful, with workmen ambling along the main road, and an occasional carriage and pair, not in the hurry one sees to-day, for life then was more leisurely. Surrounding the village were corn fields and gardens, and on the the main road from the railway bridge were hedges until one came to Lacey's bakery on the same side, or the Stag Inn on the other side, with the exception of a Jacobean farmhouse and a barn opposite at the crossroads. I remember a group of cottages somewhere between the farm and and the inn, but they were derelict, all the windows were broken, and some of the slates had gone from the roof - a mournful and desolate sight. There was no mall at the crossroads, and no paving; just the road, very dusty in summer and rather muddy in the winter. After rainfall, water lay in the hollows and it was difficult to walk without collecting yellow mud from the gravel. At night there was little lighting, the lamps being few and far between, and one walked some distance in darkness. I have a vivid memory of the chirrup of the crickets in the hedges.

One, however, was not troubled to avoid motor vehicles; just an occasional horse and carriage or a farm cart passed by; different from the constant stream of charabancs and cars which every second speed along the highway to-day.

In addition to the baker's shop was a blacksmith's forge, where I have watched the horses being shod, fascinated by the sparks which lit up the dark background. There was also a boot and shoe maker.

At the beginning of a rather rough little lane which led into Stag Road was the wheelwright and carpenter's shop. I can still see the large wagon wheels assembled there and the long planks of timber.

Opposite, where the Newport road joined the Sandown road, there were hoardings for advertisements, until a large shop was built on the corner...

What I really regret is the passing of the old farmhouse. It was built on a slant, the corner touching the road, or most probably, the road was made after the house was put up. A mass of ivy covered the front except for the small windows and on a dark night, the yellow glow from them was a welcome sight. In one of the lower windows was a notice announcing fresh eggs for sale. At the back was a good-sized yard, protected by a stone wall, in which could be seen farm carts and several farming implements under a shed...

"Progress" has come, and, inevitably, the cornfields have given place to bricks and mortar. The old farm has vanished, and in its place are modern shops; the carriages have gone, and the new generation takes the motor traffic for granted, but to me the Lake I knew and liked was the village of long ago.

The illegal introduction of myxomatosis to the Island had, in fact, been quietly welcomed by many landowners and now that the disease had had such a great effect in reducing rabbit numbers, the National Farmers Union proposed that local farmers should finish the job and make the Island a totally rabbit-free area ...

January 21st, 1956
RABBITS REAPPEARING.
FARMERS ASKED TO PREVENT RABBIT PLAGUE

Mr. R. A. Stark, NFU, appealed to farmers to co-operate in making a thorough job of clearing the few rabbits which were beginning to appear following the outbreak of myxomatosis... If the golden opportunity of keeping the rabbits down which exists at present was neglected, it would not be very long before the position was as bad as ever... It is pointed out by officials in the Pests Office that in a season a pair of rabbits can produce about 100. In various parts of the Island rabbits are to be seen again and some of these have been shot and their blood examined, and it is certain that they are immune to myxomatosis. It is believed that young bred by such rabbits may be susceptible to the disease if it comes again... Three areas in the Island have been designated free areas - East Cowes, Havenstreet and Bembridge - and it is proposed that two more areas, Godshill and the West Wight will shortly be designated...

◆

In the latter months of 1955, someone in Bembridge allowed oil or paraffin to contaminate the public water supply. Through the letters column, residents complained in large numbers about the unpleasant tasting water and such was the level and strength of these complaints that the Water Board were eventually forced to bring uncontaminated water in by road. It was established that contamination was taking place between the borehole and the pumping station located at Home Farm but so far the Water Board had been unable to be more precise. Faced with growing public anger they were left with only one option...

February 4th, 1956
BEMBRIDGE WATER SUPPLY
BOREHOLE TO BE ABANDONED

The mystery of the oil pollution of Bembridge's water supply has not been solved, but at an emergency meeting of the Water Board it was decided to abandon the present borehole and give the village a new supply by the summer season at a cost of about £28,500... At a press conference the Council Clerk (Mr. L. H. Baines) said it was true that there was a small amount of oil in the water - enough to give it an unpleasant taste and smell - but the quantity was small. All analyses and biological tests showed that otherwise the water was pure. "Investigations continued day and night," added Mr. Baines, "and we have come to the conclusion that the general condition of the borehole at Bembridge is such that it ought to be abandoned"... Mr. Baines said that the Board had accepted a tender for the laying of pipes from Brading to Bembridge and these would be laid along the disused railway line. Work would start almost at once and will be completed in time to ensure an ample supply of pure water for the season... At the request of the Board's engineer, the Fire Brigade undertook to lay an emergency water supply line from St Helens to Bembridge. On Saturday the Home Office was contacted by telephone and red tape was cut to enable a mile of six inch plastic piping to be sent to the Island. During the weekend, 15 members of the Auxiliary Fire Service, who received no payment for their work, laid the line from St Helens pumping station to the storage tank at Bembridge.

———————————————◆———————————————

The fourth railway line closure in as many years was about to take place and the last ever train to run on the Newport to Sandown line was set to depart the following night. The Island's railway lines were held in some affection and the latest closure was marked by a nostalgic, almost poetic essay...

February 4th, 1956

SANDOWN-NEWPORT RAILWAY CLOSURE
AFTER EIGHTY YEARS
LAST TRAINS TO-MORROW

The white gates swing shut, halting a procession of impatient motorists, while a busy little engine puffs breathlessly into the station. A pause, then, as it chugs happily out, billowing white smoke, the gates clank clear again and the vehicles stream away.

This performance has been repeated daily for 81 years at the seven level crossings on the Newport-Sandown railway line and after tomorrow evening these hold-ups will be a thing of the past, for then the gates will close for good behind the last train and the final chapter in the history of the line will end.

... The Southern Railway absorbed the three separate Island companies in 1923... and private ownership ended in 1948 when the lines passed to the British Transport Commission.

"SANDOWN FOR CARISBROOKE CASTLE"

Competition for passenger traffic was intense and to offset inconvenient sites, imposing, but wildly inaccurate claims were made. For instance Sandown was hopefully styled "for Lake, Carisbrooke Castle and Parkhurst." Many a stranded passenger must have pondered the truth of this assertion as he completed his journey by four-horse coach... Unjust fares were a grievance against the old companies too. Until 1914 there were no third class tickets and travellers were charged 3d. and 2d. a mile for first and second class fares respectively. These high charges provoked a Punch cartoon showing a poster at Ryde Pier Gates advertising "IW Railways - 12 miles in 12 hours for 12 shillings."

COLOURFUL VARIETY

The railways have always provided a colourful and distinctive collection for the enthusiast and up to 1914 a strange variety of vehicles could be seen on the rails... The engines on the Central Railway were a rich red and some, such as the "Cowes," were resplendent with copper-top funnels and polished brass domes... The four famed "Terrier" engines worked the Sandown line. Unlike other Island locomotives they whistled in the conventional manner, the others being fitted with hooters.

FAREWELL

Changes came but they were never striking and to-morrow, when Islanders say farewell to their fourth branch line in two years, there will be little material difference between the scene then and eight decades previously. The old tale of the engine going off the track at Newport and train not leaving Ashey until "the stick" had been carried on horseback from Newport is still remembered, and locals may repeat the legend of the dog which fell out of the carriage at Whippingham and was awaiting the train on its arrival at Havenstreet...

Whether an avid engine spotter or an impatient motorist, there will be few who will not regret the final closing of the gates at Pan, Shide, Blackwater, Merstone, Horringford, Newchurch and Alverstone tomorrow. There is a Lilliputian air about these austere but friendly platforms with their few travellers and shining milk churns which captures the imagination and recalls past days. The affectionate pride of the Islanders in this over-criticised and ill-fated railway is shared by many visitors who good-naturedly termed it "quaint" and although the wheels of the last train will be urgently repeating their final message to the metals "I'm the last, I'm the last" to-tomorrow evening, Islanders should be grateful for many years of faithful service.

The final day of service arrived...

February 11th, 1956

NEWPORT-SANDOWN RAIL LINK SEVERED
LAST JOURNEYS ON SUNDAY.

From a vantage point on the downs above the Arreton Valley on Sunday night a watcher would have seen, travelling along the valley, a row of lights, dwarfed by distance to the size of a glow-worm. Pausing now and again it would have been followed after a brief interval by another, heading in the opposite direction. Over the last 80 years with the exception of war-time blackouts, the site has been commonplace, but our watcher on Sunday would have seen it for the last time. As the station staffs extinguished the oil-lamps lighting the wayside platforms, and left for their homes after signalling through the last trains that evening, the Newport-Sandown line passed into history[*].

At Sandown and Newport, there were scenes of animation as members of the public, augmented by visiting enthusiasts, made final sentimental journeys, but there was little rejoicing among the railwaymen, as for some the closure meant the wrench of transfer to mainland posts, or in many cases, continuing Island service in less remunerative grades.

DEPARTURE SCENES

... There was little ceremony at Newport where the most unusual feature was the large number of passengers. Normally at that time something like 10 may be expected - in the evening Station Fireman K. Sterne was kept busy, in the absence of a booking-clerk, writing tickets for those who had decided to make a final trip. Well over 100 tickets were issued to various stations on the Sandown line in addition to those who had booked in advance... Local passengers included Mr. Harold Biles, of Newport, and his son Mr. David Biles, wearing top hats and giving rousing toots on their hunting horns. Press men

See photgraph page 131.

and photographers clustered round the engine as it stopped under the footbridge and took on water, but there was little time for reminiscence as after a very few minutes Guard W. Dibden showed the green light and the engine "Seaview" puffed and rattled over the viaduct for the last time...

A large crowd gathered on the departure platform at Sandown to travel to Merstone... Cheers greeted the train as it came in from Ventnor, and the arrival was filmed for I.T.V.* As the train pulled out for Newport, about a dozen detonators exploded and there were more cheers from those on board and on the platform.

As both trains made their journeys little knots of people at the level crossings and on the platforms cheered and waved, and car-drivers - held up at the crossing gates for the last time - sounded their hooters.

MERSTONE EXCHANGE

Many passengers changed trains at Merstone where for a brief while as both trains stood on opposite sides of the platform, the scene was like a Bank Holiday rush. The platform was brilliantly illuminated as ITV cameramen recorded the scene, but the stop was brief, and to the accompaniment of more cheers, both trains drew away... At Sandown, after the passengers alighted more pictures were taken by the ITV staff, the "Last Train" board was taken down, and as the train pulled out for Ventnor more detonators exploded and the driver whistled a "Last Post."

We understand that about 30 railwaymen are affected by the closure, many of whom have worked on the Island railways all their lives. All these were offered jobs in comparable grades on the mainland but only about six have accepted and the remainder will ... have to accept downgrading. For this reason some were understandably inclined to be resentful of the lightheartedness displayed by members of the public and one said with some bitterness: "It is no laughing matter for us to be treated like this after so many years' service."

———————————◆———————————

Outside the world of the County Press, one of the defining moments of the 20th century had taken place. Fuelled by disposable incomes and rock and roll, the "teenager" had arrived, not quite fully formed as yet but the time was not far away. On the Island, while jukeboxes were beginning to appear in numerous cafes "jiving" was struggling to get a foothold in the Island's dance halls. A glance at that week's entertainments listings reveals that the dance halls were the province of, amongst others, The Music Makers, The Belvederes, The Metronomes, Eric Galloway and his Band, and Kay Cavendish on the Keys, catchphrase - " From Bach to Boogie."

In what was possibly a first for the County Press, a letter from a teenager appeared in the letters column ...

March 3rd, 1956

JIVE AND BOP

Sir, I would like to ask a question that concerns myself and many other teenagers. Will some dance promoter or ballroom manager hold a dance where jive and bop is not objected to? If he advertised such a dance I'm sure he would

* Only viewers in the London and Midlands area would have seen the report. ITV was not available in the South of England until 1958.

sell every ticket. Everywhere we go we are told "No jiving." Last week in Ryde we were told it is not respectable. If jive is not respectable some of the so-called dancing that is all hugs and hot breath must be downright indecent, and no one ever bans that. As soon as jive and bop are mentioned, our elders immediately think of dens of vice and opium. We aren't drug addicts, we are modern, we go for the modern music, and we like to jive to this music; it adds to the pleasure of listening to it. There is not much in the way of entertainment for the youth of the Island so please could someone give us "kids" a break?

RITA HOBGEN (Mrs.) Flat C. Ampthill, East Hill Road, Ryde.

ISLAND NOTES

Daily papers on Wednesday stated that during the previous night's storm hailstones as big as lumps of sugar fell in the West Wight. A Bembridge friend commented: "We had hailstones as big as particles of caster sugar, but then of course, we are more refined."

ISLAND GAS SUPPLY PROBLEMS. – When Mr. G. G. Warne, the manager of the IW Gas Undertaking, addressed the Chamber of Commerce on Wednesday he was met with a threat that many large consumers were looking for alternative means of power, energy, and heat. The new works at East Cowes are expected to be in production by the end of the year, and about three months later the works at Ryde, Shanklin, Newport, and West Cowes will cease production. A serious redundancy problem is not anticipated.

Workmen building a retaining wall for dredging spoil in the swampy ground to the south of Bridge Road, Yarmouth, have encountered what they describe as a "bottomless pit" which swallowed 1000 tons of rubble in four days.

From the first days of the motor car there had been complaints that there were too many of them. In 1956 Ryde Councillor, Commander Rees Millington spoke out...*

July 14th, 1956

"TOO MANY VEHICLES IN THE ISLAND"

At this weeks meeting of the Roads and Traffic Arrangements Sub-Committee Commander W.O. Rees Millington said that there was no doubt that there were too many vehicles in the Island and however much they enlarged the roads, the parking areas could never be provided unless they had overhead

---

* The Commander went on to find posthumous fame when he appeared in the 1995 film of the 1970 Isle of Wight Festival, "Message To Love," uttering the memorable lines, "If you have a festival with all the stops pulled out - kids running about naked, f—ing in the bushes and doing every damn thing they feel they're entitled to, I don't know that's particularly good for the body politic." Five years later, in 2000, the Commander found even greater fame when his words were sampled by the band Oasis to be used as part of the chorus of the song 'F—ing in the Bushes', a track on their album 'Standing on the Shoulder of Giants.'

parking as in New York. They had had bitter complaints from residents but they were the last people to be considered. He hoped that the regulations would be modified in the winter months. - Replying, Mr. Dorley Brown (Committee Chairman) refuted the opinion that the problem was being neglected. The problem applied almost everywhere and especially in the Island...

———————————◆———————————

THE WEEK'S NEWS

RABBITS - ISLAND A CLEARANCE AREA. – The whole of the Isle of Wight will shortly be a rabbit clearance area under the Pests Act, 1954... The Act states that "The occupier of any land in a rabbit clearance area shall take such steps ... to destroy the wild rabbits living on any part of the land." Myxomatosis has killed nearly all the rabbits on the Island and now that their numbers are so low the committee hope that all occupiers of land will do their utmost to deal with the few remaining... (February 18)

Workmen laying a new sewer across the Square at Yarmouth, have found two green glass flagons believed to be about 300 years old, at a depth of 8ft., in land which had previously been made up. The flagons, each holding about a pint, bore traces of gilt lacquer. (Feb 18)

LAST TRAIN TO BEMBRIDGE. – After two years without a railway service the presence of a train every day this week on the line between St Helens and Bembridge has aroused considerable interest. The appearance of the train was the result of the Water Board's decision to provide the new supply to Bembridge from Brading Down, hence the temporary re-opening of the much overgrown track. Pipes for the new main, brought by a vessel to St Helens Quay, have been loaded onto wagons and these, with a brake van, form the train, which must be the slowest ever to have run over the track. As it proceeds in short jerks the pipes are lowered one at a time to the side of the track. Railway enthusiasts and local residents have viewed the presence of the train with a certain sense of satisfaction, not that it portends that passenger trains will ever again run to Bembridge, but in that they are now probably seeing the last train to use the line. (March 10)

CHILDREN AND TELEVISION - MEDICAL OFFICER'S WARNING. – The Cowes medical officer of health warns parents of the danger to their children of watching television late at night. Dr. Mills says that while recognising the potential educational value of television, it was sad to see the evil effects on children in those homes where the viewing was not reasonably controlled. In many schools it was possible to pick out the children who watched television far too late. Teachers spoke of drowsy, inattentive pupils and were concerned at the evil effect uncontrolled viewing was having on the health of the child...

---

* The line from Brading to St Helens actually remained in service until November 1957 to allow scrapped rolling stock to be taken to St. Helens Quay for transfer to the mainland.

Horringford Station, at Arreton, on the Newport to Sandown railway line. Two years after closure the entire track still remained in place apart from this road crossing. (See page 126)   *[Photo, Reg Davies]*

THE END OF FRESHWATER RAILWAY STATION
The scene of desolation and demolition at Freshwater Railway Station following the tearing up of the tracks. The work has now stopped. (November 24.)

AFTER 50 YEARS. – A 50 year old family connection with the Prince of Wales Inn at Freshwater came to an end when the tenancy changed hands last week. It was in 1906 that Mrs. Elizabeth Merritt made her home there when her father, the late Mr. Tom Groves, became landlord. In those days beer was only tuppence a pint, and a favourite form of recreation among the customers was gambling for pennies on the "spinning Jenny," which was fixed to the ceiling. Most inns in the area had these gaming devices at that time, but police disapproval led to their gradual disappearance...

———————————◆———————————

Air travel to and from the Island continued to be successful. With an impressive list of destinations the services had attracted 9000 paying passengers the previous year and for the moment all the signs were that the success story was to continue...

July 21st, 1956

GROWING POPULARITY OF ISLAND AIR TRAVEL

The regular air services, which this year started on May 15th, between various parts of the country and Bembridge Airport have been considerably increased in the light of last season's experience, when about 9000 holiday-makers used these routes. During the first month this year when services were operating, the number of passengers increased by 50 per cent. On the Liverpool route the number of services has been increased from five to 10 per week, and on the Manchester route from one to five. In view of the heavy demands on the Newcastle and Leeds planes which ran a combined service last year, it has been found necessary to introduce separate services from both places. Other services now in full operation to and from Bembridge are those for London Airport, Birmingham, Coventry, Brighton, and Portsmouth. The machines making the journeys are Dakotas and Rapides...

———————————◆———————————

TOWN AND COUNTY NOTES

MOTHER LOVE. – A workman returning from his overnight employment at 5 a.m. on Wednesday saw a fox cross the road near Sheepwash, carrying a hen in its mouth. The farmer Mr. G. Osman was roused, but a search failed to find any trace of the intruder, and, strangely enough, none of the poultry houses appeared to have been entered nor their occupants disturbed. Later, in full daylight, Mr. Osman retraced the path taken by the fox by following the trail of scattered feathers. This led to a hedge about 50 yards from where the fox was seen, and, under which, sitting snugly on a clutch of 17 eggs, was a hen with nearly half its feathers missing, but otherwise unharmed. It is believed that the fox, alarmed by the workmen, dropped its prey and the hen immediately scurried back to her nest, the existence of which was unknown to any of the farm staff.

During the season 180,000 persons went on the Royal Victoria Pier, Ventnor. The peak month was August with 70,000.

A resident cut off the brush as a souvenir when a Southern Vectis bus driven by Mr. H. Hooker ran over and killed a dog fox at Thorley on Saturday evening.

◆

Television had made serious inroads into the number of cinemagoers. On the Island, the number of cinemas fell from 13 in the 1950's to 6 in the 70s, before picking up again during the 80s. The first cinema closure came in 1956...

November 10th, 1956

ISLAND CINEMA TO CLOSE
OTHER RUMOURS DENIED

Isle of Wight Theatres, Ltd., issued the following statement on Thursday : "The management of Isle of Wight Theatres, Ltd., announce that owing to the heavy burden of entertainment tax and generally increased costs of running the cinema, they are closing the King's Cinema, East Cowes, after the last performance on December 1st."

The cinema has been sold to Messrs. Saunders-Roe. The announcement will confirm rumours which have been circulating in the district for some time, but in issuing a statement, Mr. P.J. Milsom (general manager) stated : "There is no truth in rumours that other cinemas controlled by Isle of Wight Theatres are closing." Mr. Milsom also said that the Royalty Cinema at Cowes was being fully equipped for the presentation of Cinemascope films. The King's Cinema was built in 1935.

◆

As far as obituaries were concerned, the County Press was all things to all men, and a chimney sweep was as likely to be featured as a baronet was. The next two obituaries make the point. The first is for a local captain of industry, George Hibberd, who was one third of the mineral water manufacturers Gould, Hibberd and Randall...

December 15th, 1956

THE LATE MR. GEORGE HIBBERD
OVER 60 YEARS IN MINERAL WATER TRADE

A great loss to the business community of the Island has been occasioned by the death of Mr. George Hibberd, of Heatherley, Avondale Road, Newport. He had been connected with the mineral water trade for over 60 years, and at the time of his death was chairman of Gould, Hibberd and Randall Ltd., of Church Litten, Newport. His energy, enthusiasm, and a shrewd practical approach did much to build up the business to its present high standing...

Mr. Hibberd was born at Ventnor in 1880, and moved to Niton at the age of three when his father became landlord of the Star Inn. He began his career as a junior clerk in the Ventnor Post Office, but found routine office work irksome, so he joined his grandfather, Mr. Charles Hibberd, in the mineral water factory founded at High Street, Ventnor, some 30 years before and which had engaged his interest as a lad. In those days horses were used for haulage and for operating a bottle power-unit - a far cry from the mechanical methods of today. His grandfather died in 1899 and Mr. Hibberd, then only 19, assumed sole control. Under his energetic direction, Hibberd and Co. expanded, and the factory moved from North Street to West Street, at a school room still owned by the present company.

Shortly after the First World War, Mr. Hibberd bought Hervey's Farm at Niton and returned to the village in which he had spent his boyhood, intending to devote most of his time to farming and take only a detached interest in the firm. Nevertheless, he negotiated the amalgamation of Hibberd and Co. and Gould and Co. of Newport, in April, 1921, and, at his instigation, Randall and Co., were brought in in February, 1922, to form the company as now constituted; but he divested himself almost entirely of responsibility. When plans for a central factory at Church Litten were discussed in the late 1920s, however, he was persuaded to leave the farm and to move to Newport to apply his ability and long experience to its establishment... Notable for its hygienic layout, the factory is claimed to be one of the finest of its size in the country...

1957

The second obituary is for a farm worker, Mr. George Lewis, born in 1863. Ironically, despite coming from both ends of the social spectrum they had one thing in common - they had both led lives that would be unthinkable today...

January 26th, 1957

A LINK WITH OLDEN DAYS
WHITWELL NONAGENARIAN'S DEATH

A lifetime of devoted service to the land ended with the death on Saturday of Mr. George Lewis, Ash Cottage, Whitwell. Mr. Lewis was 93 in November. He started work as a carter's mate at the age of eight and did not completely retire from farming until he was 81. He personified true yeoman stock and could recall the days when although work was hard, times were often happier and people more contented. Mr. Lewis was born at St Lawrence in 1863 when his father was carter at Bank End Farm and after a short time at Sheepwash, the family moved to Week Farm, where Mr. Lewis started as a carter's mate at 2s. a week. His father's wage was 9s. a week. For several years, Mr. Lewis was employed as a carter at Old Park Farm by Mr. Spindler and in addition to performing duties, carted stone and pipes to build several well-known properties in the Ventnor district. On leaving Old Park, he commenced an association with Ash Farm, Whitwell, which was to last for 45 years and in which he faithfully served Mr. and Mrs. T. Reynolds and their family. He was an expert thatcher, using the old familiar crowns for his ricks. He also thatched the farmhouse and buildings and won several certificates for his proficiency... He tended his horses with great affection. He was one of the few remaining Islanders who used the broad Island dialect and although he had been to Ryde and Portsmouth, he had only been to Freshwater once and knew little of the West Wight. When the Reynolds family disposed of Ash Farm in 1938, Mr.

GODSHILL ELECTRIFIED

Lewis retired on reaching the age of 75, but continued in a part-time capacity owing to the shortage of labour. During the last war he was in the employ of Mr. R. Russell, of Whitwell Farm and Mr. T. W. Attrill, of Dean Farm, until he was 81... He had resided in the same house for 61 years and regularly attended the Methodist Church...

Skiffle had arrived in Britain. It was the advance party for rock and roll and its standard bearer was Lonnie Donegan. Clean cut and wholesome, Donegan performed American folk and blues songs such as "Lordy, I shall not be moved" and earnestly sang of being "Alabamy Bound" while dressed in tuxedo and bow-tie. Almost considered mainstream by the older generation he posed no threat to the status quo and as if to confirm his respectability, when he appeared at the Commodore Theatre in Ryde a County Press reporter attended and gave his performance a worthy, almost scholarly review...

February 2nd, 1957

LONNIE DONEGAN AT RYDE
LARGE AUDIENCES GREET FAMOUS SKIFFLE GROUP

Capacity audiences of young people applauded the exciting music of Lonnie Donegan and his Skiffle Group at the Commodore Theatre, Ryde, on Sunday. Famous for his unusual voice, Mr. Donegan also plays an electric guitar, and is supported by two other guitarists, a bass player and a drummer, who comprise the skiffle group. Their carefree manner hides masterly and accurate treatment of American folk songs and the brilliant rhythm and frenzied pace of their music is infectious. The measure of their popularity can be gauged by the fact that over 2600 people attended the two performances. Their numbers included "The Cumberland gap," "Bring a little water, Sylvie," "Alabamy bound," "Long, long, long gone," "Don't you rock me, Daddy-o," and the particularly popular "Rock Island line." Most of these were preceded by the story of the song told in Mr. Donegan's imitable style. This contemporary, tense music is new to Island theatres and the enthusiasm with which it was greeted by the young people certainly warranted the innovation. The supporting programme was effectively provided by an eight piece group, the Dean Maddison Orchestra, who played a variety of more generally accepted popular music including a Rogers-Astaire Medley, "Baby Doll," "Intermission Riff" and a rock 'n' roll interlude including "Garden of Eden," and "R-O-C-K."... Keeping the programme at a lively pace and amusing the audience was compere Mr. Tommy Godfrey, principal comedian in "Aladdin" at the Commodore Theatre recently.

Bannister's rope works at Cowes had been in existence for 200 years servicing the local ship and boat building industry. It had recently passed into the hands of J. S. White, the Cowes shipbuilder...

February 9th, 1957

ROPE-MAKING AT COWES
LONG RECORD OF THE BANNISTERS

It was only natural that a healthy rope-making industry should grow up in Cowes nearly two hundred years ago. The port was the centre of the shipbuilding industry in the Solent, when busy yards at Lymington, Hamble, Beaulieu, Basildon, and at Cowes, built "The Wooden Walls of Old England." Of the eight hand roperies which carried on their operations in Cowes two centuries ago only one remains today - Henry Bannister's - keeping alive the glory and service of an ancient industry. Although Bannister's is officially recorded as established in 1820, there is ample evidence to show that the family carried on rope-making many years before that time... It was in about 1820 that the demand for ropes for outfitting the many yachts, commercial sailing vessels, and men-of-war, being built in the Solent area, led to the establishment of the rope works on its present site. A rope-walk 1000 feet in length was constructed in what is now a completely built-up part of the town and subsequently it became necessary to build a humped-back road bridge over the ropewalk building to provide a route from the railway station to the ferry plying between West and East Cowes.* Bannister's trade was mainly with the very exacting members of the Royal Yacht Squadron, thus the emphasis was always on beautifully finished ropes of high-quality. Many examples of these ropes, made during the last century, are possessed by the firm, and among them are some of the sheets made for the royal racing yacht Britannia... Recently, Henry Bannister and Co., has become a wholly-owned subsidiary of J. Samuel White and Co., Ltd., the well-known shipbuilding firm, and it is their intention to continue the successful policy of making high-quality ropes for specialised use

---

NEWS IN BRIEF

VENTNOR LANDMARK TO DISAPPEAR – A prominent landmark† for nearly 20 years will disappear in the next few months with the removal of the six radar pylons from the top of St Boniface Down, Ventnor... They are being taken down because, with the advancement of modern radar equipment, they are of no further use... The original pylons, erected in 1938-9, provided a radar detection screen for the south-eastern part of the country... In November, 1947, a newspaper and mail plane on its way to the Channel Islands crashed into one of the towers and two airmen were killed... The work is expected to take about three months. (January 19)

HUNGARIAN REFUGEES AT NETTLESTONE. – Life among the refugees at the Hungarian camp at Nettlestone has been brightened in the last few days by interest in two domestic events, a marriage and a birth, the marriage being the first to take place since the refugees arrived in December.

CONDITIONS AT NEWPORT MARKET CRITICISED. – Answering questions on marketing at a well attended meeting of Gurnard Ratepayers'

---

* Bridge Road, Cowes. The "hump" in the road was removed in 1969.
† See photograph page 145.

Association ... Mrs. Roger De Quincey, who with her husband farms at Kings Manor, Freshwater, criticised the treatment of animals at Newport market. Mrs. De Quincey said that animals in the Island were on the whole very well looked after, but an exception to this was Newport market which was "a blot on a fair Island." She added that never had she been charged so much to have calves treated so badly. They were tied up by the neck and gave the appearance of being half strangled. She had learned that to be with one's own cattle was the only way to ensure that they received reasonable treatment...

I.T.V. STATION FOR THE ISLAND - SUGGESTED SITE ON CHILLERTON DOWN. – The Independent Television Authority announces that it is hoped to erect a station in the Island in the first half of next year. Application has been made for a site on Chillerton Farm... The station would occupy about two acres of a 23-acre field and would be about 3 miles from Newport and about 3 miles from the B.B.C. transmitter at Rowridge... Advertisements would shortly be issued inviting applicants to supply programmes...

———————————◆———————————

There was a widespread collapse in egg sales in the early 1950's and in response the government created the Egg Marketing Board in December 1956. Just a few weeks later the Island's egg packing station embarked on a publicity campaign to persuade a reluctant public that their eggs were fresh...

February 23rd, 1957

NEW LAID EGGS FOR ALL
PROTECTING THE ISLAND'S BREAKFAST

Mr. P. C. Barton, manager of the I.W. Egg Packing Station, Ltd., of Newport is a man with a mission - to break down the prejudice which exists against the stamped egg. Too many people, he considers, think that stamped eggs cannot be fresh; yet there is no reason why the Islander should not enjoy a new-laid egg for his breakfast, in spite of the suspicious rubber stamp. If that stamp is numbered "105," it is a guarantee that the egg has come from an Island farm, and has been delivered, fresh, to an Island shop... The prejudice (probably justifiably, Mr. Barton admits) arose from the war years of ration and restriction, when it was not always possible to ensure that eggs reached the shops in strict rotation and perhaps harassed packing station staff were not as careful as they might have been... The Island Egg Packing Station has been in existence for about 16 years and for the last three years it has been released from Ministry control, functioning as a private wholesale firm... the station deals with 700 Island producers - about 95 per cent of the total number. Their lorries call at each farm once weekly, and other consignments are brought in by the farmers. The eggs do not stay in the station longer than 72 hours; the period is often much shorter. There is thus an average lapse of between 5-10 days from hen to shop, which, Mr. Barton states, justifies the claim for freshness... For only about two months of the year (late July and August) Islanders may not be able to obtain "105" eggs. Production is then at its lowest and holidaymakers swell the population. During that period the Island station receives only about 40,000 eggs a week, and to meet orders from shops they are obliged to augment stock by importing from the mainland... The weekly average of Island eggs coming into the station is 180,000 and the figure increases to a peak of 234,000 weekly.

———————————◆———————————

TOWN AND COUNTY NOTES

At Cowes Council meeting on Tuesday Mr. B.F. Venner described as "rude" posters in Newport advertising a meeting of ratepayers and residents to discuss the new rates, which state: "They've got their hands in your pockets."

THE SHIPBUILDERS STRIKE - OVER 2000 OUT AT COWES ... The shipbuilding strike will enter its second week to-day. In the Island over 2000 men are involved, most of them at Cowes. The majority are employed by Messrs. J. Samuel White and Co., and the remainder are spread over a handful of small boats and yachts builders. Cowes has been unnaturally quiet this week.... many workers have been strolling the streets or congregating in the clubs... From remarks made by a cross-section of men, it seems evident that the majority are averse to the strike. Mr. C.R. Reed (A.E.U. district secretary) said that no one liked a strike - least of all himself - but he pointed out that the trade unions elected their leaders and should have confidence in their leadership...

A green linnet flew through the open top deck window of a Newport-East Cowes bus while it was in motion near Whippingham on Tuesday. A passenger succeeded in capturing the bird and released it through a window.

FAIRLEE HOUSE TO BE DEMOLISHED. – When the Finance Committee report stated that no planning objection was to be raised to the demolition of Fairlee House, Mr. Minns asked for the reason. Ald. Chandler replied: High cost of maintenance, deterioration of the building through not being occupied, impossibility of finding a tenant, inadequacy of the sewers, and the awkwardness of converting the high rooms for housing. Ald. Purdy said that lead had also disappeared from the roof. Ald. Chandler said that steps had been taken to make it possible for the lead from the roof to be identified - if more were taken. - The report was approved.*

CARISBROOKE RAILWAY STATION DESTROYED - POLICE ENQUIRING INTO THE CAUSE -- In less than half an hour on Wednesday evening Carisbrooke Railway Station and the railway house were destroyed by fire. The alarm was given by telephone at 7.56p.m., but 20 minutes earlier children were seen running away from the building. Two appliances reached the building by driving along the disused railway track. The property has been derelict since the closure of the branch railway line in September 1953 and had become a playground for children. Police are making enquiries into the cause of the fire and are questioning children.

* See photograph, page 145.

Up until the mid-1970s the Island was unusually well catered for in terms of venues for pop and rock stars. The trailblazer was the Commodore Theatre in Star Street, Ryde, home to many rock and roll performances over the years...

March 30th, 1957

ROCK 'N' ROLL AT RYDE
TOMMY STEELE ENTHUSIASTICALLY WELCOMED

At the Commodore Theatre, Ryde, on Sunday evening one of the stars of the rock 'n' roll craze, Tommy Steele, appeared on the stage twice and received an enthusiastic reception from an audience of 2500, mostly young people from all parts of the Island and about 300 from the mainland. Tommy Steele's meteoric rise to fame within recent months has been a feature in the entertainment world. He appeared in the orthodox attire of this modern style of dancing, a check shirt, jeans and soft shoes, accompanied by his four "Steelemen." The remarkable spell he holds over juvenile audiences was illustrated by the rapturous applause he received. He had only to flick the lock of hair on his fair head or tap his foot and the audience was in ecstasy, while the enthusiasm they showed as he left the theatre amounted to adulation. There was a foretaste of this at Bembridge airport, where he arrived in a specially chartered aeroplane at about 5p.m.* A crowd of about 100 youngsters darted towards him, as he went to enter a waiting car, demanding his autograph. Police officers, who arrived in two cars, kept control. At the Commodore crowds of youngsters besieged the theatre entrance in the hope of securing his autograph. He spent the night at Yelf's Hotel and left on Monday morning. Supporting items to his programme were given by the Scutt Brothers, Tommy Godfrey, Jean Ford, the Dean Maddison Show Band and the Four Skiffs. Before flying to the Island Tommy Steele had taken part in an afternoon charity performance at the Albert Hall. Tommy Godfrey, who was MC, had on the previous day returned from Germany where he had been touring with the Tony Hancock show.

◆

Sabrina was a 21-year-old Stockport girl who for a brief period in the late 1950's enjoyed enormous fame as Britain's answer to Jayne Mansfield, the American actress and was, in the newspaper parlance of the day, a "sex bomb" or "sultry siren." She was also described as a singer and actress, both fairly slender claims as in truth she was actually rather more well known for her 42 inch bust.† She enjoyed a meteoric rise but after a few years her star waned and she moved to Hollywood, where apart from one brief unsuccessful attempt to rekindle her British career in the late 1960s, she remains to this day. At the height of her fame she came to the Commodore Theatre in Ryde...

June 1st, 1957

SABRINA AT RYDE
SKIFFLE AND ROCK 'N' ROLL PROGRAMME

High spirited entertainment was the order of the day at the Commodore Theatre, Ryde, on Sunday, when Sabrina and popular recording stars, the Vipers Skiffle Group topped the bill in a programme of skiffle and rock 'n' roll.

---

* See photograph, page 145.

† Harry Secombe in a 1956 Goon Show, as a record request show host says, "Mrs Gladys Quimby would like to hear Sabrina sing.... So would I."

The compere, George Moon, kept the show moving at a lively pace and set an appropriate atmosphere. Leon Bell and the Bellcats, a group comprising electric guitar and banjo, tenor sax and drums, started the programme and appeared again in the second half, when the drummer stole the limelight with some cheeky clowning. Playing a large selection of skiffle music almost non-stop, the Vipers Skiffle Group brought the first half of the programme to a close. Masters of this type of music, the group of three guitars, bass, and washboard gave by far the most polished performance in the show. Stealing the show in quite another direction was young Jim Dale and his Dalesmen. The possessor of a pleasant singing voice, he endeared himself to the audience by his modest surprise at the reception he received. Sabrina, who wore a tight fitting red dress, sang several popular songs, including "I want a man, not a mouse," "It's better in the dark," "S'wonderful," "Persuade me," and "I can't give you anything but love." She was accompanied by pianist Miss Ann Seymour and the Bellcats. During the song "Persuade me" she persuaded a brave but bashful young man from the audience onto the stage, and as she sang "Diamonds are a girl's best friend" she threw four bracelets to the cheering men.

———————————◆———————————

Owning and operating an ITV station in the late 1950's was so lucrative that in 1957 the owner of Scottish Television, Lord Thomson, uttered the immortal words "Independent Television is a licence to print money." Commercial television was about to arrive in the South of England and with its affluent population the South was the second most profitable television region after London and was known within the industry as "South Bank-on-Sea." Not surprisingly, when the ITV franchise for the South was advertised, there was keen interest...

July 6th, 1957

ISLAND I.T.V. STATION
KEEN COMPETITION FOR PROGRAMME CONTRACT

There has been keen competition for the programme contract for the new I.T.V. station to be broadcast from Chillerton Down which is scheduled to come into operation in the spring or early summer of next year. It is considered to be one of the most attractive I.T.V. regions outside of London. It has attracted far more applications for the contract than any of the existing stations, including London. There were 29 requests for application forms and on the closing day (June 12th) the authority had received 10 firm applications for contracts to provide programmes. With the opening of the Isle of Wight station the national I.T.V. coverage will be raised to 40 millions, or 80 per cent of the population of the United Kingdom.

———————————◆———————————

The ancient crafts were disappearing fast. County Press contributor George Long, made an attempt to record some of those still in existence...

September 28th, 1957

INTERESTING ISLAND CRAFTS
BY GEORGE LONG, F.R.G.S.

Perhaps our oldest Island craft is that of the smith, and in years gone by there was a smithy in every village... The mechanisation of agriculture, and the coming of the motor car and lorry, have greatly reduced the number of horses in use. This means far less work for the smith, so that today there are very few smithies left in the Island and some of these do general ironwork - such as the making of ornamental iron gates - which several do very skilfully, instead of shoeing horses. As to the village smithy, I am afraid there are very few left, but I have discovered three. The picturesque smithy at Blackwater is one of the oldest in the Island, and Mr. William Orchard, the proprietor, is still working at the age of 83. Another veteran is Mr. Hayles of Binstead. I found him working at his forge, and he told me he had a record of 60 years continuous work. Mr. Toms, of Newchurch, is the third of my trinity. His forge stands beside the steep hill running up to the village church. These fine old men are an example to all of us; long may they flourish.

AN ANCIENT CRAFT

The thatcher is engaged in another useful and ancient craft... A newly thatched roof requires further attention every seven to ten years, but I have seen none which appear to be in urgent need of repair... The thatchers to-day say they have great difficulty in getting good thatching straw. The combine harvesters have a tendency to split the stalks and worse still, the farmer sometimes burns the straw instead of harvesting it... Like most tourist resorts, the Island has its potters and weavers, as it is an attraction to visitors to see the work done by hand. Mr. Lester, of Freshwater, has a pottery studio in Freshwater, Niton, Seaview and Shanklin, where customers can see this fascinating craft. Miss McKechney has a hand-loom shop at Brading, where cotton and wool fabrics and furnishings are made.

HIGHLY SKILLED JOB

A very useful Island craft is the making of lobster pots from osier rods. This is a highly skilled job. A well-made lobster pot is a veritable work of art, strong and symmetrical. There are a number of fishermen along our coasts who still make their own pots. A good worker can make three osier pots in a day, and it is a useful job to fill up slack times in winter, when it is too rough to put to sea. The Wheelers, of Blackgang, were formerly well-known for their excellent pots, but they have now ceased production. I was fortunate enough to see another member of this well-known Island family, hard at work making a lobster pot. This is Mr. Wheeler, of Steephill Cove. He is a very skilled maker of pots, in which he is ably assisted by his partner, Mr. Cook, of Brighstone, and also makes pots on a commercial scale and sells them to fishermen along the coast. Another interesting hand-made job is the holley or hulley, which is skilfully fashioned from hazel rods. It is shaped like a torpedo and is four or five feet long. Fishermen use it as a cage to float in the sea and keep their captives alive...

"WATTLE AND DAUB"

My last example is the hurdler, who makes hurdles for sheep folding, from hazel rods. I found one of these at work in the woods between Wootton and East Cowes one winter's day. He told me that he can make a dozen hurdles in a day, but he loses time in wet weather... The hazel rods are split and woven together to form the hurdle. Until fairly recently country cottages were made of these hurdles, daubed with clay, inside and out, to keep out wind and rain. This type of construction is known as "wattle and daub."

———————————◆———————————

A few weeks later Mr. Long turned his attention to the remaining water mills of the Island...

October 19th, 1957

SOME WATER MILLS OF THE WIGHT
BY GEORGE LONG, F.R.G.S.

There were water-mills working here when the Domesday book was compiled but the origin of milling goes back many centuries before this. It was the milling and storing of grain that made city life possible and gave security against famine; in short the mill was the mother of civilisation. Up to a century ago, water-mills were very numerous in the Island, even the smallest brook seems to have had one or more, but with increasing competition many of the smaller mills have gone out of business. Thus the town of Newport, half a century ago, had three important mills driven by the modest stream of the Medina. Two of these mills are still flourishing as fine modern mills using electric power. The first is Ford Mill and the second - a little higher up - is Leigh Thomas and Co.'s Pan Mill... St Cross Mill, near the foot of Hunnyhill, has given up milling and is now part of a brewery, and Shide Mill, a couple of miles upstream, is now empty and unused. The Lukely stream at Carisbrooke is even smaller than the Medina but for many years it drove the enormous wheel of West Mill. The wheel is still in working order but is no longer required, as the three-storey mill building is now a wholesale grocery warehouse.

There is another big mill with an interesting history at Wootton Bridge. It is unique in the Island because it is not driven by a river, but by the mighty surge of the tide. The causeway which carries the Newport-Ryde road through the village also acts as a dam to hold back the tidal water above the mill. The mill has been derelict for some years but when it was working it operated in this way. Sluices were opened at low water to allow the rising tide to fill up the basin above the mill. They were closed at high tide and the water thus penned up flowed back into the estuary through the mill wheels and so drove the mill. Thus Wootton Bridge possessed almost unlimited power, but like all tide mills suffered one serious disadvantage. Its working was entirely controlled by the state of the tide and it could not begin until three and a half hours after high tide and then could only run for five and a half hours. This working period, twice in 24 hours, might come at any inconvenient hour imaginable yet the miller could do nothing but wait for it.

When I consulted an old, large-scale map of the Island, every little brook

Tommy Steele, the rock and roll star (wearing windcheater), and his company arriving at Bembridge airport on Sunday for their appearance in the evening at the Commodore Theatre, Ryde. (March 30)

LOCAL LANDMARK DISAPPEARS
Demolishing the last of the radar pylons on St. Boniface Down, Ventnor. (June 22)

THE FLYING-BOAT DISASTER
The tailpiece of the flying boat remains intact, although the rest of the machine disintegrated. Soldiers and firemen are seen searching the debris. (November 23. See page 147)

seemed to have one or more mills, most of which are now ruinous or have vanished altogether, but I have discovered four village mills which are still flourishing. Each is driven by a stream so small that a tall man could stride across it without wetting his feet... Where streams are copious and the fall is slight, an undershot wheel is used which works by the push of the stream flowing under it. In the overshot wheel the water falls on top of the wheel and adds the force of gravity to the impulse given by the current of the river. The big wheel at Yafford Mill, near Shorwell, is a good example of this principle... Yafford Mill was busily working when the Domesday book was compiled, and was still going strong when I visited it in August...

Brighstone Mill no doubt originally had an overshot wheel, but today is furnished with a modern turbine which is even more economical of power. This mill specialises in cattle food. Yafford Mill does this too, and makes wholemeal flour as well. We can get an idea of the power which can be drawn from tiny streams by looking at the Calbourne stream which flows through lovely Winkle Street. In the course of two or three miles before it meets the sea at Newtown, it drives two mills. Calbourne Upper Mill is very similar to Yafford Mill and like it, has an overshot wheel. The Lower Mill has a turbine to make the most of the power available. Below the mill the stream flows across the lane, forming a picturesque water-splash or ford. I wonder how many Island residents have ever found these delightful old mills?

---◆---

ISLAND NOTES

The announcement that Russia had successfully launched a satellite[*] made Mr. W.G. Sherratt, radio dealer of Newport, drop everything, including breakfast, to get to his workshop... A phone call to the BBC in London confirmed that signals from the satellite were being received... and equipment was hurriedly assembled to listen... At 7 a.m. on Sunday excellent recordings were made. Faint signals were first heard as the satellite approached the British Isles, and for two minutes the signals were so strong that they might have been coming from the local TV station. In about eight minutes they died away completely as the satellite covered the distance from England to Italy in three minutes! (October 12)

NEWPORT-FRESHWATER RAILWAY BRIDGE DEMOLITION. – A familiar sight to travellers on the Newport-Cowes Road, the railway viaduct over the stream and highway at the bottom of Hunnyhill, Newport, will soon disappear. Following the removal of the railway track, Messrs. Jolliffe of Cowes commenced the work of taking down the bridge on Monday and the job will take several weeks... The ironwork is being sent as scrap to the mainland but one section of the bridge will remain in the Island, however, as it has been purchased by the Ryde Town Council for possible use as a footbridge from Ryde Esplanade Station to Quay Road... (December 7.)

---

* The launching of 'Sputnik 1,' the world's first satellite, was a major coup for Russia. Launched on October 4th, it began the space race. It broadcast an audible "bleep" as part of experiments in radio signal propagation from the ionosphere. The signals lasted 22 days, and the satellite itself three months, before burning up on re-entry.

Wootton Creek was partly frozen over on Tuesday morning following the most severe frost of the winter so far. (December 21.)

GOOD NEWS FOR COWES. – Messrs. J. Samuel White and Co. yesterday received news that their tender had been accepted for building two passenger steamers for the Channel Islands service... It will mean ample work in the shipyard until the middle of 1961. (December 21.)

Perfect reception of London ITV programmes is reported from a site overlooking the Needles, and Horsebridge Hill at Newport.

THE SATELLITE DOG. – Sir, horrified protests have been made against the imprisonment of a dog within the latest Russian satellite.* Moscow radio is reported to have stated that apes will shortly be sent up. It is most unlikely that Russian Communist scientists will be influenced by humane considerations but it is all to the good that such protests are being made... We must ensure that no scientist within the British Commonwealth is permitted to copy the Russian experiment.

A. MAURICE TOMS, The Tiny House, Ryde. (November 9.)

———————————◆———————————

At the end of 1957 came what the County Press described as "the Island's worst peace-time disaster" when a flying boat en-route from Southampton to Madeira crashed into a chalk pit on the side of Shalcombe Down killing 45 people. The cause of the accident remains unknown, the only hard facts emerging being that both No. 3 and 4 engines on the starboard wing had stalled and that at the time of impact the plane was banking steeply to the right, possibly as a result of that loss. There was also some puzzlement over why the aircraft was in that area at all, the usual route involving passing over the Island near the Needles. Whatever the cause, the end result was horrifying, the graphic County Press report making grim reading. The event was given extensive coverage that week which is reflected in the size of this item, which is a précis of those many and lengthy reports...

November 23rd, 1957

FLYING-BOAT DISASTER – DEATH ROLL OF 45
SOLDIERS BRAVE INFERNO TO SAVE OTHERS

The Island's worst peace-time disaster occurred at 10.50 p.m. on Friday week when the giant flying-boat Sydney, outward-bound from Southampton, crashed into a chalk pit at Shalcombe Farm, near the Calbourne-Freshwater road. The aircraft burst into flames and the eight members of the crew and 43 passengers lost their lives in the holocaust as the aircraft and 2000 gallons of petrol blazed like a volcano. Two more of the passengers died later in hospital bringing the death toll to 45.

The flying-boat, a Short Solent owned by Aquila Airways, was on a flight

---

* Sputnik 2 carried a canine passenger, a small terrier named Laika. Believed for years to have perished on re-entry, it was disclosed in 2003 that she actually died of heat exhaustion just a few hours into the mission and in any case, was to be painlessly euthanased with poisoned food just before re-entry.

from Southampton to Las Palmas and Madeira via Lisbon, with 50 passengers going on holidays, including three honeymoon couples who were among those who died in the flames as would-be rescuers watched helplessly*.

Local residents co-operated magnificently with the rescue services, and at least half the survivors owe their lives directly to the selfless courage of two Army officers and a senior N.C.O. of the Junior N.C.O.'s School, R.A.S.C., Freshwater. Time after time the three men braved the inferno, dragging out dead and injured, until, with their own clothing alight, they were finally driven back by the terrific heat.

Throughout Sunday, particularly in the afternoon, thousands of sightseers flocked from all parts of the Island to view the scattered wreckage. A large force of police officers, assisted by members of the motoring organisations, were kept busy dealing with a record flow of traffic. As dusk fell, a cordon guarding the upper lip of the chalk pit, on which the wreckage lay, turned back a number of adult souvenir-hunters attempting to creep past them on hands and knees.

EYE-WITNESSES' STORIES

Major W.J.F. Weller, officer commanding the junior N.C.O.s Regimental School, R.A.S.C. at Golden Hill Fort, Freshwater, told the "County Press" that at 10.45 p.m., accompanied by Lieut. J.R. Sherburn and Q.M.S. W. Reid he was sitting in a vehicle about 200 yards up the road from the chalk pit. Along with other officers he was awaiting the completion of a night exercise in which 36 trainees were taking part. After two or three minutes they heard an aircraft approaching. The engine sounded uneven. He estimated that the plane was flying at below 100 feet. All the cabin lights and navigation lights were clearly visible. The aircraft banked steeply to the right and crashed into the disused chalk pit. He sent a driver to telephone for help and with his two companions ran to the wreckage which was flaming furiously. At that time the tail portion of the plane was not on fire. As they ran towards the plane they heard cries for help and found seven persons lying near the wreckage, badly burned. Two women walked away from the rear of the aircraft apparently unharmed...

THOUGHT IT WOULD HIT HER HOME

Mrs. Brenda Bruce, of Chessell Farm, said she was in her bedroom when the noise of the approaching aircraft became so loud that she feared it would strike the farmhouse. From the window she saw it flash by, a few feet overhead, with those inside clearly visible in the cabin lights. Then came a loud crash... A local farmer, Mr. H. Kitson said he heard the plane roar low overhead. Then came a loud bang. He said: "That's it," pulled on his boots and ran out of the house half clothed. Quick as he was, he found Mr. Bert Tyrrell, a shepherd, already on the scene helping to get people away from the blaze, which he described as "like a volcano." He helped Mr. Tyrell carry away living and dead on hurdles. The soldiers gave their greatcoats and tunics to use as padding for the hurdles and coverings for the injured...

HEROIC SOLDIER RESCUERS

All who were present united in praise of the magnificent work done by the soldiers, chiefly by the two officers and Q.M.S. Reid. From what they told "County Press" reporters it is obvious that Major Weller's statement, quoted above, is a masterpiece of modesty. All three dashed into the blazing debris,

See photgraph page 145.

dragging out the dead and injured, and ignoring the terrific heat. Some of the victims were screaming in agony with their petrol-splashed clothing blazing like torches. Q.M.S. Reid said "If ever a man deserved a medal it was Lieutenant Sherburn. He was last in the plane, standing there with his shirt blazing and tugging away at a seat containing a woman and child. I rushed to his aid and between us we got the seat and passengers clear, but unfortunately they were dead. From then on the position was simply hopeless; it was obvious that anyone left in the blazing machine was dead."... As all the passengers were strapped in their seats it was necessary either to cut through the straps or tear the seat away from its mountings.

GRIM SEARCHES

The County Fire Brigade and the police were on the scene very promptly and a lorry load of troops from Golden Hill Fort, Freshwater, was sent to the scene immediately the alarm was raised. They helped the police and firemen in their grim task of searching the wreckage. Some of the earliest recovered victims were taken in private cars to St Mary's Hospital, where a complete ward was vacated to make room for the stretcher cases. During the night 17 bodies were recovered and taken by Army lorry to the rifle range at Albany Barracks, which was used as an emergency mortuary. The soldiers and firemen resumed the grim task of searching the wreckage for bodies at dawn and by midday on Saturday all 43 had been recovered. The utmost difficulty was experienced in extricating the last few bodies, which were buried under the engines which fell on them as the wreckage disintegrated. The engines had to be dragged clear by teams of men hauling on ropes, which frequently broke under the strain... As the hours passed access to the still smouldering pyre became more and more difficult because the thousands of gallons of water which had been pumped on the wreckage after the use of foam turned the approach lane into a quagmire. At 4 a.m. the metalwork was still red hot and it was daylight before it had cooled sufficiently to be handled.

SUNDAY CROWDS

Residents of Chessell and Brook, who had attended a moving memorial service in the Parish Church on Sunday morning, expressed disgust at the holiday atmosphere pervading the scene in the afternoon when thousands of sightseers flocked to the area from all parts of the Island. Police had anticipated a large number of motorists and had taken precautions. More than 200 cars and motorcycles were parked and there was a non-stop stream of traffic past the entrance to the pit, where a view could be obtained of the giant tailplane towering above the charred remains of shrubs and trees. Viewing the milling throng, which included many young children and even babies in arms, one Brook woman commented: "They are simply ghouls. All it needs now is an ice-cream stall and a hot dog stand." As dusk fell people were seen approaching the site from the top of the downs. Some adult souvenir hunters attempted to get through a cordon on hands and knees, but all were turned back. Mrs. Bowyer (wife of the rector) described such behaviour as "utterly disgusting."

"ENGINE TROUBLE" MESSAGE

Aquila Airways announced on Saturday that shortly after take-off at 10.41 p.m. the pilot radioed that he was having trouble with No. 4 engine and that he intended to return. One of the survivors Mr. Arthur Mangham described how they were late starting. They should have taken off at 9.30 p.m. but did not taxi out until 10.08 p.m. There was no fog. The engines were revved up and cut down several times. Each time he thought they were taking off. It was his first trip and he insisted on sitting by the window to watch the take-off. There followed more revvings-up of the engines and finally, after more than half an hour of taxi-ing they were airborne. "A few moments later the plane dropped. It started to climb again and then dropped again. It made me grip the arms of my seat... We went on for about five minutes, repeatedly climbing and dropping and an officer came in and told us 'Things are a bit sticky.' But gave a thumbs up sign, grimaced and turned back into the crew's portion of the plane. The officer seemed white and tense, and quite frankly I was already looking around for a way out. He had just gone out of the cabin when the plane dropped again. There was a grinding noise, which kept on for a minute or two, and then everything went blank."

"JUMPING INTO BLACK VOID"

Mr. Mangham added: "The next thing I knew was smoke and the smell of something like burning varnish. My wife said 'Kick the window out.' I went out first, and that was the worst experience of the whole trip because I was jumping into a black void and did not know whether we were on land or water. My wife followed me and we rolled down a bank. I pulled my wife away because I was afraid it was going to explode and then I went for help." Later Mr. Mangham helped to place his wife on a hurdle, which was used as a stretcher and was helping to carry it to the roadway when he asked two young Scouts (Robert Pacey, 14, of Roseland Cottage, Calbourne, and Graham Barnes, 13, of Five Houses, Calbourne) to lend a hand as he was just about all-in, and they did so.

THE LAST FOUR SEATS

Taking up the story, Mr. Hewatt, a friend of Mr. Mangham, said that they and their wives were occupying the last seats in the rear of the plane. Before the crash there was no warning of danger. The plane appeared to be on an even keel, but he agreed that the 10 minutes of flying was very rough and that Mr. Mangham's description of it as "like being on the big dipper" was correct.

LOCAL SERVICES ADEQUATE

Island authorities were annoyed at some national newspaper reports, which stated that scores of police, firemen and doctors were flown to the Island from the mainland. Nothing could have been further from the truth. A "County Press" representative who spent most of Friday night at the scene writes: "The Island services proved more than adequate and all branches co-operated magnificently." The Newport Corps of the Salvation Army ran a mobile canteen at the scene of the disaster from 9 a.m. on Saturday until nightfall on Sunday and during that time distributed free to rescue and salvage workers 1000 cups of tea, 500 cakes, 200 packets of biscuits and several tins of potato crisps, all of which had been given.

1958

In April 1951, Edwin Holbrook of Porchfield, then aged 84, set down his recollections of life in and around the village, copies of which have long been in circulation on the Island. In 1958 he sent an edited version to the County Press...

January 11th, 1958

A NONAGENARIAN'S RECOLLECTIONS
MEMORIES OF NEWTOWN, PORCHFIELD AND NEWPORT

Mr. Edwin Holbrook, formerly well known as a carrier between Porchfield and Newport (the last to use a horse-drawn van) recently celebrated his 90th birthday at the home of his son-in-law and daughter (Mr. and Mrs. F.J. Fallick) at 59 Clarence Road, Newport. He formerly resided for many years at Bethel Cottage, Porchfield. He has a wonderfully retentive memory and the skill to record his recollections, as a diary of his life, which he wrote at the age of 84, strikingly evidences. "I have had the pleasure and privilege of reading the life story of this worthy veteran," writes "Vectensis," and he has culled the following extracts from no fewer than 64 pages of quarto typescript copied from the diary by Mr. Holbrook's grand-daughter.

OLD NEWTOWN FAMILY

For more than 200 years members of the Holbrook family lived at Newtown. At one time they were engaged in making salt at the old saltern on the banks of Newtown River and were the owners of two good-sized sailing boats, in which they traded, mostly between Newtown and Swanage and Portland, carrying salt on the outward trips and returning with Purbeck and Portland stone. When I was a small boy in the 1870's I remember the last survivors of these seafarers, Tom, Jim, and Reuben, and their vessel, the Wellington, anchored in the river.

CHILDHOOD DAYS

I was born at Durrants Farm, Porchfield, the youngest of a family of five sons and one daughter. In 1871 my parents moved to what was then known as Dirty Lane*. A more fitting name could not have been chosen, as only farm wagons and carts could pass that way and in the winter there were ruts two feet deep filled with water. My father could not read or write - he went to school for only two days. My mother was more fortunate, having attended the Church of England School at Carisbrooke for several years, and I well remember my mother teaching my father to read and write. After much patience and great perseverance on the part of both he was eventually able to read quite well. The only books I ever saw him read were the Bible, Bunyan's "Pilgrim's Progress," the chapel hymn-book, and the "Bible Christian Magazine," but he liked my mother to read extracts from "Fox's Book of Martyrs."

LOCK'S GREEN SCHOOL

Before the church school was built at Lock's Green a dame school was carried on by a daughter of the late Mr. Benjamin Ford, at Bethel Cottage, the house which I later purchased and was my home for nearly 50 years. The urgent need for better educational facilities was keenly felt and mainly through the efforts of Sir John Simeon of Swainston, who was MP for the Island, Mr. H. Hughes, of

---

* New Road, Porchfield.

Thorness, Miss Ward, of Northwood House, Cowes, and my father-in-law Mr. H.E. Mew, of Porchfield House (who gave stone quarried in one of his fields, still known as Quarry Field), the Church of England School was built in 1869-70... I attended the school from 1872 to 1879. We had to pay twopence a week, which had to be taken each Monday. Before entering in the morning the children lined up outside and marched in, the girls curtseying and the boys saluting as they passed the head teacher. Then we sang a hymn and recited the Lord's prayer. Reading, writing, and arithmetic took up most of the time, but the lessons in grammar, history, and geography were very good. Reading was monotonous as the only books provided were the standard schoolbooks, and we read the same things over and over again. At that time there were between 70 and 80 children attending the school, some walking two to three miles.

LOW WAGES

Workmen's wages were very low, those of farm workers in particular. Skilled tradesmen - carpenters and bricklayers - received from 24s. to 25s. a week; farmworkers, 14s., usually with a rent-free cottage, but for carters and cowmen it was a seven-day week, and the only time off was a few hours on Good Friday and Christmas Day. Women were glad to do any work on the farm for a few shillings to help buy food for their children. I remember five women, who, in bitterly cold weather, went into the fields during February and March to plant beans with a dibber for a few pence a gallon. They were lucky if they earned more than 1s. 4d. a day.

PARISH DOCTORS AND THE WORKHOUSE

The conditions under which many old people in the country lived at that time were distressing. Their great horror was the workhouse. I have known old men crippled with rheumatism walk, with the aid of two sticks, for miles from home to crack stones by the roadside for a few shillings a week to keep them out of the workhouse. If country people were ill the only doctor for them was the parish doctor. Before the days of bicycles, if anyone was ill someone had to walk or run to Newport for the doctor, and it was often the afternoon of the next day before he came to see the patient. Sometimes, in serious cases, he was too late. In the 1870s the parish doctor for the Porchfield district was Dr. Miller, of Newport. He had no conveyance and made his rounds on foot.

When old folks or anyone out of work were in want they had to apply to the Board of Guardians for help. The amount of relief allowed was a shilling and a four pound loaf of bread a week. The relieving officer called with the shilling and the bread was supplied by Mr. Buckler, a baker of Shalfleet, but the people of Porchfield had to walk two miles for it.

The workhouse van was a rather large vehicle with thick, stiff springs and heavy iron tyres. It had a canvas tilt and was drawn by a half-bred horse. The driver was a workhouse inmate, and old people being taken away were helped up a short step-ladder after the tail-board had been let down.

TOLL-GATES

I remember when a toll-gate was across the road at the top of Hunnyhill, Newport, almost opposite the Britannia Inn. Later the boundary of the borough was extended and the gate removed to Forest House corner. The argument between the public and the Highway Commissioners over tolls went on for a long time. All vehicles with wheels under three inches wide were charged 3d. or 6d. according to size and weight. The matter was brought to a crisis when a farmer instructed his carter, taking a wagon load of corn to a Newport mill, to refuse to pay the toll at the Forest Gate, and, if necessary, he was to hitch one of his horses to the bar and pull it away. This the carter did and I remember seeing the broken gate lying by the roadside. Soon afterwards highway rates were introduced, and the tolls discontinued.

COUNTRY CARRIERS

Before the railways came, and for a considerable time afterwards, the only means of transport available to country people were the horse-drawn carriers' vans. The women of the villages usually went to town once a week to do their shopping and were quite content to sit under the tilt for an hour or more each way, chatting to pass the time and thoroughly enjoying themselves. When I was a lad working at Vittlefields Farm the carriers who passed were Chambers, who drove a four-horse coach from Freshwater; Simmonds, whose coach was smaller with three horses; William Whittington, from Yarmouth; and Robert Drake, from Wellow. Mr. James Blake, of Yarmouth, a miller and corn merchant and the last mayor of the ancient borough, always had an inside seat in Chambers' coach, which carried eight inside and 12 on top. Chambers had a long grey beard and wore a grey top hat. I bought the carrier's business between Newtown and Porchfield and Newport from my brother-in-law, Mr. W. Smith, in 1902, and carried it on for 24 years. Among the many amusing experiences I recall was one connected with the second marriage of a former vicar of Newtown, the Rev. H. Rice Venn. He returned from a holiday with a second wife, much to the surprise of everyone. One old lady would not believe it, and she asked me to bring her the "County Press" on the Saturday morning. As I was leaving her gate she said "Better bring me two copies, then I shall be sure it is right if it is in both." It was, and the old lady was satisfied! Another surprise was when, on leaving the "Noah's Ark" public house at Newtown one night after delivering goods I had brought from Newport, I discovered that a man, dead drunk, had been put into the back of my van. I took him home, but saw to it that such unwelcome visitors were not put into the van again...

MACHINERY COMES TO THE FARM

It was at Colemans farm, Porchfield, that I last saw thrashing done with the flail. Probably there are some people who do not know what a flail was or how it was used. It was two short rods, one about 4 ft. and the other about 3ft. long, joined end on with leather loops. The man using it held the longer rod and swung the shorter one over his head and banged it down on the corn spread thinly on the barn floor. It was a job requiring skill; one could easily get a crack on the head if not careful. In my early days I remember seeing the first horse-powered thrashing machine working at Locks Farm. Later the steam engine supplied the power and I recall seeing the first steam thrashing unit going along Forest Road with a man walking 50 yards in front carrying a red flag.

WEATHER FREAKS

The only tornado which, as far as I know, ever occurred in the Island happened between 6 and 7a.m. in either 1878 or 1879. I remember the storm, although a boy at the time. It came in over the downs and passed near

Colemans Farm with an awful rushing sound, taking off the roofs of the farm buildings. At Nodes Farm, Northwood, it picked up a large straw rick and carried it out over the Solent. The track of the storm was only about 125 yards wide. Fortunately no one was injured... I also remember the greatest of all Island snowstorms in January, 1881, when all roads were completely blocked with an average depth of six feet and drifts up to 15 or 20ft. When walking to work at Vittlefields Farm on the morning after the storm with another farmworker we were able to take a straight line, struggling through over the covered hedges. We had to go to feed the animals. The severe weather lasted for about 14 days. In the meantime country people had to struggle through the snow to Newport to get food and often there was little except bread...

TOWN AND COUNTY NOTES

STARLINGS DRIVEN SOUTH. – Yesterday morning, at about eight o'clock, a huge flock of starlings was seen flying over Newport in a south-westerly direction. The birds were so numerous that the closely packed flight took about two minutes to pass, and occasionally an exhausted bird was seen to fall. The starlings were obviously heading for warmer climes.

AN ISLANDER'S NOTES BY VECTENSIS. – Some of my readers were, no doubt, surprised to see in Saturday's "Daily Express" that, according to one of that newspaper's staff reporters, Islanders are known as "corkheads." The terms "calf" or even (in Naval circles) "savage" have long been in common usage, but this is the first time I have encountered "corkhead*."

GODSHILL FARMER'S WIFE ATTACKED BY FOX. – Mrs. Attrill, of Smart's Cross, Godshill, wife of Mr. Frank Attrill, a smallholder, was attacked by a fox when she went to milk the cows at about 6.30 a.m. yesterday. The animal sprang out at her from the hay in the stable. She beat off the first attack with milk buckets, but the fox returned to the attack twice more and jumped on her chest, causing scratches. She ran indoors suffering from shock, and her husband went out with his gun and found the fox still in the hay and apparently ready to spring again. He shot it.

The unusual sound of a train passing through the Arreton Valley was heard on Tuesday, when a locomotive, a crane, and a goods truck collected platelayers' huts and material from the line side. The train came from Sandown, as the metals over the Horringford crossing have been removed. The line was closed two years ago. (February 8)

SMUGGLERS HIDEY HOLE FOUND AT BROOK. – An interesting discovery this week has produced a new link with smuggling days along the Channel coast of the Island. Workmen engaged on alterations to No. 2 Myrtle Cottages,

---

* County Press editor, Walter Sibbick, who penned the Vectensis column, was born on the Island in the late 1880's. It is inconceivable that the word 'corkhead' had somehow passed him by all those years. It does not appear in W.H. Long's 'The Isle of Wight Dialect,' published in 1886 nor in the 1889 'A Glossary of IW Dialect.' It seems to be a twentieth century invention.

Brook, found a six-gallon brandy cask and three glass bottles or jars of four, five and six gallons capacity in a chimney hidey. The casket is in perfect condition and the jars are uncracked, but the woven withies around the two large ones have rotted. The glass is dark green. The containers were found behind a bend in a chimney stack between the main building and a lean-to, which is being demolished. No entrance to the hiding place was apparent. Mr. J. C. Morris, owner of the property, who lives next door in Rectory Cottage, estimates that the bottles and cask have been stored away for at least a century. (January 25)

———————————◆———————————

Obviously, two pounds was two pounds in the Fifties...

February 8th, 1958

ALONE IN THE DARK

If you have ever wondered what it is like to sit alone in a dark and empty cinema at midnight with only a demon for company, Mrs. Doris Dyer, of 6 Surbiton Grove, Ryde, can tell you. She was chosen from some 100 who replied to an advertisement in last week's "County Press" for a woman to sit alone in the stalls of the Commodore Cinema on Monday and watch the screening of "Night of the Demon," an X certificate film. Afterwards, Mrs. Dyer, with the £2 reward in her purse, confessed that she would think twice before doing it again. "I am not squeamish," she said, "but under those conditions it was definitely frightening." She gave a vivid description of the film, which lasted 80 minutes, and added, " I never dared to close my eyes, even at the worst parts." Mrs. Dyer does not go to the cinema very often but has enjoyed "X" films before - in company!

———————————◆———————————

In 1845 John Dennett of the British Archaeological Association committed to paper the local legend of "Newmans Cross." Possibly apocryphal, he introduced the story with the words "as I believe it has never been recorded, and is now nearly forgotten, I may be excused for preserving a memorial of it here." 150 years later, it is included here in the same spirit...

February 15th, 1958

AN ISLANDER'S NOTES
BY VECTENSIS

I had not known until this week that back in the 1700's a design of crossed swords, cut in the turf and carefully preserved, could be seen on Bowcombe Down. This was disclosed in a record of the British Archaeological Association's meeting held at Winchester in August, 1845. Among the papers read thereat was one by John Dennett, telling the grim story of why the crossed swords were cut in the turf. It reads as follows:

"At a fence which terminates Bowcombe Down we enter an enclosed lane, on each side of which are several fields that have been enclosed from the down within the memory of persons now living. Before they were ploughed up there were to be seen on the higher parts of one of them a representation of two

The Campaign for Nuclear Disarmament

THE HYDROGEN BOMB IS AN ISSUE WHICH CANNOT
BE EVADED. IT INVOLVES THE FUTURE OF MANKIND.
WHERE SHOULD THIS COUNTRY TAKE ITS STAND ?
THE CASE AGAINST OUR PARTICIPATION IS A POWER-
FUL ONE. IT SHOULD BE HEARD, UNDERSTOOD AND
EVALUATED. IT WILL BE STATED BY :—

MICHAEL FOOT
J. B. PRIESTLEY
A. J. P. TAYLOR

at **THE SANDOWN PAVILION**

on **WEDNESDAY 23rd APRIL**, at 7.15 p.m.

with HIS WORSHIP THE MAYOR OF NEWPORT in the chair.

ADMISSION 1/-.   TICKETS LIMITED TO CAPACITY OF HALL
See local posters for availability of seats

swords across each other, cut in the turf, and upon them the names William Roach and Richard Newman. These cuttings were kept from sheep damage by the shepherds who attended the flocks on the down. The persons whose fate was thus commemorated were two officers, probably of the militia of that period, as both are Isle of Wight names. They had been taking refreshment together, either at the Crispin or the Castle Inn, at Newport, and were to have proceeded from thence to Yarmouth. While they were at the inn a dispute arose between them, but all angry feeling appeared to have subsided before they left the house; however, one of them having occasion to quit the room for a few minutes, left his sword on the table, and the other, taking advantage of his absence, broke the blade and replaced it in the scabbard. They soon after left to go on to Yarmouth apparently as good friends as usual. While on their way the quarrel was renewed and at the spot mentioned they drew on each other, and the one who's sword had been broken, finding himself thus betrayed, rushed on with such exasperation that each met his death by the other's hand. This occurred about the year 1741, and as I believe it has never been recorded, and is now nearly forgotten, I may be excused for preserving a memorial of it here. The above particulars have been often repeated to me by an old servant of my father's named Benjamin Redstone, who has died since these lines were written, in his 84th year, and also by Thomas Lacey, who died in November, 1844 in his 89th year, having resided the whole of that time in the cottage in which he was born. The spot in question is by some still called Newmans Cross."

THE WEEK'S NEWS

YOUTH'S VARIED OFFENCES – David B—, of Manor Road, Pan Estate, Newport, was summoned for committing an indecent act in the street. - P.C. Arber said that while in plain clothes in South Street he saw defendant, who was with another youth, commit the offence. He told the defendant who he was and B— replied "Do you want to make something of it?" Defendant refused to give his name and address, saying when asked, "It might be Tommy Steele." Witness later saw defendant in another part of the town and ascertained his name. Fined £2. B— was also fined £2 for riding a bicycle without lights.

"ONLY TWO EMPTY SHOPS IN NEWPORT" – Speaking at the Newport Town Council meeting, the Mayor of Newport said auctioneers and estate agents were appreciated more in Newport than anywhere else. Thanks to them, there were only two empty shops in the borough; hence their prosperity. Empty shops anywhere in the Island meant despair.

SOUTHERN TELEVISION TO OPEN ON AUGUST 30th – Low-power tests for the new Independent Television station, which will be known as Southern Television will be made from the station in the course of the next week or so and the station is expected to come on full power for testing purposes on August 1st. Studios are being prepared in premises previously known as the Plaza Cinema, Southampton.

SEQUEL TO FLYING BOAT CRASH – Complaints by residents that the water supply tasted strongly of chlorine has brought to light an unusual sequel to the flying boat crash. Following investigations, the IW Water Board has lodged a claim with Aquila Airways on the basis that the water supply in the Shalcombe area has been polluted by aviation spirit from the crashed aircraft... The fuel had seeped through the chalk and entered the galleries in which the water is stored. An alternative water supply was brought into operation. To date over 80 gallons of the spirit have been drawn off and there is still more to come. (February 15)

———————————◆———————————

In readers' letters over the years, Cowes had come in for more complaints than almost any other town on the Island. Amongst other things it had been referred to as aloof, snobbish, cliquey and greedy. It was now, perish the thought, being called "dreary"...

August 9th, 1958

COWES - A VISITOR'S IMPRESSION

Sir, I have just been reading the letter in your last issue about the lack of amenities for visitors in Ryde, but compared with Cowes, Ryde is a giddy Southend. When I arrived last week, I asked a resident what there was to do here. She replied : "If it is hot you sunbathe on the Green; if it is cold, you walk up and down the High Street; if it is wet you shelter in Woolworths and in the evening you either stay indoors or go to a pub." I thought this was a joke, but found it to be a very truthful statement of fact. Apart from one small picture house and dozens of small pubs, there is, quite literally, no place to go. This is my first visit to Cowes, and, can you wonder, it will be my last. I have visited almost every seaside holiday resort on the South Coast and I can honestly say that I have never had a more dreary holiday than in Cowes.

A.M. MOORE, 33 Gloucester Terrace, Bayswater, W2.

———————————◆———————————

The Seely family were about to sell off what remained of their estate at Brook. The potential bidders were assembled at the Newport auction rooms when with just minutes to go, it was announced that the entire estate had just been sold to a Yorkshire property company. The sale would still proceed but with a different vendor...

August 9th, 1958

BROOK ESTATE SALE

A century-old link with the esteemed Seely family was severed on Thursday when the Brook Estate, owned by Lord Sherwood came under the hammer at Newport. It was about 100 years ago that Mr. Charles Seely, Nottingham colliery owner and ancestor of Lord Sherwood, came to the Island and acquired large areas of land and much property. The estate first began to break up in 1925 when the greater part of the outlying farms were sold, many to the tenants, and in this week's sale the last 2498 acres changed hands. The sale aroused considerable interest, the large gathering at the Unity Hall including prominent Island landowners, farmers, investors, estate agents, solicitors and tenants... Mr.

Watson of auctioneers Way Ridett announced that four lots, totalling 28 acres in the Compton Bay area, had been withdrawn and sold privately to the National Trust at a modest figure, which links up with the coastal strip recently acquired by that body... The properties offered included four dairy and mixed farms, 1250 acres of forestry land, a village inn, 10 cottages, and 14 beach chalets, with a rent roll of about £3140... The most popular sales, completed to applause by a packed sale room were where tenants secured their own properties. The highest price of the day, £8150, was paid by Mr. Kingswell, of Cranmore, for 71-acre Brook Farm and 13 acres of woodlands and 40 acres of arable land all with vacant possession... Brook Hill House and 52 acres of grounds, together with two acres of woodland, failed to raise a bid. Brook House (the mansion divided into flats) and 15 acres of gardens with workshops, was withdrawn at £2400... Dunsbury Farm, of 320 acres, opened at £7000 but was withdrawn at £10,000... An area of 406 acres of forestry land, mostly tenanted by the Forestry Commission and 780 acres of forestry, down and farmland, and lots said to contain some excellent shooting, were acquired for a total of £4200 by Sir Robert Hobart on behalf of the Langdown Estate Company... Hanover House, Brook, with shop and Post Office, was withdrawn at £1050... A 72-acre area of mudland and saltings at Yarmouth was sold for £500 to Mr. R. De Quincey... The vacant Hulverstone School was withdrawn around the £800 mark. The Sun Inn, Hulverstone, leased to W. B. Mew, Langton and Co., failed to attract a bid, as did 14 holiday chalets at Brook.

TOWN AND COUNTY NOTES

Grape seeds planted at Christmas 1956 have produced 12ft. vines in a Yarmouth greenhouse.

NOTES BY VECTENSIS. – A display in the window of Messrs. Duke Bros. Ltd., builders' merchants, of High Street, Newport is exciting much interest, particularly among older residents. The focus is on craftsmanship ancient and modern, and two old relics are featured. One, which came into the hands of Mr. J. E. Duke (director) only last week, is a lantern bearing the name "Salisbury Arms" in blue lettering on white glass. The Salisbury Arms Inn was formerly at 7, High Street, where the showrooms are now situated, and the lantern was suspended from the iron bracket on the wall close to the attractive bay window. It was evidently oil burning.

NEWPORT'S "HOLE IN THE HEART" – A major operation is being carried out on the heart of old Newport. Messrs. Cheek Bros are using bulldozers and other modern demolition devices to clear away ancient structures to make room for a bus station which will end the congestion in St. James's Square. The premises fast disappearing comprise the old storage buildings, stables and houses running from the Nodehill end of South Street through to Orchard Street... As was to be expected, with bulldozers literally crushing old buildings to pieces, no interesting relics have so far been discovered.

"WIGHT MAN'S CLOTHIERS" SHOP GOES.

This photo, taken about 60 years ago, is of one of the oldest business premises in the centre of Newport, which is being pulled down to make room for a bus station. It is of the clothier's shop in Nodehill, started by Ernest Whitcher in 1865, and now continued by Frank E. Whitcher, Ltd., in premises near the Guildhall, to which the business was transferred four years ago. The picture shows the founder, chatting with one of his customers in a pony trap, and the late Ald. Whitcher is standing behind him. (August 16)

Messrs. Cheek Bros. are clearing away ancient structures to make way for a new bus station which will end the congestion in St James's Square.   [*Reg Davies.*]

For over 60 years Ryde had two piers; Ryde Pier, which is technically three piers joined together, and the smaller Victoria Pier. Built in 1863, Victoria Pier was the Island terminus of the Gosport ferry service from Stokes Bay until 1875 when it became a 'bathing station.' An elderly reader shared his memories of the days when one took a bath on the pier...

August 16th, 1958

AN ISLANDER'S NOTES
By VECTENSIS

"Old Rydeian" sends me the following reminiscences : "... What a change has taken place on the Ryde waterfront ! In the 1880s there was no sand, it was all mud and stone, although a few wood groynes existed. It was not until vast quantities of chalk were dumped near the boating slipway and later when the Western Esplanade was made that sand collected and made bathing utterly different. There were two piers, the 'Long' pier as now, and the 'Short' pier, or 'Victoria,' which ran about 300 yards out from where the huts now end; I was always sorry that this pier was dismantled during the First World War. Originally a commercial pier, it was getting dilapidated in my time, but had a complete bathing establishment for ladies and gents, together with hot 'ozone iodised' baths. Dashwood, an old tar, and his buxom wife, looked after their clients well. There were three what might be called bathing pens, both for ladies and men, no mixed bathing being then dreamt of. Ladies wore heavy knicks and skirt, but the men wore the smallest of slips. One pen at high tide might be 7ft. deep, No. 2 4ft., and No. 1 say 2ft. deep. Outside the pens it would be 12ft. deep, so it was a real swimming place, and had running boards, diving platforms at various heights, and there were about 30 huts in which to dress. We often bathed from May until November. The time of bathing was limited to tides. In addition to the bathing here, the town council erected a simple shelter for men only, which was popular as the 'halfpenny' stage, this being the amount one paid to be respectable!"

Rock 'n' roll was here to stay and young hopefuls were being signed up by record companies almost daily. In 1958 a singing milkman became the Island's first pop star when 17-year-old Terry Perkins from Newport won a local talent contest and changed his name to Craig Douglas. He went on to have nine top 40 hits but like many other acts of the time his career was eventually cut short by the Merseybeat boom in the early 1960s. His pleasant singing voice stood him in good stead and led to a long cabaret and cruise liner career which continued until 2010, when he retired due to ill health...

August 23rd, 1958

SINGING MILKMAN
YOUNG NEWPORTONIAN MAKES DECCA RECORD

If 17 years old Terry Perkins, of Newport, lets his mind wander from his job as a milk roundsman on Friday it will be little wonder, as he enters on that day the ranks of recording vocalists and the Decca Gramophone Company are putting on the market his recording of two songs, "Sitting in a tree house" and

"Nothing shakin'." If the record proves popular Terry, whose voice and style have been frequently likened to that of ballad singer Pat Boone, will have opened the door to television performances and top stage shows. Terry is an unassuming young man with a friendly smile. He is one of eight children of Mr. and Mrs. W. A. Perkins, of 14 Prospect Road, Newport... On leaving school Terry went to work as a milk roundsman for Mr. P. Strickland, of Pitts Farm, Calbourne. He started on the ladder to success as a singer in November of last year, when he won a talent contest at the Medina Cinema, Newport. It was there that his voice and personality attracted the attention of Mr. Robin Britten (managing director of Southern Cinemas, Ltd.) So impressed was he that he arranged for Terry ... to have an audition with a prominent London theatrical agent and he made his stage debut at the Empire Theatre, Portsmouth. By now the recording companies were beginning to take an interest and Terry found himself in the favourable position of having offers from Decca and EMI. Decca offered a two-year contract with a minimum of three records in the first year, and this was the one, on Mr. Britten's advice, that he decided to accept...

PRACTISING HARD

Since the opportunity of making a name in show business arose not a day has passed without Terry practising. He leaves for work in the morning at 8.30 a.m. and does not return home until about 6p.m. After tea and a change of clothes he catches the 6.50 bus to Ryde for rehearsals at the Commodore Theatre. On his days off he usually goes to London for singing lessons and then Mr. Britten takes him to a top rate variety show so that he can study the technique of the stars. Terry is modestly reticent about his progress, except to express his gratitude to Mr. Britten for his help, to Mr. Strickland for giving him days off to go to London, and to his accompanist, Vic Lewis, with, of course, a big "thank you" to "Mum," who persuaded him to enter the Medina Cinema contest. To-morrow Terry is appearing at the Commodore Theatre's evening shows, which star the well-known vocalist group "The Mudlarks." He has adopted the stage name Craig Douglas and made the recording in that name.

———————————◆———————————

Southern Television was about to come on the air. There had been keen competition for what was to prove a very lucrative franchise, the eventual winner being a consortium formed by the Rank Organisation, DC Thompson (owners of the Beano), and Associated Newspapers (owners of the Daily Mail). Southern Television enjoyed a profitable existence until 1982 when they lost their franchise to TVS ...

August 23rd, 1958
ISLAND'S CONTRIBUTION TO INDEPENDENT TELEVISION
CHILLERTON DOWN STATION OPENS NEXT SATURDAY

Next Saturday Island television viewers and those in a large area on the mainland, will have the choice of an alternative service, when the Independent Television Authority's new transmitting station at Chillerton Down comes into operation. Thus, much speculation connected with the selection of the site, followed by anticipation, as daily the giant mast seemed to spring up a few feet towards its height of 750ft., now approaches realisation. The station will commence sending out full programmes on Saturday next... The programmes will be provided by Southern Television Ltd., with offices and studios in Southampton, and they will be originating both local programmes and material for transmission throughout the independent television network...

———————————◆———————————

The big night arrived and Southern Television took to the air. Into people's homes came "Take Your Pick," "Emergency - Ward 10" and within 18 months, "Coronation Street" while children were delighted by the appearance of "Popeye" and "Robin Hood." Broadcasting two television channels from different transmitters meant two aerials on everybody's roof which meant it was easy for neighbours to see at a glance who had ITV, and who did not...

September 6th, 1958

SOUTHERN TELEVISION
MIXED RECEPTION OF OPENING TRANSMISSIONS

In more ways than one there was mixed reception at the start of Southern Television's programmes on Saturday. According to estimates based on the number of conversions and modifications carried out by local dealers and reports received by them, only about half of the Island's tele-viewers saw the programmes. There are 15,650 television licences issued in the Island - roughly one set to every five residents. Dealers say that there was a last-minute rush to have sets modified*, despite the fact that they had been advertising since last December. Approximately only half of the sets had been adapted to receive the signal from Chillerton Down. Many people thought they could get the alternative programme simply by switching over and were disillusioned. One of the reasons for the public holding back, according to a Newport dealer, is that reception of Southern Television broadcasts seems to vary almost from house to house. An aerial which is suitable in one house may be quite useless on the opposite side of the road. A few lucky viewers have been able to receive signals without further alterations to their sets or aerials, but many have been faced with not only modification of their set, but the installation of an aerial which could cost from 30s. to £15 extra.

DEAD AREA

Many parts of the Island cannot receive the signal no matter what is done to their sets. Ventnor, Bonchurch, St Lawrence and the Undercliff area, are affected... Within a few minutes of the programme starting at 5.30 p.m. on Saturday apologies were being offered for a breakdown. Other small breaks occurred on Monday. The general opinion is that the quality of the picture is not yet so good as that of the BBC transmitter at Rowridge... Comments on the content of programmes also vary. Some people, having become accustomed to the BBC's more sombre style of presentation, switched off because they found the new style too brash. But the majority of seekers after light entertainment were well pleased with the alternative programme. Island celebrities - Mr. and Mrs. J.B. Priestley, and Mr. Uffa Fox - were among those interviewed on the deck of the Caronia at Southampton, and star of the first variety show was Gracie Fields. On Sunday afternoon the Island's transport and other problems are to be featured...

---

* Earlier sets required a visit from an engineer to install the tuning coils required for reception of the new channel.

What will you see on Southern Television on opening night?

Take a look now at our studio preview

IT'S 8.0 p.m. on August 30th. The great night. The night you've been waiting for. Southern Television's Opening Night. You've switched your set to Channel 11 (transmission began at 5.30—but now it's 8.0 p.m.). Just what will you see?

"Southern Rhapsody" A wonderful show to remember. Packed with laughs and entertainment. Packed with glamour. Whatever you do—*don't miss it.*

Who are the Stars? We've asked David Langdon to sketch them for us. Take a look at them. From left to right they are: *Gracie Fields*—the immortal, incomparable 'Gracie'. *Line Renaud*—glamorous French singer. *Clive Lythgoe*—famous concert pianist. *Gary Miller*—young singer who's quickly making his way to the top. *Eric Winstone* and his Orchestra—one of the foremost recording orchestras in Britain. *Alan Melville*—writer, wit and TV personality who'll be introducing the show. And of course, Girls. Lots of them. Lionel and Joyce Blair with their Glamorous Dancers. A bevy of Bathing Beauties and the Bournemouth Girls Choir.

Enjoy every Minute of this programme. Now you know who the stars will be. Don't miss them. Let the whole family watch the show. Make a special point of staying in on the great night. On August 30th. At 8.0 p.m. *When the curtain goes up on the Opening Night of Southern Television—the South of England's own television station.*

Is your set ready? Don't risk missing the great Opening Night programme. If you haven't already done so, SEE YOUR DEALER IMMEDIATELY about adapting your set for Channel 11. You will still be in time if you see him NOW. Remember all sets, whether multi-channel or B.B.C. only may need some attention.

SOUTHERN TELEVISION opens
THIS SATURDAY
and the great opening night show starts at 8 p.m.

CHANNEL   ELEVEN

SOUTHERN   TELEVISION

ISLAND NOTES

THE CONSERVATIVE CANDIDATE - MR. MARK WOODNUTT RECOMMENDED – Only one name will be submitted as prospective Conservative candidate – that of Mr. Mark Woodnutt, aged 40, of The Pines, Swains Lane, Bembridge. The search for a candidate began many months ago when Sir Peter Macdonald, KBE, the Island's MP for 35 years, announced that he would not be seeking re-election. Should Mr. Woodnutt be adopted, the Island will have as a candidate a man who has a detailed knowledge of the Island and its problems, as evidenced by his able chairmanship of the Finance Committee of the County Council.

The aurora borealis was clearly seen from Ventnor on two successive nights before the exceptional storm on Friday week.

CRAIG DOUGLAS GAINS BBC CONTRACT – On October 11th Craig Douglas, Newport's young singing discovery, starts his career as a professional entertainer in earnest, when he takes part in the first of six programmes on the BBC television show "Six-five Special." It is most unusual for an artist to be engaged for so many appearances on this programme, a feat which obviously shows that a bright future lays before the likeable Craig. His popularity is illustrated by the sales for his first record "Sittin' in a tree house," and by the amount of "fan mail" which he has received since his television debut... On Saturday Craig's recording was played on the radio programme "Pick of the pops" and the previous Tuesday it was heard on "Housewives' choice." Yesterday he appeared on the Southern Television programme "Cool for cats." (September 20)

The staff at Welcome Beach, between Lake and Shanklin saw a strange object on the sands when they arrived on Wednesday morning. 100 yards away, in the Hope Beach direction, was a Southern Vectis bus stop sign "Stage 29."

DEMOLITION OF NEWPORT GASWORKS. – Demolition work started at this site only about four weeks ago... One of the most interesting of the demolition operations was the spectacular felling of the old boiler-house chimney stack. Craft had to be moved in the river and the road cordoned off. The gib of a 10 ton excavator was applied to the side of the 85 foot high stack by way of a few seemingly gentle stabs... The chimney came down cleanly to disintegrate into a mass of hundreds of tons of masonry and brickwork with clouds of brick-dust, reminiscent of the days of the blitz. (November 8)

A Ryde woman who lost her dentures while swimming at the weekend noted the spot and returned at low tide, when she retrieved them from a mass of seaweed.

Many of Saunders-Roe's contracts came from the Ministry of Defence. Unfortunately this sometimes left them at the mercy of politicians, and a change of Government or shift in Government policy could mean an abrupt change in the company's fortunes. For the past few years Saunders-Roe had been engaged on a government contract for the design and manufacture of the SR 177 jet fighter, but even as the first one was under construction at East Cowes, the government decided that fighter aircraft were to be phased out and replaced by ground-to-air guided missile systems. It meant an instant end to all work on the SR 177, and the contract was cancelled on Christmas Eve 1957, leaving 1500 men redundant.

However, the company was nothing if not diverse and found compensation in other projects. Although their main customer was the aeronautics industry, over the years they had successfully manufactured computers, flight simulators, helicopters, decompression chambers, widespan roof sections, radio towers and even prefabricated petrol stations for use in Africa. Another string to their bow, again as a result of a government contract, was the manufacture of space rockets...

September 13, 1958

ISLAND MOVES INTO THE SPACE AGE
SAUNDERS-ROE'S PART IN PRODUCING BLACK KNIGHT ROCKET.
TESTS CARRIED OUT AT THE NEEDLES

The Island's sympathy with Saunders-Roe, Ltd., in their ill-fated post-war Ministry of Supply projects – the giant Princess Flying Boats and the S.R. 177 fighter aircraft – gave place to widespread pleasure and satisfaction on Sunday, when it was announced that their latest enterprise, the Black Knight space rocket, had been successfully fired at Woomera, in Australia. The only thing marring the general sense of satisfaction is that it is unlikely to have much effect on the redundancy problem in the firm's aircraft construction departments. A Saunders-Roe spokesman referred to the splendid teamwork which had gone into the development of Britain's first space rocket, and said everyone concerned was extremely pleased at the result. Mr. Maurice Brennan, the firm's chief designer, led the team responsible for the construction of the rocket. The powerful liquid-fuelled engines were designed by Armstrong Siddeley motors and all the testing was carried out at the Needles rocket site by a team of technicians led by Mr. Paul Leyton (chief rocket development engineer) whose home is in Freshwater. Since the first information was released, the Minister of Supply (Mr. Aubrey Jones) has stated that work is now proceeding on the development of a two-stage rocket which could be fired to a height of 1500 miles, as compared with that of about 300 reached by the Black Knight. Referring to reports that the development of the rocket had cost not less than £48 million, Mr. Jones said that the real figure was between £4 and £5 million, and it is understood that that figure covers the production of 24 such rockets.

JUBILANT TECHNICIANS

The news was received with jubilation by the technicians at the Needles rocket motor testing site, where the Black Knight has undergone months of rigorous testing. These technicians put in more than 90 hours' work apiece during the final week to ensure perfection before the rocket left the site early on the morning of June 23rd. During the long months of testing and adjusting, members of the technical staff who were to handle the launching at Woomera studied the rocket's behaviour on the firing testbeds at the Needles. Others were flown to and from Australia to familiarise themselves with the conditions under which Black Knight would make its debut. Six members of Saunders-Roe's staff were stationed at Woomera, and a seventh travelled there for the firing.

THE NEEDLES SITE

The testing site on the Needles promontory was opened about two and a half years ago. At first local opinion was strongly against the project, as it was feared that the noise from engines on test would drive visitors away. The site was so carefully constructed and screened, however, that the noise was directed out to sea, and the only indication that testing was taking place was an occasional column of smoke above the cliff edge. Far from being a nuisance the establishment has brought a welcome influx of trade into the area.

THE LAUNCHING

… After rising vertically from the launcher, the vehicle is controlled to climb for several thousand feet, after which it is directed into a climb path towards the target area. From the point of engine cut-off the missile coasts upwards in "free fall" to an apogee of several hundred miles, and then descends until it reaches the fringes of the atmosphere above the down-range target area. Measures of the behaviour of the rocket engine, the control and guidance together with its environment and other phenomena are continuously made throughout flights and relayed to ground receivers by transmitters installed inside the missile...

NOSE CONE RECOVERED

The shattered nosecone of the rocket was found near the spot where it was expected to land, and the remains were reassembled by scientists who said they were delighted with the results of the test. The rocket is believed to have reached a height of more than 300 miles, and examination of the portions recovered is expected to provide much information on the manner in which it stood up to the terrific heat generated by its passage through the atmosphere.

◆

More local history came to light when a long standing resident of Lake died...

November 1st, 1958

"GRAND OLD MAN" OF LAKE
DEATH OF MR. R. SNUDDEN

By the death of Mr. Robert Snudden, the district has lost the last survivor of its original businessmen and one of its most greatly esteemed residents. He was 83. Bob Snudden could be regarded as the grand old man of Lake, on the history of which he was a great authority... Mr. Snudden was one of the few remaining Island born and bred individualists and to get him talking of his early recollections was an interesting experience. Lake in his younger years was very sparsely inhabited and its gravelled narrow roads ran between hedgerows and trees. When he built his shop, there was no other building on his side of the road between that and an old farmhouse, dated 1704, at the other end of the village. This old farmhouse was in existence until the beginning of the first world war when it was pulled down. Mr. Snudden often talked about the toll gate with its wooden fronted cottage which stood at the Newport road junction nearby and

of the young "bloods" of the Island driving through the gate at top speed in their gigs, pairs and fours-in-hand to avoid paying the toll. The toll was 3d. one horse and 6d. for two, with a ticket to frank the owner through the next toll gate eight miles away. Another of his reminiscences concerned a swampy tract of land at the bottom of Lake Hill about where the present war memorial stands. The swamp surrounded "Granny Gale's" cottage, reached by a small bridge, and in wet weather this became a veritable lake, which was possibly the origin of the name of the locality. The only other shop apart from Mr. Snudden's was Lacey's bakehouse on the other side of the road by the side of the forge, where the village blacksmith plied his trade. There were no schools nearer than Brading in his boyhood days and those who wanted schooling had to walk there. Mr. Snudden was a boy of seven when the great snowstorm of 1881 cut Lake off from the outside world. Flour ran short at the bakeries and when soldiers from Parkhurst were sent to clear the railway, village men volunteered to cut their way along the road to the station and bring back supplies. As the snow froze people walked along the tops of the hedges some five or six feet above the roads and over the tops of gates...

1959

In conditions of great secrecy, Saunders-Roe had gained yet another Government contract, this time to explore the potential of machines that rode on a cushion of compressed air. Being of the opinion that there was no military potential for the application, the government eventually handed the project over to the National Research Development Corporation who went on to fund further development. An invention which had started life as a mock-up using tin cans and hairdryers went on to become a full-sized reality and the publicity machine began to roll...

January 24th, 1959
"FLYING SAUCER" PROJECT AT COWES
UNUSUAL SAUNDERS-ROE CONTRACT
The first man-made flying saucer to take to the air is likely to be produced at Cowes and tested over the waters of the Solent. This was announced at the week-end in the national press, when it was stated that the revolutionary Hovercraft designed by Mr. C. S. Cockerell had reached a stage where a piloted version may be flying in a matter of months. The aircraft is designed to ride on a cushion of compressed air a few feet above the surface, and originally the device was on the secret list. Messrs. Saunders-Roe, because of their unrivalled knowledge of seaplane construction, and the excellent test facilities which they have available at East Cowes were selected to conduct preliminary experiments. These were subject to security regulations and were carried out on behalf of the Ministry of Supply.
NO MILITARY VALUE
In the course of the experiments it became clear that whatever the benefits

which might accrue in civilian applications, the device had no military potentialities. As a result the project was taken off the secret list last autumn and since then Messrs. Saunders-Roe have continued their experiments on behalf of the National Research Development Corporation. Press reports released at the weekend stated that the corporation had been working against time to take out patents before competitors in other countries did so, but that the delay due to the secret list restrictions had all but cost this country the lead in what some scientists believe will become a new form of transport. Messrs. Saunders-Roe state that experiments are progressing but that the production of a piloted version is by no means imminent. The Hovercraft differs from the usual conception of a vertical take-off aircraft, which needs immense power as it is necessary for the downward thrust to equal the weight of the machine. The Hovercraft requires only a fraction of that power, and estimates indicate that an engine of 150 brake horse power will be capable of lifting a weight equivalent to that of an average sized car. The present average British car is powered by an engine giving about 100 brake horse power.

NEW APPLICATION OF WELL-KNOWN PRINCIPLES

It is understood that conventional jet turbines would provide sufficient power to build up the air cushion through ducts. A flat under-surface is an essential requirement, and even with the largest machines envisaged, capable of carrying 1000 passengers, a pressure of only three-and-a-half ounces per square inch would provide all the support necessary. There is nothing new in the principle involved, its application having been the only difficulty... America appears to be the first country to have brought the principle into general use although it has not so far been applied to aircraft. More than a year ago the latest type vacuum cleaners were designed so that the machine glided along an inch above the carpet and at the Chicago Motor Show, the Ford Motor Company are at present demonstrating a wheel-less scooter operated by a jet of compressed air..

———————————◆———————————

To the horror of many if not most Islanders, land opposite Newtown had been earmarked as a potential site for a nuclear power station. There was a storm of protest and the County Press letters column became the Island's forum for complaint. Standing almost alone among the protesters, (local trades union leaders were also in favour) was the Island's Conservative candidate and soon-to-be MP, Mark Woodnutt, who declared himself firmly in favour of the project...

February 21st, 1959

SITES FOR NUCLEAR POWER STATIONS
INVESTIGATIONS TO START AT HAMSTEAD

The Central Electricity Generating Board are to carry out detailed investigations at Hamstead - between Newtown and Yarmouth - to find out whether the necessary facilities are available for a nuclear power station. The investigations will include ground surveys, trial borings, and hydrographic surveys and will take several months to complete. Large quantities of easily accessible water are required for cooling purposes and sites near the sea make large cooling towers unnecessary. The board stated on Wednesday that there was an urgent need to explore ways of expanding power generating capacity in this area to meet the constantly growing demand for electricity... Six nuclear power stations have yet to be sited somewhere in the southern part of England to meet the government's plan for 12 operational stations by 1966... The landowner and farmer most closely affected by the proposal is Lt. Col C.R.H. Kindersley, D.S.O, M.C., of Hamstead Grange who is emphatically opposed to the idea. He told a "County Press" representative that he intended to fight it as hard as he could... He declared that both Lower Hamstead Farm and Hamstead Farm would be ruined... The proposals have come as a rude shock to Island yachting enthusiasts, who are already perturbed at the rapid increase in the industrial development of the Solent area...

"A REALLY BIG FISH"

Mr. Mark Woodnutt, prospective Conservative candidate for the Island, said he welcomed the news that the Central Electricity Generating Board were considering a site at Hamstead for a nuclear power station. "I have known about the proposal for about eight months," he said, "and although I am surprised that the information has been released so soon, I welcome it. It is part of our policy to bring industry to the Island. It is a real big fish if we can catch it." Negotiations were going on to bring other industries to the Island, and he had every hope of one factory coming here which would employ over 300 people.

------------------------◆------------------------

Fourteen year old Jennifer Lale of Alverstone wanted to tell the world a little about her village and so she sent a letter to the County Press. It was a spirited, sometimes waspish account; an historical essay that perfectly captured the flavour of life in an English village in the 1950's...

April 4th, 1959

ALVERSTONE VILLAGE

Alverstone is just a small village, roughly about three to four miles from Sandown if you were to go by the small bus, but if you walk along the tattered railway line you would take about 20 minutes and the distance is just over one mile. In the year of 1954 rumours were spread that the train would be taken away and that the station would be closed down. This has proved true and we are now greatly honoured by a small coach which the bus company call a bus. The bus service is dreadful, we have eight bus duties a day, and we have no buses at all on Sundays, so instead of going out we have to stay at home and watch the television. There was once the old Mill at home, but it is no longer used now. By the Mill runs the River Yar. This is one good point of which we are very proud of. Although it is now falling away and the water wheel is old, dilapidated, and green with age, we still get a lot of people to see it in the summer (when we get any). On the river are boats which the public can hire and enjoy perhaps an hour's boating or more. If you were to travel the whole way up the river you would end up at Newport but owing to the lack of river diggers the furthest that one can get is Newchurch. We are known as a farming

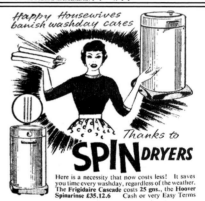

village although there are only seven farms around about and there are only 23 houses, of which two are empty. We have the huge population of 73.

In the summer the Alverstone Tea Gardens are open but even they close at about 7 o'clock. The people of Alverstone are no people for drinking beer and so there is no pub. The nearest one is either a nice walk to Lake to the Stag Inn or a walk to Newchurch to the pub there. On Thursday nights there was once a club for the young ones, but that has been closed down as there were not enough people that went. We had great fun and played different games, including table tennis, darts, the male of the youth played billiards and snooker, while others danced modern "rock" and "old-time" dancing. Every Tuesday night there is a whist drive at 7.30, and the old folk turn up from as far away as Ryde, Shanklin, and Lake. Every other Sunday there is Church in the Hall. The Vicar of Brading comes over to take the service. Sunday-school is taught the Sundays it is not church.

Carnival time we enter in the carnivals. This year we entered in Sandown and Ryde and were awarded first in both and were runners-up for the best entry in Sandown. This year we went as "Market Day." There was once a post office at Alverstone but that has been taken away, although we still have a letterbox.

By now you may think we are not very modern and that we walk about holding candles, but we have the electricity and also we have three road lights, of which two are in working order.

The houses in Alverstone are mainly old, and from the outside they all look it, but inside most of them have been redecorated... The week-ends at home are rather fun; there is a gang of us who go about together. If it rains we troop into one of our houses and play a game of cards or do something to keep us out of mischief. We all went carol singing last year at Christmas and we collected three pounds, which went towards the Sunday-school party.

We have one market gardener in the village who is kept very busy as he has to supply some flowers for the whole of the village folk. The oldest resident is Mrs Plumbley, who is 87, and the youngest is a baby of about two months now. Here I will end, and if you want to know any more you must come to Alverstone and see for yourselves what a quiet place it is, but at the same time see how friendly we all are.

JENNIFER LALE (Aged 14).

Editor's note :- Jennifer Wendy Lale, of Anzac Farm, Alverstone, is in Form 4B at Fairway County School, Sandown.

◆

Between 1955 and 1962 about a quarter of a million Afro-Caribbeans were encouraged by the British Government to settle in Britain. They faced a hostile reception from some quarters, and there were 'race riots' in Notting Hill in 1958, leading to two outcomes; the subject of immigration became a national talking point overnight and secondly, the Notting Hill Carnival was born.

Even on the Island not everything was sweetness and light...

May 2nd, 1959
RACIAL DISCRIMINATION
Sir, there is always a great stir in England when racial discrimination takes such an appalling form as it did recently in Little Rock, Arkansas,* and as in South Africa to-day, yet I am repeatedly faced with a doubt as to the genuineness of the true feeling here. Does a "vacancy" sign in the window mean whites only? During the Easter holiday two groups of coloured students called at my home seeking accommodation. They were cultured, with manners far superior to most of their opposite types here, yet they explained that they had called at establishments all around the town, and in each instance were informed that the places were full. I directed them to where I felt sure they would be welcomed, but, on phoning to confirm this, found that once again they had been turned away. My husband and I felt most distressed, as we had no room for them, but fortunately I saw them still wandering, and with the help of my daughter a good friend prepared rooms for them, and I hope we were able in some measure to dispel the hurt suffered. When they called on us before leaving the Island to thank us, we felt more than rewarded for our trouble. This was their first visit to the Isle of Wight. They may not pass this way again, but I hope that although they must have known that had their skins been white they would have been welcomed with open arms, they will not think of Island hospitality too unkindly. H. S. Ryde.

TOWN AND COUNTY NOTES
OFFER TO SELL RAILWAY TRACKS TO COUNCIL. – The Roads Committee are considering an offer from the British Transport Commission to sell to the council the disused railway tracks and other property between Town Gate, Newport, and Freshwater Railway Station, and between Coppins Bridge, Newport, and Sandown Railway Station (exclusive of the lines where they remain in position and of certain bridges).

NEWPORT BUS STATION. – At the monthly meeting of the Newport Town Council on Wednesday the mayor stated that the completion date for the proposed bus station at the junction of South Street and St James's Street, was now June, 1960.

COWES VICTORIA PIER. – The old Victoria Pier, Cowes, which has not been open to the public since the war, is to be taken over by private enterprise. Mr. William Dobson, of York, was prepared to take a five-year lease of the pier... Mr. Evans said he was sure one day they would all thank Mr. Dobson, who had saved the pier at the eleventh hour and fifty-ninth minute.

---

* On 3rd September 1957, the Governor of Arkansas used the National Guard to stop black children from attending the high school in Little Rock. As a result, President Eisenhower sent Federal troops to escort the children to their classrooms forcing the white population of Little Rock to integrate their school. The white residents described the Federal troops as "an army of occupation."

To the delight of Saunders-Roe, the hovercraft had captured the public imagination.
Newspapers excitedly referred to it as a "flying saucer" and its first public appearance,
keenly attended by reporters from all over the world, was more successful than
Saunders-Roe could have dared hope for. The machine gave a flawless performance
without the slightest technical hitch and the pilot confidently manouvered around the
concrete slipway to the delight of all present. The quick demonstration on the slipway
was all that had been planned but the journalists wanted more, and persuaded the
company to allow the hovercraft to take to the water. It was towed out into the mouth of
the Medina where by immense good fortune, the passenger liner Queen Mary happened
to be passing by, in the Solent. It was a heaven-sent photo opportunity and to the delight
of the Saunders-Roe management the next day's newspapers all carried the iconic image
of the hovercraft speeding along in a jet of spray, silhouetted by the Queen Mary...

June 13th, 1959

SUCCESSFUL HOVERCRAFT TRIALS AT COWES

The Saunders-Roe Hovercraft, an all British invention which possesses many
exciting possibilities that may well revolutionise transport, made a successful
first appearance before an admiring crowd at Cowes on Thursday. It was the
long-awaited SRN 1 ... Rigid security measures had added to the nationwide
interest and speculation about the invention. On Thursday at a Press day many
of its secrets were revealed to 260 journalists and photographers from British
and foreign newspapers and technical publications, TV, radio and films.

After they had inspected the machine it was demonstrated on the concrete
slipway and later made its first free flight over the sea off Cowes. Large crowds
lined the East and West Cowes shores to watch the hovercraft as it skimmed
low over the sea in a cloud of fine spray thrown up by its air jets. Aircraft and
many small boats converged on the scene during its half-hour test. The
watchers saw a thrilling comparison as the Hovercraft was silhouetted against
the towering sides of the Queen Mary as she passed from Southampton, a
comparison which was depicted in the T.V. films in the evening programmes...
Mr. Stanton-Jones, Saunders-Roe's young chief designer, told the "County
Press": "The prototype bears no relationship to what future hovercraft will look
like - they will be as different as Stephenson's Rocket is to present-day railway
engines." ... A 400 ton hovercraft would require only a quarter of the engine
power per tonne of an aircraft, and could carry nearly twice the payload. It
could carry passengers and freight at high speeds of 70 to 120 knots. It was
likely to find its first practical application in fast ferries over medium distances,
making possible, for example, a 10 to 20 minute journey between England and
the continent. A 100 ton cross-channel passenger ferry was visualised to cruise
at 19 knots. It would be about 130 feet long and capable of carrying 300
passengers with luggage... Yesterday the hovercraft demonstrations were
prominently featured in every national newspaper. Descriptive names of the
new craft differed, but all were unanimous in their acclamation of this notable
achievement by Saunders-Roe, which promises to bring enhanced industrial
prestige and prosperity to the Island.

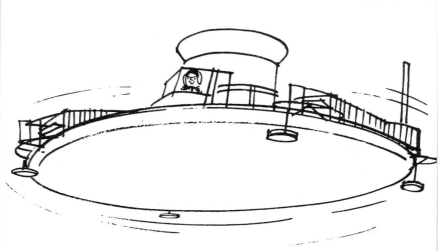

WE FUEL THE WORLD'S FIRST FLYING CUP AND SAUCER

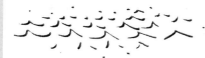

Let's establish one essential fact first. Mere flying saucers never really stirred us tea drinking British. But the British built prototype Hovercraft SRN1 does, because it's very properly shaped like a tea cup and saucer.

What of the Hovercraft's future? Enthusiasts predict that it will bring about a revolution in transportation. The Hovercraft makes, and rises on, its own cushion of air, and then skims on it over the surface of land and sea.

The possibilities of the Hovercraft stretch the imagination. It needs no ports or airfields. And its efficiency increases with its size. The makers are already thinking in terms of a large Hovercraft ferry weighing a thousand tons and up, skimming at speeds of 100 knots.

The prototype SRN1 is fuelled and lubricated by Shell. Which is what you might expect, since we have always looked after, fussed over, and generally mothered the pioneers of air transportation.

YOU CAN BE SURE OF

In the summer of 1959 a national print dispute led to the County Press printing staff going on strike for six weeks. Rather than face a loss of £600 a week the management and remaining staff donned aprons to produce a paper during each of those weeks...

July 4th, 1959

HOW WE FACED THE STRIKE
TEAMWORK BY BOSSES AND BOYS
[By the Editor]

We have had many letters and verbal messages of congratulation from readers on producing a 12 page issue of the "County Press" last week in spite of the fact that all the fully trained members of our printing staff obeyed their union's instructions to withdraw their labour owing to the dispute over wages and hours. They did so after the issue of June 18th... Many of those sending congratulations expressed surprise and wonder as to how we managed to produce a paper... We therefore tell the story of our achievement, not in any spirit of conceit or boasting, but to give our readers and advertisers information they obviously wish to have, and also to pay a well deserved tribute to the eight young apprentices on our staff who were not involved in the dispute with the unions and who splendidly rose to the occasion to play a most creditable part in an achievement of which the directors, executives and staff of the "County Press" are extremely proud.

FORESIGHT

... Lt Col C. W. Brannon (son of the founder) set an inspiring example by going to the Intertype Works at Slough for two days where he had instruction in working the typesetting machines with which our news composing room is equipped. Last week he took off his coat, rolled up his sleeves, and joined the enthusiastic young team of apprentices in setting up the type for the news and advertisements which appeared in our last issue. There were many problems to be solved, inevitable when unaccustomed hands had to work these intricate machines, but persistence and enthusiasm triumphed. Other apprentices tackled the exacting task of making up the pages of type, a job usually done by men with years of experience but now undertaken by senior and junior apprentices ... One with only 18 months training set up his first display advertisement, that of Messrs. Wadham's, furnishers, and made an exceedingly good job of it.

TRIAL AND ERROR

When the typesetting problems had been solved there still remained the more anxious work of casting the plates for the rotary press and running the huge yet delicate machine. That task was undertaken by the deputy manager (Mr. George Moth) and his assistant (Mr. Richard Bradbeer). With the benefit of hints from a representative of the firm who supplied the equipment, who came to the Island specially for the purpose, they proceeded by trial and error to master the molten metal and plate production and the roaring monster - the rotary press... When the page cylinders and wheels of the machine began to revolve the most anxious moments of all came. For a time it was progress by fits and starts, but gradually they got the monster under control, and it roared steadily away until 30,000 copies had been printed. Other available members of the staff lent a hand

The two ton elephant Candy, latest arrival at the Isle of Wight Zoo, Sandown, thirsty after her long journey from Stratford-upon-Avon, enjoys a pint of beer supplied by Mrs. Harris, wife of the licensee of the Fort Tavern, Sandown. (Aug 1)

The Saunders-Roe Hovercraft made a successful first appearance before an admiring crowd at Cowes on Thursday. Many of its secrets were revealed to 260 journalists and photographers from British and foreign newspapers, TV, radio and films at a Press day. (June 13)

in the final distribution activities. The writer, after one of the most trying weeks in his 57 years' service, tidied up his desk and joined the packers, endeavouring with more or less success to recapture his youthful dexterity in putting wrappers around some of the thousands and more papers which are posted each week to subscribers.

Refreshed by Mews' ale and pork pies, the band of workers plodded on until the job was done, and what may justly be described as an historic issue of the paper was ready for the newsagents on Saturday morning...

———————————◆———————————

NEWS IN BRIEF

SAUNDERS-ROE TAKEOVER – Westland Aircraft, the well-known firm of helicopter manufacturers of Yeovil, are taking over the whole of Saunders-Roe of East Cowes... The merger will result in the formation of one of the largest helicopter manufacturing groups in the world outside the USA... The new company will, of course, take over the further production of the Black Knight rocket and missile and the hovercraft research vehicle... There are still possibilities for the use of the three giant Princess flying boats which now lie cocooned at Cowes and Calshot as they may be wanted for atomic propulsion test purposes by the US Navy.

ANOTHER HIT FOR CRAIG DOUGLAS – Craig Douglas, the young Newport ex-milkman singer, is now firmly established as a recording star. With his record "Teenager in Love" remaining in the hit parade last week at number 13, and his latest offering "Only Sixteen" shaping for equal success, his record sales during the last four months are approaching the 200,000 mark.

NEWTOWN HAS ELECTRICITY – Electricity was switched on in Newtown this week, the last village in the Island to be connected to the mains... The old borough street layout remains practically unchanged to-day. High Street, Gold Street, Broad Street, Church Street, and others remain partly as mere grassy tracks... It was therefore more than usually important that overhead cables along the old streets should be avoided and accordingly the whole scheme has been carried out with great care by the Southern Electricity Board. (August 15)

Tommy Steele, who is camping "somewhere in the Isle of Wight" after his Russian visit, arrived in Sandown on Sunday to visit his friend Johnny Goossens, who is appearing at the Copa Cabana Club, and was soon recognised. He tried to get away from the club but was soon surrounded by scores of teenagers, including members of the Carousel Club.

———————————◆———————————

There are many stories of unofficial night-shift activities at J.S. White's shipyard in Cowes, some true, some not so true. The one about shipyard workers fishing with an arc welder is quite clearly genuine...

August 1st, 1959

AN ISLANDER'S NOTES
by VECTENSIS

Shipyard workers at Cowes have found a new and easy way to supplement their family budgets with fresh fish - without angling for them. At certain states of the tide in hot weather, shoals of mullet drift by in the Medina. When this coincides with the lunch break, the men row out, taking with them the business end of electric welding equipment. With the power switched on they wait for the mullet. When they move close to the boat the welding torch is touched to the water, the fish are stunned by the shock, and are then picked out of the water. Fish up to 7 or 8 lb. have been caught in this way. The electric shock method of capture is used by river boards and fisheries when they require to rid a river of coarse or unwanted fish. If left, the fish soon recover from the shock. Such methods are regarded with disdain and disgust by the angler, but the finer points of the sport have probably always been disregarded by some people. As a boy I was guilty of catching trout with a fine wire noose, and during the First World War the troops used to throw Mills bombs into the French rivers and gathered the fish stunned by the explosions.

———————————◆———————————

Councillor Fred Smart had become the chairman of Cowes Council, a position which meant that in the course of his duties he would be expected to hold official receptions in his chambers at Northwood House. Rather unwisely perhaps, Mr Smart had announced that his political beliefs would not allow him to spend public money entertaining people who were "on a higher social scale than himself." His remark coincided with the release of the film 'I'm All Right Jack', a comedy which poked fun at class distinction and Britain's poor industrial relations. The national Press picked up the story and made merry with Mr. Smart's beliefs. The County Press were not so amused and spoke out...

August 8th, 1959

COUNCILLOR SMART AND COWES WEEK

Daily newspapers this week have quoted Mr. F. Smart, chairman of the Cowes Urban District Council, as having "frankly stated" that there was no official reception to the officers of visiting warships and prominent yachting people at Northwood House during this year's yachting week (in contrast to previous years) because "it would be on his conscience if he spent public money entertaining people on a higher social scale than himself." He is also credited with saying that he did not respond to an invitation to take tea on the Royal Yacht Squadron lawn "as he knew he would not feel at home among the members, because he is a shipyard worker." Such explanations are unfortunate. If Mr. Smart did not wish to take part in such social courtesies he was entitled to decline to do so, but to emphasise class distinction as a reason was foolish. Is not the office of leading citizen in the world's premier yachting port sufficient social standing, and is there any other sport where such standing has been more disregarded in recent years than in sailing?

Over the previous twenty years most of the Island's airports had closed, almost bringing to an end the days of regular air services to and from the Island. At Cowes the former Somerton airport was about to gain an important new lease of life. The site had been chosen by Decca as the location for their new radar factory, beginning an association which continues to this day...

September 5th, 1959

DECCA COMPANY'S PLAN FOR SOMERTON

Mr. M. Gibson, General Works manager of Decca Radar, Ltd., who have taken over what was formerly Somerton airport, spoke at Newport Rotary Club on Wednesday about the company's plans for development on the 60-acre site. "We are opening up in the Island," he said, "and to-day I have been informed that we take over with effect from to-morrow (Thursday) and move contractors onto the site. We hope to make immediate use of the area. "Our intentions are to clean up the area and buildings on the site and operate it not later than the first week in October. We shall employ 50 or 60 people in the beginning, but we shall drive very hard for the first 6 to 12 months. We have to do this because we are a commercial organisation, and we have to see if roads and transportation and the labour situation and housing are all right. Every indication we have had to date is that we have got here what we want, thanks to the courtesy of all the people I have met on the Island." Mr. Gibson said it would, of necessity, be a fairly long-term plan, and will extend over 10 years. If things were satisfactory a great deal of it would be in the first five years. Recently they planned development on a new radar set. 300 were to be built, but they were all sold before the first one was completed and another 2000 were needed.

MAINLY ASSEMBLY WORK

Mr. Gibson said they were an international concern. It was early yet, but they were expecting to build in the Island larger radar equipment - harbour radar, air surveillance, and interception radar. The circumstances pointed to a labour situation which could adequately take care of that type of fabrication. It would be of an assembly nature only in the first instance. The next stage would be to build up and start manufacture...

Over the years the Island has had more than its fair share of hermits. In 1959 another one came to light...

September 12th, 1959

AN ISLANDER'S NOTES
by VECTENSIS

Stanley Cotton's recent charming article on Gatcombe in the spring has brought me an interesting letter from the "mayor" of that delectable village, Mr. Arthur Williams, in which he tells the story of a local character who lived as a hermit on the downs which Stanley Cotton so vividly described. "He was Daniel Barnes, a native of Alverstone, a dignified and noble figure who died unhonoured and unsung," writes Mr. Williams. "He was known to all local residents as 'Chairbottomer Jack,' because he earned a precarious living by mending rush and cane-bottomed chairs. He was a short man with long hair

Cowes 1959

On the East Cowes side behind the sheds of Saunders-Roe, the lower grounds of East Cowes Castle are visible. The cocooned Princess flying boat is just across the river at West Cowes and at the bottom, Cowes railway station and the adjacent Denmark Road School.   [Author's Collection] and tanned face. Children were frightened of him, but he was quite harmless and too honest to steal and too proud to beg. He lived for about 30 years on the downs without any kind of shelter, although in very severe weather he would take refuge in a disused limekiln on the south side of Chillerton Down. I often saw him in my younger days. He never revealed to anyone the reason for his life of seclusion and privatisation, but there was probably some deep spiritual reason. This is confirmed by what a woman told me. She gave the hermit a loaf of bread and he placed it on the ground and said the words from the Lord's Prayer 'Give us this day our daily bread' before he thanked her. She was so touched by the act and so ashamed that she had given him bread only, that she hurriedly got some cheese and gave him that as well. He used to make his home on the spot where the ITV station now stands... Daniel was eventually found in an exhausted state and removed to hospital, where he died."

———————◆———————

THE WEEK'S NEWS

FUTURE OF NORTHWOOD CAMP SITE UNDECIDED – Concern was expressed at the condition of the site of the former Northwood army camp, whose appearance, now that buildings have been sold and removed, was felt by the council to be seriously detrimental to the amenities of the district... In answer to representations to the Secretary of State for War, asking that the site be returned to its former condition so as to conform with surrounding agricultural land ... he had replied that the site would be disposed of by public auction at some future date but there was no way in which his Department could oblige the purchaser to clear the site.

THE NAVY CALLED IN TO BLOW UP DISUSED RAILWAY BRIDGE – One of the few remaining signs of the existence of the now defunct Ventnor West-Merstone railway line, the buttresses which once supported the track over the road leading to Roud from Godshill, has this week been the subject of a demolition exercise for naval personnel from HMS Vernon... using a combination of TNT and plastic explosive which was detonated from a firing point established about a quarter of a mile away...

———————◆———————

A general election was approaching. The Island was a safe Conservative seat held by Sir Peter Macdonald for the last 35 years but he was standing down to make way for Mark Woodnutt (who was to remain the Island's MP until 1974). Standing against him for the Labour party was mainlander Alderman Amey, who declared that while it would naturally be impossible for him to actually live here if he were to win, he would, however, promise to visit the Island every three weeks. That remark, and also referring to the County Press as a horror comic, did him no favours and Woodnutt, to no-one's great surprise, went on to win the seat by a landslide. On the hustings Mr Amey was asked for his thoughts on the nuclear power station debate. Speaking at Wroxall he thought the site was unsuitable but speaking at Brading, he welcomed it...

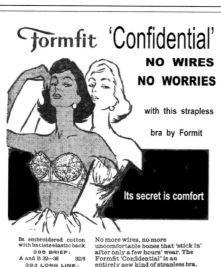

October 3rd, 1959
NUCLEAR STATION SITE UNSUITABLE
Question time mainly consisted of a lively exchange between Alderman Amey and two Wroxall electors. One repeatedly challenged the candidate on his allegiance to the Island. Alderman Amey said it would be impossible for him to live in the Island if elected, but he promised to visit the constituency every three weeks to meet the people and to discuss their problems. He claimed that was more than had ever been done by Sir Peter Macdonald. Asked for his attitude to the suggested site for a nuclear power station at Hamstead Alderman Amey said he had visited the site and it had struck him as a wilderness. This brought a retort from the questioner that those who wished to preserve the area as a bird sanctuary would not appreciate that remark. Ald. Amey said whether the site was right for a power station or not was one to be decided locally. He did not know the opinions of the residents; he had only received one complaint and that was from a man at Salisbury! Asked if he had not read the views expressed in the "County Press" Alderman Amey said he did not read "horror comics." Challenged further on the point, Alderman Amey said he thought the site at Newtown was unsuitable...

BRADING During question time he was asked what his feelings were over the proposed nuclear power station. He said, "I would welcome it."

Editorial same issue:
"HORROR COMIC"
Asked at a Ventnor meeting if he had not read the views expressed in the "County Press" on the proposed nuclear power station at Hamstead the Labour candidate (Ald. E.C. Amey) replied that he did not read horror comics. The only justification we can think of for such a description is that the "County Press" includes in its columns reports of Ald. Amey's speeches.

◆

As the Fifties came to an end, so did a long established Newport business...
November 14th, 1959
THE PASSING OF PADLOCK HOUSE
OLD ESTABLISHED NEWPORT BUSINESS CLOSES
The sale by auction as we went to press yesterday of the remaining stock-in-trade of the ironmonger's and locksmith's business carried on at 146 High Street, Newport, by Mr. W. A. Hayles, marked the end of one of the borough's oldest established businesses, and the close of a personal association with trading in the town extending over 69 years. The giant padlock, which for over half-a-century has hung over the entrance as the sign adopted by the business - "Padlock House" - will soon disappear, as Mr. Hayles has leased the premises and, with his wife, has moved into a bungalow at Carisbrooke. They are looking forward to retirement free from the shop bell, which has largely governed their lives since they were married 52 years ago. Mr. Hayles, who is 81, entered the business established by his father at the age of 12, when it occupied premises at

41 High Street. It was moved to 146 High Street about 20 years ago. Among the changes since his early days, Mr. Hayles said perhaps the most striking was the revolution in lighting wrought by electricity. His father used to contract to light public halls and similar places with oil lamps, and the stock of oil lamps numbered about 2500. Of the many business changes Mr. Hayles has witnessed in the High Street, between the Guildhall and St James's Square, he recalls no fewer than 14 at the premises now occupied by Boots the chemists.

Yesterday's Papers, Volume 6, covering the 1960's, will be published in late 2011.

ISLE OF WIGHT REVISITED

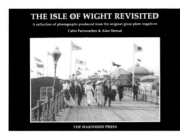

Most of the photographs in this book were taken nearly a hundred years ago. Some are older and date from the 1890s while a few are from the 1920s. All the photographs were taken on glass negatives and apart from a handful, have not been seen since the day they were first printed. Over the passing years, the glass negatives have lain untouched in their boxes until now. All the photographs in this book have been produced by returning to these original glass plate negatives to produce stunning new prints from them, modern technology allowing them to be carefully and sensitively restored with a degree of sophistication unimagined by the photographers. The result is a unique collection of photographs of the Island, all of the highest quality. By Colin Fairweather & Alan Stroud.

Oakwood Press. ISBN 978 0 85361 642 9 Hardback **£19.95**

RYDE REVISITED

Postcard collectors on the Isle of Wight will be familiar with the name of William R. Hogg. This book celebrates Hogg's work by reproducing over a hundred of his photographs, in large format and in the highest possible detail, to a degree unavailable until now. Without exception they have all been produced from Hogg's original glass negatives. Mr Hogg would be pleased and proud to see his photographs published today; his work was of the highest standard, technically and aesthetically, and it deserves to live on. We feel privileged to have been able to breathe new life into Mr Hogg's photographs and to present them to a new audience.

By Colin Fairweather & Alan Stroud.

Oakwood Press. ISBN 978 0 85361 660 3 Hardback **£19.95**

ISLAND VOICES

In the early 1980s, the authors carried out a series of recorded interviews with Islanders talking about their working lives and childhood in the early part of the 20th century. All were in their seventies or eighties at the time of recording and some of them are speaking of Island life over 100 years ago. Between them they tell of the day-to-day running of a village mill, launching a lifeboat with the aid of horses and even the social standing of a telephone engineer in the 1930s. Nine Islanders recount the intimate details of everyday life that that no-one will ever live again.

By Alan Stroud & Colin Fairweather

Now and Then Books. ISBN 978 0 95650 76 0 0 **£11.95**

YESTERDAY'S PAPERS Vol 1:   *Life in Late Victorian England, 1884 - 1901*
With the passing of time, journalists' work originally meant to have a life of only seven days, has become a valuable history resource. These first-hand accounts of the day-to-day life of Victorians, written with few inhibitions and often in the smallest and most revealing detail, provide a history not found in textbooks. This is the Victorians writing about themselves, uncluttered by today's attitudes and opinions with no other agenda than to provide a straightforward account of the week's news.

Oakwood Press. ISBN 978 0 85361 671 9   **£11.95**

YESTERDAY'S PAPERS Vol 2 :   *Life in Edwardian England, 1901 - 1918*
Volume 2 dips into the County Press archive to present a selection of cuttings from 1901 to 1918 which give a flavour of life on the Island covering the Edwardian era and World War I. By their very nature all the items have historical interest. Some of them are amusing while some of them are not so amusing. On occasions they have a foot in both camps. This is pure and undiluted history; Island news, told every seven days, as it happened.

Oakwood Press. ISBN 978 0 85361 684 9   **£12.95**

YESTERDAY'S PAPERS Vol 3 :   *Life in England between the wars, 1918 - 1934*
While the Victorian way of life was a whole world away from today, the same is not true for the inter-war years. Much of what is familiar now was familiar then. By the 1930's the car, the telephone, electrical appliances of every type and even air travel, had become a part of everyday life for those able to afford them. For many others the 1930's were not so cheerful. Long-term unemployment became a way of life for thousands, especially on the Island.

Oakwood Press. ISBN 978 0 85361 693 1   **£13.95**

YESTERDAY'S PAPERS Vol 4 :   *Life on the Island, 1935 - 1949*
For the second time in many people's lifetimes, Britain and Germany went to war. With its shipyards, aircraft manufacturers and proximity to Portsmouth's dockyards, the Island was an important military target and suffered heavy bombing raids. Overnight the County Press found itself at the centre of Island life, recording the highs and lows of Islanders' lives week after week; accounts of the lives of long-suffering, but always resilient, Islanders

Now and Then Books. ISBN 978 0 95650 76 1 7   **£11.95**